Praise for

Crushing the Cancer Curveball

"*Crushing the Cancer Curveball* combines the wise perspective of lived experience and detailed research on options and serves as an important guide to help women navigate the complex landscape of breast cancer risk, treatment, and recovery. Kaufman's approach is to empower women to learn through stories and arm them with knowledge so that they can be more engaged in their care and know what questions to ask."

—Dr. Laura Esserman, Alfred A. de Lorimier Endowed Chair in General Surgery, UCSF; Professor, Departments of Surgery and Radiology, and Affiliate Faculty, Institute for Health Policy Studies, UCSF; Director, UCSF Breast Care Center; Co-Leader, Breast Oncology Program, UCSF Helen Diller Family Comprehensive Cancer Center

"Joelle's passion for living, even in the face of breast cancer, is infectious. She shows us how positivity and perseverance can convert a challenging and terrifying experience to one of personal growth, relationship strengthening, and appreciation of life."

—Dr. Merisa Piper, Assistant Professor, UCSF, Reconstructive Breast Surgery

"Joelle's story and how she became the best possible patient helped me better understand the diversity of priorities for individual patients. I look forward to making *Crushing the Cancer Curveball* part of our highly encouraged readings for young researchers and friends interested in cancer research and care."

—Dr. Peter Kuhn, USC Professor, Director of the Convergent Science Institute in Cancer (CSI-Cancer)

"Joelle's unique cancer story is one that is meant to be told and shared. A truly comprehensive road map to managing the emotional and medical ins and outs and ups and downs of the patient experience. This comprehensive resource leaves readers with an increased capacity to process, communicate, and manage this often overwhelming and life-changing experience."

—Dr. Sadie Philips, Psycho-Oncology

"Joelle's perspective and self-advocacy during her cancer journey were truly inspirational to witness. She has now channeled her experience, curiosity, and knack for efficiency into a comprehensive guide for those facing a cancer diagnosis. It will offer solace and guidance to individuals feeling isolated and unsure of their next steps. At Sharsheret, we often receive calls from such people with a new cancer diagnosis, seeking direction and a sense of community; many in search of a practical guide. Joelle's book will meet these needs with insight and pragmatism."

—Aimee Sax, MSW, Sharsheret Support Program Manager

"The word 'practical' tends to mean boring, but Joelle's book is dynamic. Those facing breast cancer can find hope as well as solid, useful information. Those who face a different type of cancer can gain much from her 'lessons learned.' It's a must-read for cancer patients, as well as family and friends. Thanks, Joelle, for your bravery, honesty, and wisdom."

—Elda L. Robinson, author of #1 international sellers
A Simple Cup of -Ty and *One More Thing . . .*

"Joelle Kaufman has hit the ball out of the park in her very personal and unique survivor's guide through breast cancer detection, diagnosis, treatment, and recovery. Her strength, resiliency, determination, and invaluable lessons learned will have an enormous positive impact in guiding, empowering, and bringing hope and inspiration to the many women facing the same diagnosis, along with their families, friends, and healthcare providers."

—Dr. Harriet Borofsky, Medical Director of
Breast Imaging for both Riverview Medical Center
and Bayshore Medical Center

"*Crushing the Cancer Curveball* is unique in that it is a deeply honest and detailed account of Joelle's personal cancer journey and also a practical, useful resource to help patients and their supporters navigate a new breast cancer diagnosis."

—Jo Chien, MD, Professor of Clinical Medicine;
Medical Director, Breast Oncology; Helen Diller
Family Comprehensive Cancer Center,
University of California San Francisco

Crushing the Cancer Curveball:

A Playbook for the Newly Diagnosed
and Their Family and Friends

by Joelle Kaufman

Crushing the Cancer Curveball:
A Playbook for the Newly Diagnosed and Their Family and Friends
by Joelle Kaufman

> 71,770 words on 20 August 2024
> Category: Adult
> Genre: Non-Fiction—Health: Women's health; Diseases & Physical Ailments: Breast cancer

This book is intended as a reference volume only, not as a medical manual. The information given here is designed to help you make informed decisions about your health. It is not intended as a substitute for any treatment that may have been prescribed by your doctor. If you suspect that you have a medical problem, you should seek competent medical help. You should not begin a new health regimen without first consulting a medical professional.

Published by River Grove Books
Austin, TX
www.rivergrovebooks.com

Copyright © 2025 Joelle Kaufman

All rights reserved.

Thank you for purchasing an authorized edition of this book and for complying with copyright law. No part of this book may be reproduced, stored in a retrieval system, or transmitted by any means, electronic, mechanical, photocopying, recording, or otherwise, without written permission from the copyright holder.

Distributed by River Grove Books

Design and composition by Juan Gabriel Diaz Rodriguez
Cover design by Juan Gabriel Diaz Rodriguez

Publisher's Cataloging-in-Publication data is available.

Print ISBN: 978-1-63299-936-8

eBook ISBN: 978-1-63299-937-5

First Edition

To Mom, for thriving more than forty years after.

To Tracey, for always being there.

To Ariel and Emma—may science stop this journey with me.

To Neal, Jessica, Heather, Michele, Julie, Shira, Ben, Taylor, and everyone on my team—you light up my life. I hope every breast cancer patient has people like you.

Contents

Introduction 13

Part I:
Prevention **18**

1. Foul Ball 19
BRCA1 gene, Diagnosis, Genetic testing, Prevention

2. Curveball 29
Diagnosis, Prevention

3. Close Call 33
BRCA1 gene, Diagnosis, Prevention

4. Safe at Home 41
Prophylactic surgery, Breast reduction surgery, Self-advocacy

Jessica G.'s Journey 49
Diagnosis, Advocacy, Financial impact, Support system, Treatment scheduling, Side effects management

Batter Up: Prevention 55

Part II:
Diagnosis **58**

5. Little League 59
Initial diagnosis, Family impact, Emotional response, Genetic risk awareness, Screening importance, Childhood coping mechanisms

6. Cancer's Home Run 65
Diagnosis confirmation, Emotional impact, Family communication, Treatment plan changes, Support network activation

7. Dugout Comradery 71
Diagnosis, Family support

8. Team Sport 79
Diagnosis, Family support

9. Dead Ball
Diagnosis, Support groups 85

10. The Emotional Swings of Cancer 91
Mental health, Support groups

11. On-Deck Circle 99
Advocacy, Lymph nodes, Oncologist, PET scan, Port

Alysia's Journey 109
Lobular breast cancer, Delayed diagnosis, Self-advocacy, Medical dismissal

Josie's Journey 117
HER2-positive breast cancer, Side effect management, Work-life balance, Family impact, Hair preservation (cold capping), Treatment adaptations

Heather A.'s Journey 123
Triple-positive breast cancer, Treatment scheduling challenges, Self-advocacy, Sex, Lifestyle changes post-diagnosis

Batter Up: Diagnosis 131

Part III:
Treatment **134**

12. Beanball 135
Financial impact, Oncologist, PET scan, Treatment

13. The Mental Game 145
Distraction techniques, Anxiety management, Medication management, Pre-treatment preparation, Self-advocacy, Communication with medical team

14. First Inning 153
Carboplatin, Chemotherapy, DigniCap, Immune system, Infusion, Oncologist, PET scan, Port, Side effects, Taxol, Treatment

15. Batting Rituals 163
Advocacy, Aromatherapy, Carboplatin, Chemotherapy, Cold capping, DigniCap, Exercise, Infusion, Mental health, Nausea management, Oncologist, Port, Side effects, Taxol, Travel, Treatment

16. The Fans 173
Family support, Financial impact

17. The Batting Helmet 185
Carboplatin, Chemotherapy, Hair loss, Nausea management, Side effects, Taxol, Treatment

18. Treatment Teammates 199
AC, BRCA1 gene, Carboplatin, Chemotherapy, Infusion, Side effects, Support groups, Taxol, Triple-negative breast cancer

19. Home Run.. 211
Treatment success, Emotional response to good news, Communication with medical team, Pathological complete response (pCR), Transition to post-treatment life, Celebration of milestones

Jacqueline's Journey..219
Triple-negative breast cancer, Unexpected diagnosis, Penguin cold capping, Treatment side effects, Emotional coping, Single patient challenges, Fertility concerns, Support system, Career impact, Personal growth, Mentoring other patients

Tracey's Journey 225
AC, BRCA1 gene, Chemotherapy, Family support

Batter Up: Treatment... 237

Part IV:
Surgery 244

20. Batting Practice... 245
Breast reconstruction, DIEP flap, Mastectomy, Travel

21. Game Time... 257
Breast reconstruction, DIEP flap, Lymph nodes, Mastectomy

Andrea's Journey... 267
Advocacy, Breast reconstruction, Mastectomy, Surgery

Cindee's Journey 279
Stage-IV cancer, Metastatic cancer, Breast reconstruction, Mastectomy, Surgery

Lesley's Journey 285
DCIS (Ductal Carcinoma In Situ), Bilateral mastectomy, fertility, Nurse Navigator

Batter Up: Surgery 290

Part V:
Recovery..292

22. The Ninth Inning 293
DIEP flap, Exercise, Lymph nodes, Surgery, Travel

23. Next Season's Curveballs 299
Immune system, Radiation therapy, Recurrence, Triple-negative breast cancer

Susan's Journey 307
AC, Cold capping, Genetic testing, Hair loss, Radiation therapy, Recurrence, Side effects, Support groups, Taxol

24. The Win 313
Survivorship, Travel, Triple-negative breast cancer

Batter Up: Recovery 320
Conclusion 325
Acknowledgments 333
Endnotes 339
Index 341
About the Author 345

Introduction

Nothing can prepare you for the gut punch of hearing a doctor say, "I'm sorry, you have breast cancer." Your world stops spinning at that moment, and you're left gasping for breath, desperate for a lifeline. That's where *Crushing the Cancer Curveball* comes in.

For more than four decades, I've been in the cancer trenches—first as a caregiver to my mom, then my mom again, then my sister, then mom again, and then as a patient myself. I've seen how the prevailing narrative around cancer—reinforced by movies, TV shows, and books—tells us that a diagnosis equals a death sentence. But I'm here to tell you *that* narrative is dead wrong.

The truth is that most women diagnosed with breast cancer will survive and go on to live long, fulfilling lives. **The five-year survival rate for localized breast cancer is a whopping 99 percent.** Let that sink in. Ninety-nine percent of women with early-stage breast cancer will still be here in five years, and most will be thriving. Five years is considered a meaningful milestone because, for most cancers, if a patient survives five years after diagnosis without a recurrence, their prognosis for long-term survival improves significantly. Even clinical trials have a five-year endpoint for studying new treatments.

Localized breast cancers are by far the most common diagnosis, and early detection is today's only approach to identifying breast cancer early. If you don't read another word of this book, know the importance of doing the following:

- Learn about your personal risk for breast cancer. There are several risk tools available online (I'll link to them at www.joellekaufman.com). As for 2024, you can join the Wisdom Study (www.wisdomstudy.org) if you are between the ages of thirty and seventy-four and have not had breast cancer. It's free, primarily online, and committed to finding more effective screening methods for breast cancer and making sure women at high risk are aware of options for risk reduction. Participating in this and other studies will help you and every woman you love.
- If you are over forty and eligible for a mammogram, discuss your risk profile and appropriate screening interval with your doctor. Then put reminders on your calendar to schedule a screening and make it happen.
- If you are told you have dense breasts, make an appointment with an expert in dense breasts to explore your risk and screening options.

- If you have a strong family history of breast cancer, especially with onset at young ages, ask your doctor about genetic testing, including polygenic risk, and more frequent screenings, which could include bilateral MRIs. Everyone's risk profile is unique, and you should discuss what's best for you with your doctor.
- For goodness' sake, touch your breasts regularly because 50 percent of women found their tumors themselves. In the I SPY 2 personalized medicine trial of 2,750 women with stage II-III breast cancer, 85 percent were not found by screening. You need to know what they feel like so if you feel anything different, you can notify your doctor immediately.[1]

Because one in eight women in the United States will be diagnosed with breast cancer in their lifetime, despite spectacular survival statistics, it is still the second largest cancer killer of women. According to the American Cancer Society, it is estimated that in 2023, about 43,250 women will die from breast cancer in the United States. And it's racially unfair, with the mortality rate being 42 percent higher for Black women compared to White women. **Early detection is the key to reducing or eliminating breast cancer risks.**

This book will guide you whether you're a newly diagnosed patient, caregiver, or healthcare provider. You'll hear not just my hard-won wisdom but throughout the book are Journey chapters that share the stories and insights of survivors who have walked breast cancer's path. Their stories will make you laugh, cry, and see their strength reflected in yourself because *Crushing the Cancer Curveball* doesn't shy away from the tough stuff.

It celebrates the unexpected gifts that can come from a cancer journey, such as clarity, deepened relationships, and a renewed appreciation for the preciousness of life. It's about more than just adopting someone else's story; it's about the power of authoring your own.

In *Crushing the Cancer Curveball*, you'll learn:

- The first three things to do after being diagnosed with cancer to set yourself up for success.
- How to assemble a rockstar medical team to get the best personal treatment.
- Techniques for processing complex emotions and communicating your needs to loved ones.
- Strategies for preparing for and minimizing the physical and financial side effects of cancer treatment and surgery.
- Tips for transitioning back to your full, fabulous, post-treatment life.

Everyone knows someone who will, is, or has faced breast cancer. Cancer is one of life's curveballs, and like curveballs in baseball, it is possible to hit it out of the park. This book provides insights and lessons learned across the five phases of cancer: prevention, diagnosis, treatment, surgery, and recovery. The chapter names build on the baseball analogy but the topics covered in each chapter are listed in the Table of Contents. Read it end to end, delve into the section that meets your current needs, or use the Index or Table of Contents to go directly to the content on the specific topics that interest you. Learn what to ask, do, and anticipate for every stage of the cancer journey, supported by personal stories illustrating how others implemented different approaches. If you are supporting someone with cancer, I highly recommend Chapter 16—The Fans—as it will give you answers to "What can I do to help?" The information in this book can help you avoid unnecessary suffering, build deeper connections with loved ones, and make treatment decisions you feel good about. It can mean the difference between merely surviving cancer and emerging with a renewed zest for life.

While there's no one-size-fits-all cancer story, *Crushing the Cancer Curveball* will help you write yours from a place of power, not fear. Step up to the plate and show cancer who's boss. Let's crush breast cancer together, one hope-filled step at a time.

Digital Resources

Part I:
Prevention

1. Foul Ball

As I grew from a teenage girl to a woman, the narrative at every medical checkup was the same. "My mother battled breast cancer at thirty-six and again at thirty-eight," I'd tell the doctor. This shadow looming over me meant that unrelenting vigilance was the theme of my life from age thirteen. My unfailing annual pilgrimage—mammograms, ultrasounds, MRIs—was to ensure that if cancer dared to lurk, we'd catch it early when it was little more than a bully whose bark was worse than its bite. Early screening—both self-exams and imaging—saves lives. Although cancer is an umbrella term for many different diseases, and even breast cancer comes in many varieties, cancer can have radically different outcomes depending on when it is detected. Radiological screenings, such as mammograms and ultrasounds, result in a lot of false positives, but they do identify 80 percent of breast cancers. Treatment is almost always necessary, but early detection makes treatments highly effective, drastically improving the odds of survival.

When it came to screening and testing, I was lucky. Until recently, eligibility for annual screening only included the over-fifty crowd. But someone up there finally caught on that forty is the new fifty, so some doctors ordered them earlier. My genetics and family history entitled me to instant testing that started when I was thirty-three. Now, screening starts ten years before your close family member's onset; for me, that meant age twenty-six. When I needed a doctor's order for an MRI, I quickly called or emailed my OB-GYN. She sent requisitions without questions. If I thought I felt anything unusual in my breasts, a mammogram and ultrasound were assured. I joked that I was a Mills-Peninsula Women's Center frequent flier. I would have the equivalent of Global Services if there were a loyalty program.

There were nights I'd wake up when something felt off in my body or I had a routine screening scheduled the next day. I'd stare at the ceiling, wondering, *Is this the day when cancer comes for me? Were the odds in my favor?* Estimated survival rates can't predict the outcome for an individual. They are a way to understand the chances of a positive treatment result. As noted on the American Cancer Society website (https://www.cancer.org):

> *Survival rates can give you an idea of what percentage of people with the same type and stage of cancer are still alive a certain amount of time (usually five years) after they were diagnosed. They can't tell you how long you will live, but they may help give you a better understanding of how likely it is that your treatment will be successful.*[2]

When I was younger, I did not expect to be shocked by cancer's arrival, even though the prospect was scary, sad, and disruptive. The burning problems I faced throughout my twenties included staying current with screening, determining when and how to tell a life partner about my genetic time bomb, and what and when to share my genetic predisposition with our children if we elected to have them. At times, I'd worry that my cancer would be detected late and there would not be good options to extend my life. I feared that I would leave behind loved ones at a young age. I prayed that my children would not have to face cancer someday.

But most days, I didn't think about cancer at all. I knew I had dealt with it before and would likely deal with it again. I tried to see every day as a gift—even the days that weren't extraordinary. I pushed the possibility of cancer out of my mind most of the time. Only on the days when there was a screening test or a funeral would the cancer elephant in the room move out from the corner and closer to the center, consuming more mental cycles. When I thought about cancer, I thought about screening and treatment advances. I planned for what I would do if cancer came for me. When we started dating twenty-seven years ago, I shared that plan with my husband, so Neal knew what he was signing up for.

Even before I had breast cancer, screening and testing saved my life.

It was October 1994, nine years after my mother's second successful treatment for breast cancer, when researchers published the discovery of the BRCA1 gene. I was in my first semester of business school. Somehow, the news about this gene and its unusual prevalence among Ashkenazi

Jewish women, like me, broke through the grind of case studies, classes, and study groups to catch my attention. A wave of relief flooded me. I'd always wondered why my mother developed breast cancer at thirty-six, and now I had an answer.

At the time, I wasn't aware that even among Ashkenazi Jewish women, most breast cancers are *not* BRCA1. Only one in five hundred women in the general population have the BRCA1 mutation; Ashkenazi Jewish women have a one-in-forty probability. And in my twenty-four-year-old mind, regardless of the evidence that my mother was the only woman in our family to develop breast cancer, I was confident that we were a BRCA1 family. Yet I did next to nothing about it.

My mother's breast cancer automatically put me in the high-risk screening population, regardless of genetic mutations. I knew to do self-exams, and when I was pregnant with my first two children, I chose OB-GYNs partially based on their rigor for clinical breast exams since the hormone surge of pregnancy can be a breast cancer trigger. Although testing was offered, I was not interested in a prophylactic mastectomy—the surgical removal of both breasts before a diagnosis of breast cancer. My memory of my mother's expanders (medical devices placed under the skin after a mastectomy to expand the skin for reconstruction) and multiple reconstructive surgeries was enough to convince me that I would have a bilateral mastectomy if I developed breast cancer, and I wouldn't do it before that point. Maybe it was fear or practicality, but I was not particularly anxious about my probability of developing breast cancer, and I didn't want to endure the risks of surgery for a disease I didn't have.

My sister Tracey's breast cancer diagnosis when she was twenty-nine confirmed my BRCA1 hypothesis. The BRCA1 gene was woven into our DNA fabric like an unwanted heirloom. My sister had the BRCA1 mutation. My mother was then tested and had the mutation, too. Mystery explained—except we have no idea where the cancer hid before my mom's diagnosis. My maternal grandparents never had breast cancer. Their parents and their parents' siblings, my great-grandparents and great-aunts and uncles, didn't have any breast cancer diagnoses or deaths. It's a genetic mystery. Although, screening is a twentieth-century advancement, and my ancestors could have carried the gene without knowing.

I still didn't get tested. My husband and I had two boys and wanted a third child, so I was sure I wouldn't act on the genetic confirmation if I tested positive for the gene. Illogically, I figured I was already older than my mother or sister were at their cancer onset, so perhaps I had dodged the genetic bullet. In any case, I was disciplined about screening. Every year, I had a mammogram, ultrasound, and bilateral MRI in addition to at least one clinical breast exam and usually more. My original primary care physician, Dr. Barry Oberstein (of blessed memory), used to do a breast exam whenever I saw him. One time, I was having a strange stiffness in my elbow, and he did a breast exam as part of his assessment.

I asked him, "Why a breast exam?"

He replied, "You will never visit this office and not get a breast exam. I will not be the doctor who missed it."

I chose to celebrate my screening exams as my biannual "I don't have cancer day" and looked forward to seeing my doctors. Twice a year, I held a mini-celebration—a cakeless, songless party to celebrate my peace of mind—assurance that I stood tall, arms akimbo against the genetic specter haunting my family's corridors. Unequivocally, it was a great day and a day when I was confident that my genetics weren't wreaking havoc on a cellular level. That was the mindset I created to mitigate anxiety and rumination by staying present to what I knew on that specific day—that I didn't have cancer.

Occasionally, there was a shadow on an image that the doctors wanted to biopsy. Twelve percent of screening imaging results in a biopsy. Most of those biopsies are negative, but false positive results are expected. While about 12 percent of 2D screening mammograms are recalled for more workup, only 4.4 percent of those recalls, or 0.5 percent overall, conclude with a cancer diagnosis. The frequency of my screening increased the frequency of my biopsies.

Biopsies are invasive and uncomfortable. My breasts were dense and sensitive, so even the MRI-guided biopsy was unpleasant. The core needle biopsy was positively torture, resulting in a grapefruit-sized bruise on the side of my breast that lasted over a month, and I am a rapid healer. In the spring of 2006, after another negative MRI-guided biopsy, I changed my mind about BRCA1 testing. If I tested negative, I wouldn't need this level of screening and would have a higher threshold for biopsies. Maybe I could stop using my breasts as pincushions.

Unfortunately, I tested positive. The BRCA1 gene was part of my genetic makeup.

The doctor likely expected me to be upset about the results, but they only confirmed a belief I'd held for more than a decade. I felt especially sad for my parents that they didn't have a single child (of two) who didn't have the gene. My mom still feels guilty about passing the gene on, even though I've assured her I'd rather exist, have her as my mom, and have the gene than any alternative.

Instead of feeling afraid, I felt empowered. I learned that in addition to my 80 percent lifetime probability of breast cancer, I also had a 40 percent lifetime probability of ovarian cancer. Granted, no one in the family ever had ovarian cancer, to the best of my knowledge, but before my mom, no one had ever had breast cancer, either. Unlike breast cancer, ovarian cancer has no viable screening. The conservative recommendation was that I should have my ovaries and fallopian tubes removed as soon as our family was complete, and preferably before age thirty-eight. Statistically, not only would my ovarian cancer risk fall below 5 percent, but my breast cancer risk would be halved to 40 percent. That's a significant reduction.

The downsides of having my ovaries and fallopian tubes removed at thirty-eight were the sudden crash into menopause and a reduction in the years my bones and heart were protected by estrogen. If I had the surgery, I would be eligible for hormone replacement therapy, provided it didn't include estrogen. While I thought early menopause would be uncomfortable, I expected it to be manageable. My weight-bearing exercises and cardio would compensate for the bone density issues and heart risks. The surgery is done laparoscopically as an outpatient and is free from serious risks.

Although I was thirty-seven at the time, I decided to have my ovaries and fallopian tubes removed after we had our third and last child. One of the lessons I learned from my mother's, sister's, and grandmother's cancer curveballs (Grandma didn't have breast cancer, but unfortunately, her second cancer was terminal) was to find a surgeon who specialized in the precise procedure I needed. This recommendation assumes financial and healthcare flexibility that isn't available to everyone. Still, I was lucky to live in a robust healthcare market in Northern California and found a gynecological oncology surgeon who was happy to take my case. He asked if I would permit my OB-GYN to scrub in, and I also welcomed her expertise. OB-GYNs can perform salpingo-oophorectomies. I scheduled the surgery for eight months after my daughter was born—right around my thirty-eighth birthday. My parents planned to visit California and could take our sons to the mountains for fun. My husband, daughter, and I could join them after my surgery, where I could recover on the couch, and Mom would handle feeding the troops. Everything would fall into place nicely.

Leading up to the surgery, I wondered how I would feel *on the other side*. Would I have a sex drive? Would sex be any different? Would I struggle with hot flashes? Would I experience menopausal weight gain? No one can tell you how your body will respond to the removal of organs, and hormone replacement therapy is different for every woman. I knew that the possibility of a late-stage diagnosis of ovarian cancer was something I didn't want to consider. Whatever was on the other side of surgery, I'd survive. For the curious, the answers to my questions were: Yes, I didn't lose my sex drive; no, sex wasn't all that different; yes, the hot flashes sucked; and yes, menopausal weight gain is real.

I haven't regretted my decision. I've spoken with numerous women considering the same surgery for similar reasons, and I am happy to share that my laparoscopic, bilateral salpingo-oophorectomy was possibly the biggest non-event of my healthcare resumé. My wisdom teeth being removed was more uncomfortable than this surgery. The surgery was quick, and afterward, my belly was moderately bloated for a few days, accompanied by the feeling of having been punched.

When I met with my surgeon for the four-week follow-up exam, he said, "I rarely get to say this, and I hope you don't mind, but you don't have cancer, and I hope I never see you again." That sounded like a fabulous plan. While the ball had come at me hard, I'd hit it into no-man's-land. I had the BRCA1 gene, but knowledge is a powerful tool. I took what I learned from medical screening and testing and used the information to make rational, educated decisions that improved my survival odds.

You can, too.

Five-year survival stats leap up to a cheering 99 percent when breast cancer gets a premature eviction notice. These are the stakes where early detection shines. When breast cancer is caught early enough, treatment becomes less a behemoth and more a season in your saga—lived, learned, and left behind.

LESSONS LEARNED

☐ Breast cancer *screening* is a preventative measure conducted before a breast cancer symptom arises. Screening tests include mammograms and ultrasounds. Breast cancer *biopsies* are done when a symptom is discovered via regular screening or a doctor's physical exam. Both can save your life, so ensure you book regular breast cancer screenings and have symptoms tested as soon as possible.

☐ The results of breast cancer screenings and tests allow you to make rational, educated decisions about your health.

☐ When breast cancer tests are needed, there are several types of tests conducted by medical professionals. These can include mammograms (breast X-rays), ultrasounds, MRIs, and biopsies. For the best care, if possible, research and meet with doctors who specialize in the specific test or procedure recommended by your medical professionals.

☐ There are hormonal and genetic links between breast cancer and ovarian cancer. If you have the BRCA1 gene, you have a 45 to 85 percent risk of developing breast cancer, and your lifetime odds of having ovarian cancer are 10 to 45 percent, according to Johns Hopkins Medicine.

☐ Although the scientists studying breast cancer are still learning more about this disease, the BRCA1 gene *can* be detected. If you have a family history of breast cancer, perhaps this test would provide you and your medical professionals a leg up.[3]

2. Curveball

My life was peppered with off-speed pitches, including being pregnant, unemployed, ventures losing funding, jobs doing things I didn't believe in, and the everyday curveballs everyone sees. The cancer curveball seemed relegated to family history as we approached the twentieth anniversary of my mother's first cancer diagnosis, and she was still active and thriving. My sister, Tracey, and I were screened for breast cancer regularly, but otherwise, cancer was not something we worried about.

In hindsight, we were naïve.

Tracey got engaged on February 14, 2003, and her destination wedding in Cabo was planned for the next Valentine's Day. My husband and I were blessed with our second child, due in mid-November. Plans for the wedding were concrete, so I learned when and how to get a passport for a newborn. My sister and her fiancé trained and completed an Ironman triathlon in August 2003. Everyone loved spending time with my son Ben. He was a toddler then and excited about the new baby. We all looked forward to a weekend in Cabo to celebrate Thom and Tracey's nuptials.

Three months before their wedding, I was thirty-nine and a half weeks pregnant. My mother called twice, so I knew something was wrong. The suspicious breast lump that Tracey had had removed was malignant. I didn't know about the lump because she and her doctors thought it was no big deal. Yet it was.

I was right; we are a genetically cancerous family. Everyone is born with a genetic makeup; genes pass from one generation to the next. Genes have a say in more than eye or hair color. Some make us susceptible to diseases and health conditions. A predisposition to cancer can be inherited.

My sister's surgeon didn't have the grace or sensitivity to wait five minutes for Thom to get home to be with Tracey when he gave her the news via a phone call. She was devastated. We all were. We saw the curveball release with no idea how fast it was moving or what trajectory it would take. We waited for pathology reports, oncology appointments, and a treatment plan. Even with a lifetime of experience, we were shocked this was happening to her at twenty-nine. And we had no idea what this meant for their wedding.

My doctor wanted me screened by a radiologist immediately. That's when I met Dr. Harriet Borofsky, the founder and chair of the Mills-Peninsula Women's Center.

"Hi," she said, "I'm Harriet, and we'll take excellent care of you." Harriet covered my belly with a lead blanket.

I had to contort to ensure each enormous breast was properly X-rayed. "My twenty-nine-year-old sister was just diagnosed with breast cancer. What can you possibly see so close to delivery? The baby is due any day now."

"Well, I can see a lot more now than when your milk comes in and it's a white-out. And while the odds are very, very low that you have cancer, they're not zero, and we should get a baseline. Do you plan to nurse, and for how long?"

"Twelve months."

"Breastfeeding is wonderful," Dr. Borofsky said.

Because my breasts are naturally dense and I was almost forty weeks pregnant, Harriet also performed ultrasound exams. Although mammograms are an outstanding technology, they miss the ball around 20 percent of the time. Like me, those with dense, mysterious breast tissue play a game of hide-and-seek with detection technology. And let's not even get started on lobular cancers—those sneaky ninjas can bypass a mammogram's searchlight altogether. That's why a trusty MRI is like the superhero sidekick we need, though it's got a price tag worthy of Bruce Wayne. I exhaled with relief when Dr. Borofsky told me she didn't see anything suspicious and asked me to make an appointment when I stopped nursing.

Shortly after that, we joyfully celebrated the birth of my son, tinged with the sadness of knowing Tracey had to face the cancer curveball twenty years after my mother had. And it wasn't going to be easy.

LESSONS LEARNED

- [ ] No one can prepare for cancer. The news is always a shock, even if you have a family history of cancer. All you can do is keep calm and cover your bases.

- [ ] It's always a good idea to screen for breast cancer when a close family member, like a sibling or parent, is diagnosed with breast cancer. Breast cancer can be genetic.

- [ ] When pregnant, ultrasounds and mammograms provide medical professionals with a solid baseline to compare future tests. Ideally, screening should be done before the breasts are ready to lactate.

3. Close Call

My confidence faded in late 2021 when my doctors saw a suspicious mass during a routine screening test. *Was cancer finally coming to call? Were my cancer-free days over?* My doctor scheduled an MRI-guided biopsy, and I braced for the physical and mental discomfort.

In the week between the biopsy and the pathology report, my sister, Tracey, and I discussed my uncertainty. I was concerned about a positive cancer result after three or four false alarms. I had a bad feeling about it. I worried I had pushed my luck. Dr. Harriet tried to reassure me, noting that even for people with the BRCA1 gene, 75 percent of suspicious areas are nothing. Tracey thought it would be helpful, informative, and anxiety-reducing if I consulted a plastic surgeon to discuss the possibility of a prophylactic mastectomy, even though, in the past, I'd been against preventative surgery that removed my breasts. Meeting with the surgeon would give me knowledge about my options for surgery and reconstruction, including pain, loss of sensation, recovery time, and likely aesthetic results. She offered to join me for the appointment.

As someone who likes having control and information, I took Tracey's advice. Her cancer experience made her a valuable source. I booked an appointment with a plastic surgeon who performs the deep inferior epigastric artery perforator (DIEP) flap procedure, where surgeons harvest belly fat to form breasts and do microvascular surgery to connect the blood supply to the new breasts. This type of reconstruction did not use any implants or expanders. Instead, the DIEP flap used only my tissue to reconstruct breasts. Doing a nipple-preserving mastectomy would keep my nipples for my reconstructed breasts instead of 3D tattoo nipples. Based on my research, this type of surgery had the fewest side effects and the most natural results of all the breast reconstruction options.

Tracey came with me to see Dr. Buntic. He had my medical details from my doctor, and we discussed my genetic history and the biopsy while my sister parked the car.

"I have the results of your biopsy," said Dr. Buntic. "Do you want to know?"

I was stunned and silent—an unusual state for me. I hadn't heard the test results were in.

Dr. Buntic didn't know me, but he read my expression and smiled. "They're good," he added, scanning the paperwork before him. "Do you want to know?"

"Well, if you put it that way …"

"You don't have cancer."

It was as if an invisible boulder had been lifted from my shoulders.

My sister joined us, relieved to hear the good news, and the conversation moved to prophylactic surgery. The three of us had a productive, low-stress discussion about the pros and cons of this procedure. Dr. Buntic referred me to a breast surgeon, Dr. Susan Lee Char, because if I decided to go ahead with it, she would perform the mastectomies, and he would do the reconstruction. Dr. Buntic radiated competence and skill; I felt confident in his care. But I still wasn't sold. I would have a bilateral mastectomy with a DIEP flap if I were ever diagnosed with breast cancer, but not before. Dr. Buntic said the decision was mine, but he recommended I seriously consider the prophylactic procedure because I was strong and healthy—my recovery would be easier without having endured chemotherapy.

We left it at that. I had a lot to think about.

Months passed, and I realized I was making a mistake by ignoring my family history of breast cancer. *It couldn't hurt to learn more*, I thought. I booked an appointment with Dr. Lee Char in the winter of 2022.

Dr. Lee Char explained some of the risks associated with the procedure and ways to mitigate them. The most significant risk was that my skin wouldn't receive enough blood supply after the DIEP flap and that, instead, the skin would become necrotic, which is a medical term for "dead." *Dead skin is not a good thing.* In basic terms, necrosis is tissue death due to a lack of blood flow or oxygen. There was about a 25 percent probability of that occurring for women like me whose natural breast size was cup size D or larger. She recommended we reduce my cup size to C, heal for three months, and then do the mastectomy and DIEP flap. The risk of necrosis would fall to less than 5 percent, and my appearance wouldn't be significantly different. She also recommended the prophylactic approach.

Over the next few months, I wrestled with the idea of removing my breasts to reduce my cancer odds. *My sister and mother had breast cancer, so I might have it as well. But why have major surgery for a disease I don't have now? Screening and testing mean early detection, so isn't removing my breasts excessive?* Breast cancer didn't keep me awake at night, but the idea of removing my breasts did. I'd already sacrificed my ovaries and fallopian tubes to be safe. And this wouldn't be a minor, no-brainer surgery like the salpingo-oophorectomy. A bilateral mastectomy, also known as a double mastectomy, was a significant surgery with a lot of potential issues. The outcome wasn't guaranteed; infection and pain were concerns. Beyond the possible complications, I'd lose sensation in my nipples and parts of my breasts. *What would that mean to my sex life? What would it be like to have breasts I can't feel?* I was proud of my rack—they'd fed each of my children for a year.

The memory of my mother's breast surgery haunted me. I envisioned her in the hospital, looking worn and scared. Her surgery required tissue expanders to stretch the breast skin and chest muscles to accommodate breast implants. The process was painful, and she seemed extremely uncomfortable. I also saw my sister after her bilateral mastectomy. The skin of her reconstructed breasts was angry and red. The pain made her irritable and frustrated. She was hospitalized due to an infection the doctors couldn't control with outpatient medication.

She required a long course of IV antibiotics. And the scar tissue would be a lifelong problem.

No, thank you.

I was attached to my breasts, figuratively and literally, so reconsidering a position I'd held for twenty years was daunting. Having this surgery felt alarmist and reactive—two things I was not. I was levelheaded. I managed anxiety well and refused to be guided by fear. Volunteering for surgery when I didn't have a disease felt illogical.

But what if I was wrong?

I asked various people their opinions. My physician, friends, and family were advocates of the surgery—they wanted me alive. Tracey said, "Why would you subject yourself and your family to chemotherapy if there was a possibility of avoiding it?" But I'm tough, and I was confident that I could endure anything for a period. I knew that cancer treatment wasn't endless. And my sister had chemo amnesia; she didn't remember the worst of her chemotherapy experiences. My brother-in-law and I remembered it vividly. From my perspective, treatment would be harder on the people who loved me. The brain understands self-preservation; I wouldn't likely remember much of it. And I would be drugged.

Preventative surgery was my decision to make, and I didn't want to be pressured.

Ultimately, my sister-in-law Heather made one of the best arguments. As a cancer survivor and a physician, the woman had clout. "Why not do it now when you are healthy and can control the timeline?" she said. "Your body will find other ways to compensate for lost sensation." She argued that my body's response to the surgery would be better and complications fewer if I did this while I was young and cancer-free. Statistically, the probability of breast cancer increases with age, and chemo suppresses your immune system, so surgery after chemo brings additional risks.

During this time of great debate, several friends were diagnosed with cancer. Although most of them became cancer-free through treatment, a few did not. When my friend Dana passed at fifty-one, I was struck by how unfair it was. She was too young, too vibrant. Like Dana, I had so much to live for, including the adventure of my children's lives and exploring the world with my husband. I wondered if I was being arrogant by playing a game of Russian roulette with the BRCA1 gene.

I'm not sure what changed, but something did. Perhaps it was the working of "the breast cancer machine," where momentum gathers for surgery. Maybe it was the appeal of control—the ability to plan the surgery and recovery as I wanted. Perhaps it was the wasted emotional energy spent on tests showing suspicious masses or the physical pain caused by the multiple biopsies. After twenty years, I possibly wanted to retire from my frequent-flier status at the Mills-Peninsula Women's Center. I don't know when I decided to ditch my hold on my breasts, but I did.

The close calls were too much.

LESSONS LEARNED

- [ ] Statistically, preventative tests and surgeries for breast cancer save lives.

- [ ] Learning about preventative tests and surgeries allows you to make educated decisions. Don't hesitate to discuss your options with medical specialists.

- [ ] Allow yourself the time needed to debate the pros and cons of preventative surgery. While the decision-making process can be a roller coaster, remember that everyone's circumstances are different, and what's right for one person may not be right for another.

- [ ] Prophylactic surgery is an intensely personal decision. Only you can decide if breast removal is right for you. While the opinions of your doctors, family, and friends can provide you with perspective, the decision is ultimately yours to make.

4. Safe at Home

Once I decided to have the preventative surgery, I was laser-focused on forcing it to comply with my schedule. The lengthy surgery would involve three attending surgeons, three fellows, and at least two anesthesiologists. Advance scheduling was vital. Dr. Buntic wanted three months between the reduction surgery and the extensive bilateral mastectomy and DIEP flap reconstruction surgery. I didn't want to start until the winter holidays were over, but I wanted to be done early in the new year so I would recover enough to travel to Florida to watch our son Taylor play spring baseball during his first year at Hamilton College. Although all three kids were aware that the BRCA1 gene massively increased the probability of breast and ovarian cancer in our family, they also knew how I felt about their education and well-being. I wanted my children to stay focused on school and the extracurricular activities that kept them healthy. The reduction surgery was booked for October 2022 so I could celebrate my parents' fifty-fifth wedding anniversary and take our big family vacation in late December. The mastectomy and DIEP surgery were scheduled for January 2023.

The breast reduction was going to be a short surgery, and its purpose was to lift the breasts and eliminate enough mass and skin to minimize the necrosis risk. A few weeks before the reduction, I asked friends who had experienced mastectomies or reductions about the loss of sensation and its impact on their intimate relationships. Every one of them confirmed the reduction cut the nerves, and I would lose sensation in my nipples and lower half of my breasts. Sensation loss was to be expected. Although this worried me, I was relieved that they also noted their bodies found ways to compensate. I didn't ask for details. I was sad I might lose sensations that I had enjoyed my entire life, but I didn't feel it would make me less feminine or less sexy.

I wasn't fond of the permanent scar tissue that would be visible around the nipple area and under my breasts, or how my body symmetry might be off if my breasts weren't balanced in size or shape. These concerns led me to seek a plastic vascular surgeon who specialized in DIEP flap breast reconstruction and a breast surgeon who specialized in nipple-sparing mastectomies. Many women struggle with these physical changes. While I knew my self-confidence was strong, how could I know how I'd feel in the future?

I had to let my concerns go. I'd made the decision, so all I could do was pray the surgery would protect me, my family, and my friends from the difficulties and fears of a breast cancer diagnosis.

During pre-op, the surgeon told my husband and me that I had a great anesthesiologist, but he was "a bit gruff." The surgeon didn't want us to be surprised. When Neal and I met the anesthesiologist, we weren't surprised at all. He was Russian—not gruff, just Russian. He walked me through the process of going to sleep and waking up. Then I walked into the surgery suite and laid eyes on the massive computer system for the anesthesia and the overhead lights. *That* surprised me. I would certainly be in the spotlight. Because I'm short, the nurses brought me a step stool to climb up onto the operating table so the anesthesiologist could do his thing.

I was nervous but relieved the party was starting.

The surgery went smoothly. I remember waking up in a bed with my husband, Neal, nearby and my right arm resting comfortably over my head. Dr. Buntic pulled the curtain aside, walked over to me, and said, "What are you doing with your arm?"

Half-conscious, I said, "I'm relaxing."

Dr. Buntic smiled. "While I'm glad you can move your arm over your head without pain, stop doing it so you don't pull out the sutures."

As time passed, the medically induced brain fog dissipated. I didn't feel a lot of pain and was able to manage it with acetaminophen and ibuprofen. I was nervous to see what my smaller, "lifted" breasts looked like. They were hiding under blankets and bandages.

The reduction surgery was an outpatient procedure. When it was time to change the dressing, I decided to look. The first view is the hardest because the sutures are red and angry. Although my chest looked different, I wasn't shocked. I looked how I expected I would look, which was reassuring. I knew I would adjust to the changes in time. I also learned from my mother, sister, and father's cousin that the scars would fade to almost nothing.

I'll never forget looking in a full-size mirror when I got home after that surgery. My reflection in the mirror had changed. My abdomen appeared bigger and pouchier below my slightly smaller breasts. I knew the mastectomy and DIEP flap "tummy tuck" would help, so the pouch was temporary, but still … My breasts looked a little perkier and a little smaller. There was no sensation from the nipples down. The certainty extinguished the last flicker of hope of retaining some feeling. The "girls" were a physical asset I liked. I liked how I looked in dresses and lingerie. I remembered laughing when I put on a push-up bra at Victoria's Secret in my twenties because I looked ridiculously buxom. When I nursed my children, I marveled at my breasts' ability to sustain life. In that mirror, I looked at my changed body with sadness, resignation, and recognition that I was doing the right thing for my future. This wasn't something I did because I was bothered by how my breasts looked or felt. I did this to prevent a disease that could kill me.

Before sending me home, Dr. Buntic popped by with instructions. "You can exercise gently after two weeks," he said. "Walking and biking with limited intensity should be fine. But no weight lifting for six weeks."

I could live with that.

"Oh," he added with a smile, "the pathology on the removed tissue was benign."

I smiled back. While only a tiny part of me was worried I'd hear the opposite, all of me was happy with the news. I went home lighter in several ways.

Once life resumed, my scars faded quickly. Dr. Buntic said I was in the top one percent of healers he'd seen in his extensive career. That was likely a combination of genetics—thanks to my mom and dad—plus my long-standing investments in exercise and healthy(ish) eating. I suspected my mindset was also vital. I listened to and respected my body's needs while it healed, asked for and accepted help from my community, and stayed focused on my near- and long-term goals. I was determined to enjoy the upcoming family holiday as a liberated woman.

I was six weeks away from dodging breast cancer for good.

With my newly reduced breasts healed, my family traveled. Our immediate family went on an annual ski trip and then met with extended family for fun in the sun to celebrate my parents' fifty-fifth wedding anniversary in December 2022. Everyone was healthy, optimistic, and confident that my January 2023 surgery would also be a success. We could finally put the specter of breast cancer into a far corner of our minds.

My last regularly scheduled breast MRI was in June 2022, and it was all clear. I was feeling quite triumphant. In December, even though I would typically have a mammogram and ultrasound, I didn't schedule either. My breasts were still recovering, and they were going to be removed in January anyway.

Dr. Lee Char arranged for a mammogram and ultrasound pre-surgery. "Just in case," she said.

"Why?" I asked. "What is the purpose of pre-screening?" I was curious. When my mother and sister had cancer, they jumped right to surgery.

"It's just a protocol," Dr. Lee Char assured me. "Sometimes, though rarely, we discover something that requires we change our surgical approach."

Freshly home from our vacation, I cheerfully arrived on the third of January and was nonplussed when the radiologist needed additional pictures of my right breast. *Easy peasy. I've been here before.* After the ultrasound, the radiologist said there was a suspicious area, and they'd like to do an MRI. MRIs are the gold standard for cancer screening. My nonchalance didn't fade. *Why worry? My breasts are being removed in a week anyway.* Regardless of the biopsy results, I wasn't worried about a curveball because I already had an ironclad plan. No matter what, my breasts would be gone in a few days. Even if I did have cancer, it couldn't be advanced; I was cancer-free only months ago. And the surgery would eradicate it.

After the MRI, the Mills-Peninsula Women's Center called to say I needed a core needle aspiration (CNA) biopsy. The test could take time to organize. *Would the surgery be bumped?*

My resolve wavered, but I advocated for myself and pushed to follow the original timeline. Not only was I mentally set on the existing plan, but I also had family traveling to support me through the surgery and recovery period. Moving the surgery would be a lot of hassle. If the doctors needed to know in advance whether the suspicious mass was cancer, they were going to have to adjust to fit the original schedule.

Somehow, they found an 8 a.m. appointment for me on the fifth of January.

The CNA was more uncomfortable than I'd anticipated. The sound of the biopsy device was so loud that the radiologist warned me not to jump when I heard it. It was also excruciating, even with my high pain tolerance. When I felt brass knuckles collide with the side of my right breast, I told the radiologist, "I think you buried the lede there." I wasn't sure if the biopsy was more painful because I had been so pushy about getting it done quickly or if they were always painful.

No one mentioned the considerable and lasting pain I would have following the procedure, either. It was worth it, though: my surgery remained on track, and the disruption to my life was on my timeline.

I went through the weekend preparing myself for the surgery and recovery. Maybe I was delusional, but I think the magnitude of the extended surgery—it would take ten to fourteen hours—in addition to previous false alarms, distracted me from the possibility that, this time, it was cancer.

Besides, I didn't have time to worry. Tracey thought it would be fun to have a Bye-Bye Boobies party the night before the surgery so my girlfriends (and guy friends) could say "thanks for the memories" and send my breasts off into the sunset. My girlfriend Jessica was the master planner and organized the invitations, food, and cocktails.

I didn't know that would be my last close call.

LESSONS LEARNED

- [ ] Your mindset and timing are essential when planning a surgery. Take the lead and advocate for a schedule that works for you and your family.

- [ ] When you look at your body after breast reduction surgery, you might feel several emotions—good and bad. This emotional roller coaster is typical. Let yourself grieve the loss, knowing you've decided to improve your health.

- [ ] Follow your doctor's orders after surgery so the healing goes as planned. While infection isn't always easy to avoid, keep the surgical area clean. Stitches and staples will remain in place if you don't overexert yourself during recovery.

- [ ] Don't forget to celebrate the small stuff. Gather friends and family close to help you through potentially rough times and to celebrate life.

Jessica G.'s Journey

Not everyone has the same experience with the medical system as I've had. At thirty-seven, Jessica was a mental health professional who worked with autistic teens. She'd worked hard to lose ninety pounds and ran marathons. When Jessica first found a lump, she was shocked. Although her mother was in remission from Stage IV kidney cancer, no one in her family had had breast cancer. *Perhaps the lump is nothing?* she thought.

Unlike me, Jessica didn't have direct access to specialized care. She had to pay $1,200 out of pocket to recognize her concern as valid. She plunged into the complex web of healthcare and insurance protocols and learned the intricate dance of insurance policies and medical procedures.

In Jessica's first battle against the system, one practitioner dismissed her cancer fear as inconsequential, suggesting she had an eating disorder. She did not. And the diagnosis came soon enough. After paying for an ultrasound, the radiologist detected a possible tumor. "Well, at least I know how I'm going to die," Jessica said, trying to wrap her head around the news. When the radiologist didn't respond, Jessica morphed into fight-or-flight mode. "How do I get things scheduled?" The suggestion of a biopsy brought challenges, with the available facilities unable to conduct one of the two biopsies needed. This limitation tested Jessica's patience and underscored the logistical limitations within the healthcare system.

Jessica eventually got the tests. The biopsy was positive—she had breast cancer.

The referral to Texas Oncology was marred by incorrect information, setting off a marathon of phone calls to correct her name and birth date. The ordeal exemplified the systemic communication issues within healthcare, turning Jessica's procedure scheduling into an arduous task fueled by persistence and daily check-ins. "I'll call you tomorrow at noon and every hour after until we get the tests scheduled," she told one clinic receptionist. It was the only way to get the help she desperately needed.

This was nothing like my experience, but it is alarmingly common. The scheduling obstacles took a heavy emotional toll on Jessica. The tumor's growth during the long wait for tests and surgery added a terrifying urgency to her logistical challenges. Fear mingled with frustration as Jessica grappled with the system's inefficiencies, concerned that time might be slipping away. *Will cancer win this battle?* she wondered. The lack of communication from her healthcare providers exacerbated the emotional stress.

Despite these and many more trials, Jessica's story is one of incredible fortitude. While exhausting, system obstacles galvanized her into action. She eventually had a mastectomy, followed by chemotherapy. Her parents were present, and her dad visited twice during the chemo sessions to assist around the house. Support poured in from her circle of friends, cultivated over a decade in Texas. People brought her meals and walked her dogs when she couldn't.

"I kept running," said Jessica, sharing her story. She even managed a half-marathon while undergoing chemotherapy. Her running community organized a five-kilometer run with participants donning shirts in solidarity with Jessica. "I suspect running aided in expelling the toxins from my body," she said. Her body needed all the help it could get. She struggled with a loss of appetite. "Food was tasteless—textures unappealing. Simple tasks like drinking a smoothie took an hour. The nausea and gastrointestinal discomfort were awful. I could shed six pounds in a day due to stress-induced eating issues." During her final chemo session, a cough emerged, causing concern, but Jessica insisted on adhering to the schedule.

Radiation treatment was the most difficult. The radiation sessions initially progressed smoothly until the twentieth round intensified, leaving Jessica in tears on the treatment table. A computed tomography (CT) scan for a procedure related to her breast cancer involved her legs, confusing uncooperative staff and complicating insurance approvals. Jessica's resolve was further tested in her pursuit of reconstructive surgery. "I read a whole book about going flat," she told me. "My doctors asked why I was reading a book about breast removal without reconstruction. They didn't understand why I needed to hear the counterargument. I was choosing the surgery, but what was I *not* choosing?"

Amidst tears and frustration, only Jessica's relentless follow-up ensured she found the medical help she needed—ready to drive across the state if necessary—to save her life. She adopted a proactive stance, refusing to be passive in the face of administrative indifference. Her engagement with the system, demanding and securing her place in it, speaks volumes about her resilience. Her story, from the initial diagnosis to the final rounds of treatment, accentuates a crucial critique of the healthcare system. It highlights the need for a more responsive, efficient, and patient-oriented approach. Although my experiences were mostly positive, Jessica's scheduling nightmares and insurance hurdles underscore the broader challenges breast cancer patients face in accessing timely and accurate care.

Jessica's advice for others battling the cancer machine? "When the system is against you, focus on what matters. I used to strive for success, aiming to climb the corporate ladder. Facing cancer shifted my perspective. Now, I value a simpler, more fulfilling life. I appreciate the little joys."

Like Jessica, be your own hero.

LESSONS LEARNED

- [ ] Not everyone has access to quality medical care. Some people experience long wait times or pay large sums of money for breast cancer tests and procedures—even life-threatening medical treatments. Appreciate what you have and show empathy for those with less.

- [ ] When the system places obstacles to getting the medical treatment you need, don't give up. Instead, get organized, be proactive, and be persistent. You are your strongest advocate.

- [ ] Sometimes, you must drive far or fly to receive breast cancer treatment or surgery. This is especially true if you live in a small community with limited medical facilities or doctors.

- [ ] Don't hesitate to accept help from friends and family. When going through breast cancer testing, treatment, or surgery, remember that a cooked meal, a clean house, and help with your pets or children can make the experience tolerable.

- [ ] Engage in activities that bring joy to your life. Focus on hobbies, extracurricular activities, and passion projects to stay positive during trying times.

BATTER UP

For those on the brink of turning forty or who have swept past the benchmark—please, hear this as the chorus of every story like my own: *Discuss your personal screening plan with your doctor.* Yes, a mammogram is awkward. Yes, a mammogram is a squish-and-squirm affair. But think of it as swapping minutes of discomfort for countless days of living bold and unbridled.

Prevention can end your cancer story before it starts.

And, before cancer does come knocking, be prepared. Build an emergency fund—money saved for unexpected health expenses. Consider life and disability insurance options. If you have life insurance, explore whether it includes living or accelerated benefits you can access during treatment. A credible insurance broker can help you. Always ensure your will is current and legally designates a power of attorney. These documents specify your wishes if you are incapacitated, even temporarily. Consult an estate attorney or use online forms like the ones available on Mama Bear Legal Forms.

Knowledge really is power.

Breast cancer statistical information can be found on various government and institutional healthcare websites or sources recommended by doctors. Although survival rates depend on the stage of cancer at diagnosis, tumor size, grade, and lymph node involvement, most websites suggest that for women with early-stage, non-metastatic breast cancer, the five-year survival rate at diagnosis is 99 percent.[4] If diagnosed with Stage IV cancer, that number drops to 24 percent, so it's important to catch cancer as early as possible. Self exams and screening tests aren't perfect, but they are all we currently have to spot breast cancer.

Hopefully, someday, breast cancer will be a thing of the past. Tech developing on the horizon promises screenings as casual as your morning latte run. Imagine a time when a blood draw infused with AI magic might reveal cancer's smoke long before the flames rise.

Dr. Peter Kuhn, a University of Southern California professor, scientist, and son of a cancer survivor, is working to transform the scare into a scan with the Pink Test. This test offers a future where "the smush test" becomes used after the blood test confirms there is a tumor to be found—minimizing unnecessary smushes and false positives with their accompanying anxiety and painful biopsies. Like a prostate-specific antigen (PSA) test for prostate cancer or a cholesterol test, this blood test for breast cancer could someday save the lives of countless women. Dr. Kuhn's lab gazed deep into the cosmos of our bloodstream and found a breadcrumb trail leading straight to breast cancer's door long before it morphs into a monster. While this technology is in its infancy, it is hope, and I am honored to be an advisor to his project.

I have a lot of skin in the game. I have three children, a niece, and a nephew, who may have to step into the batter's box and face a curveball. I want them to have every possible advantage science can provide. With my sister's first tumor manifesting at a relatively young age, my daughter and niece will undergo screenings earlier than I did. Our sons will need to share their genetic risk with prospective partners. In the dynamic landscape of medical advancements, promising developments are emerging. One such breakthrough is a treatment that potentially delays the onset of BRCA1-related breast cancers for years. This drug could provide young women who wish to start families the opportunity to do so and breastfeed their children before contemplating prophylactic surgery. The advent of mRNA vaccines might even unlock avenues to rectify the BRCA1 mutation entirely, eliminating its associated risks for future generations—the horizon beckons with hope and possibilities, a testament to our collective resilience and scientific progress.

Early detection isn't just a shot; today, it's your best shot. Remember to press, prod, and pamper yourself until we see a day when screenings come without pinches and pulls. Because somewhere between awareness and action, lies the power to change the game.

Start your batting practice, my friend. Your life may depend on it.

Part II:
Diagnosis

5. Little League

I was far too young to have to learn about breast cancer. I was thirteen years old, and my sister, Tracey, was nine. It was a Sunday night in November 1983. I don't know if we cried, but I remember the fear and anxiety when my mother and father asked my sister and me to join them in the formal living room. My mother looked shattered.

Cancer was a weighty word.

From what I remember, my dad told us that Mom was going to have surgery the following day and would probably be in the hospital for six or seven days as she recovered. My parents said they weren't a hundred percent positive, but the doctors thought it was likely that the lump my mother felt in her right breast was cancerous. If that was the case, they were going to do an immediate modified radical mastectomy. They also said they believed Mom would be all right after recovering.

There was nothing my sister and I could do other than hug our mom. We didn't know anyone whose mom had breast cancer—or any other cancer, for that matter. Our grandparents were flying in to help us. All we could do was wait for the ordeal to be over. We went to school the following day.

Monday afternoon, Dad called to say the lump was cancerous. They'd done the surgery, and Mom was recovering well. The doctors were sure they got it all. The tumor was small and hadn't been there long.

The definitive diagnosis devastated me. My first thought was that my mom was going to die. Even at that young age, I knew cancer was disruptive and deadly. My second reaction was anger. It was unfair that my mother—a healthy, active thirty-six-year-old physical education and health teacher who had just returned to working full-time after thirteen years of being a stay-at-home mom—got cancer three months into her new job. She was excited to return to teaching and coaching, even teaching some of my camp friends. Although I couldn't put my feelings into words at the time, I felt cancer was robbing her of her independence and identity.

It wasn't right. It wasn't just. My mother didn't smoke. She was fit and didn't drink alcohol. My mother had a beautiful figure, and surgeons had carved up her body to remove something that never should have been there. *Besides*, I thought, *young mothers aren't supposed to get cancer.*

It wasn't long before my worries expanded to how cancer would impact my life.

My mother and I were close. She was easy to talk to and genuinely interested in my life—even the trivialities. She recognized that my teenage challenges with teachers, friends, and crushes were significant to me and, consequently, important to her. Our relationship was affectionate and fun. With my mother's cancer diagnosis, virtually everything in my life felt insignificant. *Compared to a life-threatening, body-deforming, unpredictable illness, who cares if I'm upset about a test grade or a boy who doesn't mirror my interest?* It seemed disrespectful to even talk about such minor problems. I felt guilty thinking about the logistics of my life—getting to and from gymnastics, religious school, or friends' homes. The guilt didn't make other emotions go away; it just ensured I wouldn't share them with anyone because I was embarrassed to think of myself at all. *My mother had cancer.*

My mother had to focus on survival, so my father would care for me and my sister. I was sad for my dad and afraid of how his anger about the situation would unintentionally be directed toward me. He had few other mechanisms to express his emotions. It felt inevitable that I would do or say something wrong, such as asking for a ride to my activities. I braced myself for the familiar tirade about how selfish I was and how I should think of someone other than myself. This tirade has been a weekly occurrence since I was about five. I knew it would get worse with Mom's cancer, and I wanted to protect my sister from it even if I couldn't protect myself.

I isolated myself from my classmates, whom I didn't trust to be supportive. My maternal grandparents stayed for a while after Mom's surgery, and my grandmother was a good listener. Still, she was primarily concerned about my mother, and I didn't want to worry her about my fears or issues. The person who supported me the most was Dot Haley (of blessed memory), an older woman who stayed with Tracey and me when our parents vacationed alone once a year. Mom and Dad arranged for Dot to stay with us while Mom was in the hospital. Dot was a huge personality who suffered no fools. When Dad called me from the hospital after Mom's surgery, I hung up and started crying hysterically. Dot hugged me and, in no uncertain terms, told me to pull myself together. I think I was "allowed" to cry for about two minutes, and then Dot said that was enough. She stayed with us until Mom came home from the hospital and kept the household running while asking my sister and me about our lives, but with the expectation that we would buck up and cope. Dot clearly said we were not to worry our parents because they had enough on their minds right now. I needed someone to remind me that I was strong and could handle whatever we faced. Dot was likely the first person, besides my parents, who was confident I could hit this and any other curveball.

It took a few days longer for me to start worrying about my own cancer risk and what that meant for my dreams for the future.

My plan, at thirteen, was to finish high school, go to a good college, get a graduate degree, and build a successful and independent career while also finding a loving partner and raising a family. I wanted to have children but did not want to stay home with them as my mother did. Years of observing the tension and arguments over money in my childhood home convinced me to become financially equal to my partner and economically independent of my parents. None of my plans accounted for a massive interruption in the middle of my thirties to fight breast cancer or, worse, that my life might not last the ninety years I was expecting. Suddenly, my well-constructed and orderly life plan had unknown risks. No amount of hard work and healthy living could eliminate the breast cancer risk. If it could, there was no way my extraordinarily healthy mother would be facing this disease.

Shortly after my emotional reaction, I began to seek answers to why my mother had breast cancer, her prospects, and what I could do to protect myself. I didn't know it then, but I've since learned that when I sense or see a curveball coming, I seek information—I understand everything I can as soon as possible. I found news articles in the library and magazines that claimed early-stage cancers were treatable and patients should live long lives. This data mollified my fears. My mother would be okay.

I didn't realize that this was only the initiation of our family's extensive experience with cancer curveballs, particularly with breast cancer. It would ultimately touch my mom, my sister, and me.

LESSONS LEARNED

- [ ] Cancer is a scary concept for a person of any age. Children, especially, can struggle to understand the implications of a family member's cancer diagnosis.

- [ ] Children may feel a myriad of emotions when learning about a parent or sibling's cancer diagnosis. Guilt might be one of those emotions.

- [ ] For some people, knowledge is a powerful tool for easing stress. Adults and children can benefit from reading books, articles, or doctor-recommended medical papers regarding breast cancer. Don't be afraid to ask children what questions they have. If you don't have the answer, you can ask your doctor or nurse.

- [ ] Grandparents and family members can be a great support system for the cancer patient and their children. While physical assistance like cleaning and cooking can be helpful, just listening or offering a hug can do wonders for those in need.

- [ ] When outside help is needed, arrange for someone outside the family unit to stay in your home, cook meals, clean, or run errands. Voluntary and paid services offer this kind of assistance.

6. Cancer's Home Run

Dr. Lee Char called with the biopsy results on January 9, 2023. I was on a Zoom call for work when I saw the number on my cell phone. I was eager to hear the results because I was still hopeful that I would be proceeding with the prophylactic bilateral mastectomy and reconstruction the next day. Excusing myself, I took the call.

"I'm so sorry," said Dr. Lee Char, "it's malignant."

Breathe, I said to myself, *no need to panic. Remember that you've seen this curveball before, and before getting upset, you need more information. Information will bring you comfort.* My breasts were being removed the next day, so while cancer had won this inning, I was still in control of the game. "So we do the surgery tomorrow, and then what?"

Dr. Lee Char sighed. "I'm sorry, Joelle, but we cannot do the bilateral mastectomy tomorrow. The standard of care is often to do chemotherapy before surgery. It is called neo-adjuvant chemotherapy. Administering chemotherapy before surgery shows better outcomes in scientific studies for tumors with your pathology. Your oncologist will explain your options."

I felt like I'd been sucker punched. I'd resolved to have my breasts removed to avoid cancer, yet here I was with a positive cancer diagnosis on the eve of my surgery. I ended the call with Dr. Lee Char and returned to the Zoom session to let my associates know I needed to leave the meeting.

I sat at my desk, looking around my home office, trying to process the seismic shift in my life. *Chemotherapy* rattled through my head like an old lawnmower. My memories of chemotherapy were all bad. I'd watched my mother struggle through cancer treatment twice when I was a teenager. I'd held my sister Tracey's hand through rounds of chemo that made her very ill. I remembered what chemo did to loved ones, too. The feelings of helplessness were unsurmountable. The prophylactic surgery was meant to relieve my family of such heartache.

Get it together, Joelle. I had to focus on the here and now.

I dreaded it but needed to tell my husband, Neal. I dreaded telling my parents. *Oh my, how will I tell my kids?* I felt terrible that my children were about to experience something that had dramatically shaped my life. My kids were in the house—two temporarily home from college. I did *not* want to tell them until I told their father and until I was emotionally in a place where I could face their reactions and support them. You never stop being a mom, even when you have cancer.

My head was spinning with all the things I needed to do. In addition to getting information, doing something often makes me feel better. Simply trying to slow my mind down enough to put various thoughts into priority order was nearly impossible. I needed Jessica to cancel the Bye-Bye Boobies party she organized so that my friends could offer support in a lighthearted way, but that meant telling friends what was happening before I knew what I wanted to say or had the outline of a plan. I didn't want their pity and knew that their sadness and concern for me would be hard to accept graciously in this initial shocking moment. I paced the room, trying to determine my first steps. *Heather is here.* My sister-in-law was staying with us to help me and Neal through the surgery. Heather is a physician, works in oncology pharmaceutical safety, and is a cancer survivor, so she would know what to do. "Heather!" I called out, looking for her.

When she saw me, she stopped mid-step. I didn't need to speak. She knew I was waiting for the biopsy result and could see the outcome on my face.

Heather started taking notes—writing down everything I rattled off to help me organize my thoughts. Looking at the list of priorities on paper helped me gain focus. We decided it would be best for Neal for us to walk to his office and tell him in person. Heather could answer his questions with authority. We left the house quickly, as I did not want to face my sons. They'd know something was wrong, and I wouldn't lie.

I don't remember the five-block walk. Neal's company was based in Ohio, so he didn't have any colleagues I had to greet as I climbed the stairs to his office. Heather asked if I wanted her in the room, but I needed a few moments alone with Neal. I knocked and entered.

Neal looked at me, and his eyes welled with tears. A friend of ours, Dana, had died of cancer six months earlier after a long, brave fight. She left behind a devastated husband and three sons. She was exactly my age. Neal's father had died from complications following a bone marrow transplant for cancer, and his aunt and uncle had died of cancer as well. The only cancer survivors he knew were my mother, sister, and a couple of our business school classmates.

He had to ask: "Positive?" He was sitting in his office chair, and I stood before him.

"Yes." We cried with his arms wrapped around me.

I asked Heather to join us, and Neal asked us questions. I didn't know much. I told him that the suspicious mass in my breast was cancerous, I wasn't having surgery the next day, and I would be having chemotherapy at some point. Neal was completely behind me and ready to do whatever I needed to smash this curveball and the ones we would likely encounter until this experience was completed. It was vital to him to attend my initial appointment with the oncologist.

A few minutes after I spoke to Neal, I called my sister. She was sad but not shocked. We're never shocked when it's breast cancer in our family.

While I talked to my sister, Heather texted Jessica. Jessica and I have been friends since we were both six months pregnant with our now twenty-two-year-old firstborn children. She's my chosen second sister, and there's nothing in the past twenty-two years that we haven't shared. I would not approach these difficult pitches alone like my parents had forty-plus years prior. I was going to have a lot of people in the dugout and cheering from the sidelines. Jessica texted me after Heather told her. The text simply said: *Fuck.* She handled communication postponing the party so that it didn't force me to reveal the cancer diagnosis before I was ready. *Is anyone ever ready?* I didn't want anyone else to know before telling my kids. My friends mostly guessed before I told them.

LESSONS LEARNED

- ☐ "It's malignant" is one of the most difficult things to hear from a doctor. Cancer is not called "the Big C" for nothing—it's a life-altering diagnosis, even when treatable. Be kind to yourself and those around you when you or a loved one receives a cancer diagnosis.

- ☐ When given a breast cancer diagnosis, it's normal to experience a wide range of emotions—not all good. Let yourself feel what comes to you, then focus on sharing the news with the people close to you.

- ☐ A cancer diagnosis can be especially hard for children. As a parent, your instinct to protect your kids from your breast cancer diagnosis might be natural. Recognize and respect this instinct, and when you're ready, trust your children with the news. They are probably stronger than you think.

- ☐ Don't hesitate to turn to loved ones for physical and emotional support when you receive a breast cancer diagnosis. Express your needs and wants so your loved ones know how to support you.

7. Dugout Comradery

Part of me wanted to cocoon with Neal as if the breast cancer diagnosis couldn't get past our barricade. I felt protected there. But I couldn't live in a bubble, and I knew I would need my family's support to make it through the trying times ahead.

I had to tell my parents.

Since they live across the country, I had to get them both on the phone. I dreaded the call. When my sister was diagnosed with breast cancer, my parents had a very rough time. As my mother recalls, "In 2003, during one of my many daily conversations with Tracey, she told me she had felt a lump near her armpit and had seen her gynecologist, who told her it was nothing. 'A mere cyst. We'll recheck it in a month,' Tracey had said." Neither Tracey nor my mother were concerned. My mother didn't even mention it to my father, Malcolm, because she didn't want him to worry. He tends to jump to the worst-case scenario immediately. But they knew to follow up with the doctor. By that point, my mother had survived three rounds of cancer, so she was a pro.

At Tracey's next appointment, the doctor again said, "It's nothing," but Tracey wanted the lump out. "Thank goodness Tracey pushed to have it removed," said my mother, "because it was cancer! She saved her own life!"

When Tracey called our parents to tell them the lump was malignant, my mother freaked out. She was nauseous with worry. Mom just handed Dad the phone and said, "Tracey has breast cancer." Then she left him to talk to my sister. Although he handled the news well, he, too, was very concerned. My mother was a mess. She couldn't concentrate and cried at the drop of a hat. My father didn't know what to do with her. Tracey was only twenty-nine. She was engaged and hadn't had children yet. Their child had cancer, and they were in the dugout while she faced the pitch in another state. My mother wanted to fly to California quickly to be with her baby.

When they made it to California, they accompanied Tracey and her fiancé, Thom, to an oncologist appointment to hear the prognosis firsthand. My mother was a wreck. While she had dealt with her own cancer diagnosis reasonably, hearing your child has cancer is a different matter entirely.

I didn't know how my parents would react to learning cancer had come for me. But I had to tell them immediately because I wasn't having surgery the next day as planned. The prophylactic bilateral mastectomy was canceled.

They were outstanding on the phone.

"My doctors ran a set of routine scans to prepare for my surgery tomorrow and found something on the mammogram. I had a biopsy last Thursday, and today I got the results. The mass was positive. It's only nine millimeters, which is very small, but touching a lymph node."

I explained, for the third time that day, why I wasn't having surgery, but they understood the cancer diagnosis. Frankly, even though I didn't understand why the surgery was canceled, the doctors were unanimous on this recommendation, so I followed their lead.

"Okay. Have you found an oncologist yet? Can Tracey help?"

My mother's reaction was very different from when Tracey had called with the same news. Of course, she was upset, but the circumstances were significantly different. I was older, and my family was complete. Plus, we had survived cancer several times by this point.

My mother was sure the doctors had detected the cancer very early, and I would be fine. "Secretly," my mother later confessed, "I was angry you had waited so long to schedule the bilateral mastectomy. But as Tracey pointed out to me, it's challenging to have such a drastic surgery when there is nothing wrong with you." She felt terrible I would now have to go through chemo before surgery, but she was not as frightened as she had been with our family's previous diagnoses.

"You are going to need chemo? Thankfully, we know what you need to take to avoid the nausea. Oh, but your hair?" said my mother. "I want to be there to help," my mother added. "No matter how old you are, having your mom with you provides comfort. And I need to see you will be okay."

My parents asked a few more questions and supported Neal, me, and the kids. I told them Tracey or I would keep them informed as I learned more about the treatment plan. I also mentioned we had yet to tell the kids but would do so that afternoon. This news wouldn't stay quiet for long, and I wanted to limit the number of times I needed to tell the story. It wasn't a story that got better with repetition.

My kids, like my parents, had to be told that I wasn't going to have surgery the next day and why. Knowing they would support each other, we asked all three to join Neal, Heather, and me at our dining room table. Our family associates that table with good times, laughter, and deep and silly discussions. I sat at the head of the table with my sons on the left and my daughter on the right. I dreaded this moment. In my childhood, there was *before* cancer and *after* cancer. Everything was impacted by cancer. My sense of being different was exacerbated by cancer. Now, that schism was going to be something my children would experience. I didn't want them to worry about me or worry about themselves. I didn't want my sons to feel guilty about returning to school. I didn't want my daughter to take on the responsibility of caring for me or Neal.

There was no easy way to say it, so I was swift and direct.

"The doctors found a tumor, and that means my surgery must be delayed until after chemotherapy. The tumor is small, and I can't even feel it. It was detected early, which means my outcome will be great."

Each child responded differently before they asked a single question. My eldest, Ben, was a resilient, logical, and almost unemotional child. He listened intently and logically processed the information. He asked questions about what we knew and didn't know and what would come next. He accepted my confident assertion that I was going to be okay. My big, strong middle child, Taylor, teared up as his mind raced to worst-case scenarios. He was about to head across the country for his second semester of college. He was riddled with guilt, wondering how he could leave me. My daughter, Ariel, sniffled and cried quietly, fear and sadness emanating from her face. Since I was also fifteen when my mother went through chemotherapy for breast cancer, I had an inside look at Ariel's experience. There was no way I wanted my daughter to have anything like my experience with my mother's cancer. Other than ensuring I was going to live, my highest priority was to insulate Ariel from the obligations of being my caregiver. Ben and Taylor would be away at college, but Ariel would be home. I wanted her life to be as normal as possible. Neal was wholly aligned with me.

 I gave each of my children a job to help me over the next few months. This gave them a sense of purpose, a way to participate in a circumstance they had no control over. I'd planned their projects based on their talents and personalities. Ben was twenty-one and in his junior year of college. His job was to create an uplifting soundtrack I could listen to during chemotherapy sessions. Our shared love of music guaranteed that Ben would embrace the outlet for his emotions and that I would enjoy his song selection during hospital visits. Taylor was nineteen and starting college. I asked him to write to me before each chemo session, and I would aim to travel to his spring baseball in Florida and hopefully a series at Hamilton. By writing, I was hoping Taylor would keep the lines of communication open while focusing on school and baseball. And I was looking forward to reading the letters—they'd be an excellent distraction when the chemo made me feel ill or bored. Ariel was to entertain me with her live music, sports, and intellectual interests. Most of all, all three were to live big in their lives, filling my soul with happiness.

Even though I was the one fighting cancer, I knew my kids needed support. My sister's family, plus our village of three families who had raised our children together, rose to the challenge. Ariel had been dealing with anxiety, anorexia nervosa, panic attacks, and social challenges before this news. She was making fantastic progress, feeling healthier, more in control, and using all the available tools. I didn't want cancer to set her back, and she was about to have a front-row seat to what I remembered was the worst show on earth. Providence ensured she already had an appointment with her therapist that day, a specialist in adolescent psychiatry.

In an unusual move, since Ariel usually attended her therapy sessions alone, I walked into the doctor's office and asked to speak with him first. I said, "I'm handing you a pile of shit on a tray. I was diagnosed with breast cancer today. We told the kids about it thirty minutes ago. Ariel is a wreck and yours for the next fifty minutes."

The doctor didn't flinch. He asked, "How are you doing?"

"Pretty well. I suppose it isn't a huge shock, except for the timing. The tumor is small, and we've caught it early—although it did include a lymph node, which isn't great." Cancer cells inside a lymph node suggest the cancer is spreading and could move to other lymph nodes or parts of the body.

"Okay. I hope coming to my office for this session is the best place for your daughter. I'll do my best."

"I'm sure it is, and I'm sure you will," I said. "Thank you." He was a pinch hitter, and I needed the bases loaded.

Neal and Heather picked up Chinese food for dinner while I took Ariel to her therapy appointment. Over dinner, my children leaned on each other for support and shared their feelings. Taylor asked if he could talk about the cancer with two of his close friends—sons of two of my closest friends, Jessica and Regina. I was reassured knowing my kids had a network of friends and family they could turn to. While the future was uncertain, it wouldn't be easy for us. Ariel wondered what my diagnosis and our shared genetic material meant for her future. Medical ethics prohibit testing for the BRCA1 gene until she is eighteen, so she cannot know how significant breast cancer might be to her future.

Additionally, even if she learns she has the mutation, she's too young for any screening or prophylactic treatment. While I applauded her sense of self, I didn't want my cancer diagnosis to worry her. I remember feeling guilty about my health fears while my mother was being treated, and I didn't want my daughter to struggle with the same emotions.

While cancer was our family affair, I wasn't about to let it take over. I was, and would remain, in control.

LESSONS LEARNED

- ☐ Cancer is a difficult—if not impossible—path to walk alone. Share your breast cancer diagnosis and trials with your family so they can support you during trying times.

- ☐ If you feel a lump in your breast, tell your medical practitioner. If your doctor doesn't take it seriously, don't hesitate to push for testing. It's your body; only you know when something feels wrong.

- ☐ No matter your age, if you have a good relationship with your mother, you'll always want her by your side. Chances are that your mother feels the same. If there is ever a time it's expected you'll want your mamma, this is it.

- ☐ Avoid keeping your breast cancer diagnosis from your children—no matter their age. They can even handle learning about your treatment regimen and prognosis. While every child will respond differently, and people grieve in their own way, they are bound to surprise you with their resilience.

- ☐ Consider ways to keep your children's day-to-day lives as normal as possible after your cancer diagnosis. Friends and family are crucial to making this possible. Give them jobs and things they can do to help you. Everyone benefits from positive distractions and contributions.

- ☐ Give your children opportunities to show their feelings, talk, and ask questions. They may surprise you. Perhaps they will surprise themselves.

8. Team Sport

Many people—friends, colleagues, and clients—knew about my scheduled prophylactic mastectomy, so the cancer diagnosis would come as a surprise. And I knew I didn't have long before the news spread through our tight-knit community, many of whom were still reeling from the tragic loss of our friend Dana six months earlier. While every cancer is unique, and Dana's story was different from mine, I felt I needed to control the narrative and give people guidance about how to support me, especially before I knew the answers to their questions. I elected to send a broad email:

> *Hi friends,*
>
> *Some of you may know I had to defer my surgery today. I was diagnosed with breast cancer. The tumor is small, and we found it*

early, but it's aggressive. We've created a CaringBridge account to keep people informed.

Neal, the kids, and I welcome your texts and emails. We welcome opportunities to catch up, laugh, and feel your love and support. Prayers and good vibes are welcome, too. You all know I'll need more to think about than cancer.

Please let us ask before offering horror stories, medical advice, and suggestions. We don't know much yet, and a plan is being formulated. We hope to enjoy all aspects of our personal and professional lives while ensuring my energy goes first to healing. My friend Jessica will coordinate the details when we know more about what we need.

I'm fortunate to have all of you in my life, and I'm sure we'll need your help. My diagnosis isn't a secret, and you are welcome to share the information with others who know us and would want to support us.

I appreciate your friendship, your humor, and your love.

Love,

Joelle

Although I did not post about my cancer experience on social media—my interest in being targeted with cancer-related advertising was below zero—we set up a CaringBridge account with Neal, Heather, and Jessica as the authors. CaringBridge was an excellent communication tool where friends and colleagues could access updates from the source and share their positive vibes online. It's very tiring to repeat news about a diagnosis or treatment plan. The free platform replaces repeat texts, calls, and emails with the tools to connect, share, and document a cancer experience. Posts from CaringBridge became an outlet where I illustrated how I turned my cancer curveballs into home runs.

It's hard to know what to say to a recently diagnosed friend other than, "I'm sorry this is happening to you." Suggesting that things will be okay or cheering the person on is very tempting. *You will beat cancer!* Statistically, that's probably right. But statistics don't apply to an individual. And highly educated and trained specialists will convey confidence about the probable outcome. People say things with good intentions, hoping their words will help the person feel better. But platitudes might make the recently diagnosed feel compelled to communicate when they aren't feeling well or need to focus on their health. It's best to mention you were thinking of them and sending them love. They don't have to respond, and a quick thank-you is all that is needed if they do.

In my email, I was also explicit about the information I did not want. Some people believe in diets, alternative therapies, supplements, meditation, or drug regimens. Some are talented web researchers who find credible links to studies and protocols. These are all great but let the cancer patient ask for your advice before you offer it. When a well-meaning friend sends texts or shares uninvited information, the message may accidentally infer the patient is responsible for having cancer because of how they ate, exercised, slept, or indulged. Putting someone on the defensive will not help. If they want information from the Internet, they will search for it themselves or ask for assistance. They have probably received a deluge of information from their doctors and maybe even sought guidance from close family members or cancer survivors.

What a newly diagnosed person needs from friends and colleagues is an escape from cancer. Between family stresses, doctor visits, and treatments, their world will revolve around the C-word for quite some time. They need to hear what's happening with your life, family, and work. Talking about family, current events, entertainment, or life in general distracts and reminds them there is life beyond their circumstances. Playing cards, games, and walking are opportunities to feel normal and experience joy. The trivialities of life become an indulgence. Offer messages of love and support. If you are spiritual, send your prayers. Help the person feel safe, loved, and supported. Cancer takes time to treat, and there will be many opportunities to provide help. Stay in touch.

LESSONS LEARNED

☐ Friends and family will want to share your cancer news and support you. If you want to control the narrative, clearly define your communication style, preferences, needs, and limitations.

☐ Posting about your breast cancer diagnosis on social media is a personal choice. Some people enjoy sharing their cancer journey online, and others prefer to keep the experience private. As an alternative, CaringBridge is a free online platform that allows you to communicate your health news with friends and family in a safe and secure environment.

☐ There are nuances to communicating with someone who has been diagnosed with breast cancer. If you have cancer, be clear about your communication expectations. Ask before offering advice or assistance if you are a friend or loved one.

- ☐ Breast cancer is a disease that touches people worldwide. There is a lot of information available—not all credible or beneficial. The sheer amount of information can be overwhelming to the recently diagnosed. Start by reading the info provided by your doctors or medical providers. They are experts with insight and knowledge regarding your specific circumstances and pathology. If you'd like to consider advice beyond your medical team, conduct online research or ask close friends or family for guidance. If you prefer to limit your intake of cancer-related information, let those around you know.

- ☐ The best thing you can do for someone diagnosed with breast cancer is to offer kind words, a prayer, or a distraction. Give them space, time, and your unconditional love.

9. Dead Ball

After my breast cancer diagnosis, there was a lot to organize. Downtime was appreciated so that I could escape and recenter. My husband and I decided to start watching Season 6 of *Peaky Blinders* on Netflix to unwind. One of the prominent story points is the funeral of a significant female character, Polly. They had to reshoot an unplanned storyline because the actress who played Polly, Helen McCrory—who also played Narcissa Malfoy in the *Harry Potter* film series—had passed away at age fifty-two while shooting the season. I remember reading the news in 2021 and feeling sad for her husband and fellow actor, Damian Lewis, and their two young children. She died of cancer.

I couldn't resist the draw of the Internet to recall what type of cancer it was. Even though I knew every pathology and treatment plan is unique, and not everyone becomes cancer-free, I was taken aback to learn she died from breast cancer. While modern medicine has improved our odds, outcomes are still unpredictable. Even one life lost to breast cancer is tragic.

Early detection is vital, but it's not a get-out-of-jail-free card.

Even with all my rational thinking and my confidence in my cancer trajectory, the fear of death held me tight. At 4:15 a.m., I found myself awake, ruminating—a lesson not to explore the Internet before bed. Watching the *Peaky Blinders* funeral on TV triggered emotions. I felt sure Helen McCrory had resources and most likely did everything she could to fight her cancer, and still died. She was my age and left children and a loving partner behind—just as I could.

My mind released the inevitable questions about whether the cancer treatment would work for me. *Will I say goodbye to my children, husband, parents, and friends? What about the memories I want to make with my friends and family? How long will I have to experience and enjoy life? Will my husband find a new partner? What will my children share with their children about me?* I thought of a woman I knew who'd had an early-stage cancer that was treated before it came back and didn't respond to a second round of treatment. When she died, she left three devastated daughters and a heartbroken husband. I thought of the people I knew who'd lost a parent young, before they were married, and how their parents didn't get to see them in love or building a life. Or the people who'd died before their children had children and didn't get to enjoy being a grandparent.

While I stared at the ceiling, my mind raced. *I don't want to miss out on my children's futures. I want as long as I can get.* I love sharing my life with my mom. We talk daily, and when something is exciting, like a big celebration or a trip, we coordinate and organize. *Will my children ever have that experience?* My teenage overconfidence about my mother's cancer trajectory turned out to be accurate—my mother survived. Yet this outcome is not true of many other women I've known since. Globally, breast cancer is the fifth leading cause of cancer-related deaths, with an estimated 685,000 deaths in 2020 alone. In 2023, just less than 43,000 women died from breast cancer in the United States alone.

I had to shake these negative thoughts. I had a lot to be thankful for. I was grateful my family and genetic history put every medical provider I had on high alert, which resulted in detecting my tumor early, even when it didn't exist on the MRI in June 2022—a rather unusual circumstance that made the University of California, San Francisco (UCSF) doctors and my new friend, the University of Southern California (USC) physicist who specializes in cancer care, all say, "Wow." Medical science was improving by leaps and bounds, and the odds were in my favor. Although 2020 saw 685,000 breast cancer deaths worldwide, more than 2.3 million were diagnosed with breast cancer that same year. That means the vast majority—millions—were treated and survived. In fact, for localized cancers, Stages 0 through III, the five-year survival rate is over 99 percent.

My mother and sister were two of the lucky ones. And I'm happy to say, I've had the pleasure of meeting other lucky women who are now cancer-free—many more than I know who've died.

We are not alone.

Breast cancer is the most common of the cancers, and there is a vast network of survivors. Upon hearing my cancer diagnosis, I joined a private Facebook group called the Peloton Breast Cancer Survivors. *Why not manifest where I want to be in six months?* There are various types of cancer-related groups and just as many benefits, so it was important I found the right group for me. Most meet in person or online, and some chat by telephone. People learn valuable insights regarding treatment options from people with the same or similar cancer experiences. Groups promote open dialogue so everyone feels comfortable sharing their emotions and fears with others who can relate. My family and friends rally around me, but not everyone has this support system. Besides being a hub of emotional encouragement, support groups provide coping strategies and tips for navigating the healthcare system. If you or a family member are on a cancer journey, don't hesitate to research local or online cancer support groups to help you and your loved ones.

Death is the consequence of living. Rationally, I knew I wasn't any closer to death after my Stage IIA diagnosis than I was right before it. My self-regulation skills are well developed, and I can usually catch myself when my mind starts generating a rapid list of what-ifs and maybe-nots. But thinking about Helen McCrory's death disrupted my self-control and highlighted that sometimes, despite the best efforts, things don't work out. The sadness of that possibility is balanced only by appreciation of how many things bless my life.

While it took a while, I eventually wiggled free from death's grip. I got myself back to sleep and recharged for the next day. The ball was back in play.

LESSONS LEARNED

- [ ] It is not unusual to fear death or consider your mortality when given a breast cancer diagnosis. Don't fight or suppress your fears. Allow yourself time to consider your feelings. Maybe write, record, or talk these out. Then, use whatever tools you must to return to the present. If you need help, try deep breathing while focusing on gratitude. Focusing on the good in your life and the positive things you are grateful for should help you recenter in a few minutes.

- [ ] Breast cancer is the most common of the cancers, inflicting millions of people worldwide every year. While breast cancer is a leading cause of cancer-related deaths, most people diagnosed with breast cancer survive more than five years after diagnosis. While your cancer stage at diagnosis plays a role in survival rates, the numbers are favorable, high, and perpetually improving.

- [ ] Support groups can be a valuable source of cancer-related information. They afford opportunities to learn coping mechanisms, find emotional support, and share your experiences with like-minded cancer warriors. If you or a loved one has been diagnosed with breast cancer, ask your doctor or search online for a local breast cancer support group. They meet in hospitals, churches, schools, and community centers. You are not alone.

10. The Emotional Swings of Cancer

Watching breast cancer take its toll on my mother's spirit when I was a child planted a sharp seed in my mind—this journey wouldn't just be physical. It would be emotional, too. Although I had a solid network of family and friends to support me mentally, I wasn't prepared to do it without professional help.

I considered the shared experience of a group setting. Several local support groups gathered to talk about cancer experiences, and I knew many people who found solace in that sort of setting. I was grateful these places existed but didn't think they were for me. Years of listening to cancer patients and caregivers told me my role would likely be the provider of support, not the recipient. I wanted individualized attention, a safe space to process my storm of emotions. This wasn't my first cancer journey, and I wanted to talk to experts.

So began my quest for the ideal mental health companion on my cancer journey. It wasn't a one-size-fits-all answer, and as I embarked on my research, a kaleidoscope of options unfolded.

First, there were psychologists. While most psychologists don't specialize in cancer, they possess expertise in understanding and treating many emotional and behavioral issues. Had anxiety, depression, or any other mental health concern existed before my diagnosis, a psychologist could have offered valuable support in navigating these concerns as they intersected with my cancer diagnosis or treatment. But I didn't feel this was the right choice for my situation.

Next, I learned about psychiatrists. Psychiatrists offer a deeper exploration into the psyche. They are equipped with the ability to prescribe medication, which can be beneficial if severe anxiety, depression, or other disorders require pharmaceutical intervention. While I could see how this approach could help people, I didn't think I needed a deeper dive or medication. I found that not all psychiatrists have experience with cancer patients, so finding one with relevant expertise would be crucial.

As I continued my research, I discovered psycho-oncology. Practitioners are mental health professionals specifically trained to understand the unique challenges of cancer patients and their families. They offer counseling, therapy, and coping strategies tailored to the specific anxieties and fears of cancer diagnosis, treatment, and survivorship. Since I was looking for someone who truly "gets it," a psycho-oncologist was a strong contender.

Sometimes, the burden isn't individual; it's collective. Marriage and family therapists specialize in navigating the emotional complexities within relationships. A cancer diagnosis impacts your partner, children, siblings, and parents. A psycho-oncologist can be invaluable in navigating communication, managing expectations, and fostering connection through this challenging time.

UCSF had mental health resources such as support groups, social workers, and psycho-oncologists. For me, availability was the issue. I wanted to start talking with someone as soon as I had the treatment plan, and no one there could take me on. I started searching the Internet for breast cancer therapists and found three profiles that looked interesting. I was looking for experienced professionals who attended a competitive school because I wanted someone whose mind would stay ahead of mine, and I used those criteria as a screen. I also preferred a PhD over a master's for the same reason. They were not perfect criteria, but they helped me determine the options. I sent emails and left voicemails for the three individuals. How quickly they called me back or replied to schedule a virtual meeting was a pleasant surprise. None of them were meeting in person due to COVID-19, but I felt comfortable with Zoom therapy for my cancer support. Frankly, having to do one less drive was a bonus.

The first therapist I talked with was a breast cancer survivor who redirected her practice toward breast cancer patients after her journey. She was passionate about the unique concerns and needs of breast cancer patients. She was older than me and kind. The second therapist was a psycho-oncologist. She was the first person to introduce me to the specialty. She'd spent years working with cancer patients at the California Pacific Medical Center (CPMC) in San Francisco, a nearby hospital, and knew my team at UCSF. Her father was a psychiatrist, and her entire career focused on cancer patients. She was a new mother who had just relocated with her family back to Los Angeles to be closer to her extended family. I felt comfortable with and confident in her expertise, style, and experience. Sadie was a fit.

I never spoke with the third therapist. Having chosen Sadie, I contacted the first and third therapists to thank them for their time and tell them I was working with someone else. Even before we met regularly, Sadie supported me through a night of high anxiety. Sadie and I talked every other week or when I needed an extra ear. She became a core member of my team.

My quest for mental health support didn't end with exploring conventional avenues. I knew my journey wouldn't be solely medical. I yearned for something more profound, a spiritual compass to guide me through the emotional storms. It was then that I considered faith and prayer, two often overlooked resources in the mental health toolbox.

For me, prayer has always been uncomfortable. I'm Jewish and prayers are in Hebrew, a language I don't speak. I asked my rabbi for musical prayers to incorporate into my weekly infusion routing. That was enough for me. For some, a clergy member becomes a beacon of hope and strength. Whether it's a priest, rabbi, imam, or other religious leader, they offer a listening ear, spiritual guidance, and solace in uncertainty. They understand the human spirit's need for meaning and purpose, particularly in the face of illness. Sharing your burdens with someone who holds your faith traditions dear can be immensely comforting, offering a perspective that transcends the physical and grounds you in something larger than yourself.

Prayer, too, became a powerful tool. Reciting verses from sacred texts, whispering personal pleas in quiet moments, or simply expressing gratitude for each sunrise—these acts of devotion fostered a sense of peace and calm amidst the chaos. Whether you believe in a specific deity or find strength in connecting with a higher power, prayer can be a deeply personal expression of hope and resilience. It allows you to surrender your anxieties, finding solace in something more significant than the immediate challenges. Many people of different faiths also asked me if I was comfortable with them praying for me. I welcomed their prayers and support.

Remember that faith and prayer aren't substitutes for professional mental health support. They should be complementary resources, weaving a tapestry of emotional well-being alongside therapy, medication, or other modalities. Combining faith-based practices with mental health professionals can create a comprehensive emotional well-being approach catering to your spiritual and psychological needs.

I connected with a rabbi who aligned with my beliefs, values, and level of observance. I knew she was someone I could confide in. If you don't have a faith leader and want one, explore different religious communities or faith practices to see what resonates with you. And remember, prayer doesn't have to be traditional. Find what works for you—a walk in nature, journaling, even singing hymns—anything that allows you to connect with your spirituality and find comfort.

Ultimately, the decision to incorporate clergy and prayer into your mental health journey is deeply personal. There's no right or wrong answer, only what resonates with your needs and beliefs. Remember, you are not alone on this path. Embrace the diverse resources available.

The beauty of mental health support lies in its diversity. If traditional talk therapy doesn't resonate with you or you want something more, consider exploring avenues like art therapy or music therapy. Expressing your emotions through creative outlets can be incredibly cathartic, allowing you to explore feelings that might be difficult to articulate with words alone. I continued to practice with my rock and roll band throughout treatment, which was both fun and empowering. Those two to three hours every other week, sometimes sitting on a stool so I didn't get fatigued, were an escape to an alternative reality where I was P!nk or Pat Benatar and not a cancer patient.

Remember, the critical factor is finding a haven to express yourself freely, without judgment or the fear of burdening loved ones. Whether it's a psycho-oncologist, who understands the intricate world of cancer, a psychologist who helps you unpack emotional baggage, or an art therapist who guides you through creative expression, choose someone who resonates with you, someone who creates a space to hear you.

And remember, the support doesn't have to be singular. A combination of resources might be just right. Online support groups offer community and connection, while individual therapy provides deeper exploration. Ultimately,

I found community in the Peloton Breast Cancer Survivors group on Facebook. They were a supportive, informed, and powerful community. The key is to see what works for you, what empowers you to face your emotions head-on, and walk your cancer journey with strength and clarity.

LESSONS LEARNED

- [ ] Being diagnosed with breast cancer is emotionally trying, and your mental health is just as important as your physical health. Don't hesitate to consider professional help.

- [ ] Professional mental health assistance takes many forms: psychologists, psychiatrists, psycho-oncologists, and various therapists and counselors. Each brings different skill sets and guides patients within a different medical framework.

- [ ] Doctor referrals are a great place to start, but only you can choose the mental health support you need. Research the options before deciding the best fit for you and your situation. If you need more than one, mix and match to deal with different aspects of your life.

- [ ] Aside from medical professionals, mental health support can be found through specialized groups that meet in person at local churches, schools, hospitals, and community hubs. Some focus on cancer in general, and some gather patients with a specific cancer, like breast cancer. Online forums are also available. Even seeking support from spiritual leaders or prayer can help.

11. On-Deck Circle

Once I got my head around the breast cancer diagnosis, my self-preservation instincts kicked in. It was time to act. While I knew that cancer was a team sport, I had to be the captain and the leader. No one could advocate for me better than me.

I didn't know it then, but that mindset would help me in numerous ways. Waiting for my turn at bat wasn't easy.

To start, I wanted oncologist referrals. I wanted an oncologist I could trust—someone I felt comfortable with. I messaged Dr. Harriet on Facebook, and she called, offering compassion and recommending medical associates. As a radiologist specializing in detecting breast cancer, every week she discovered three tumors that the patient or a doctor had not palpated. She knew many breast oncologists. Everyone Harriet recommended was affiliated with UCSF. The stars aligned with my desire for a National

Comprehensive Cancer Center, and UCSF had a new campus close to home. I called the offices she recommended and left messages saying I was newly diagnosed, mentioning Dr. Borofsky's referral.

Time passed, and I still didn't have an oncologist, but a friend of Tracey's connected me to another friend who was very involved as a UCSF donor. The UCSF donor asked me to write about what I needed and then he sent my note to Dr. Laura Esserman, a renowned breast surgeon and UCSF Breast Cancer Center director. After dealing with various scheduling challenges at UCSF, I appreciated how this individual expedited my care. I am in his debt and fortunate to have had his sponsorship. Part of hitting a curveball is creating opportunities for people to help you in unexpected ways. I didn't know who could help me, but I'm glad someone did.

After booking an appointment with the oncologist, I had to schedule a positron emission tomography (PET) scan. The doctors needed to know more about my specific breast cancer to create a treatment plan. PET scans are full-body CT scans with the added pleasure of radioactive sugar (glucose) coursing through your body. This process requires an hour of waiting in an isolation room until the radioactive sugar reaches all parts of your body. *Will the PET scan be positive? Will it show tumors in other parts of my body?* A positive result would mean metastatic cancer, automatic Stage IV, with much lower survival odds. Although, there are survivors as well as patients who live for years following treatment for Stage IV cancer. PET scans can also discover additional primary tumors, which add stress and complexity to the treatment plan and extend the timeline. What I knew was that I wanted a negative PET scan. I couldn't remember whether my mother or sister had PET scans or if this was a new addition to the screening protocol.

When one location didn't have availability, I asked for another. The scheduler found the first available appointment by the second or third ask. I would have to wait a few days for my first experience with nuclear medicine, but my persistence and flexibility paid off. I live in a medically lush environment—unusual and lucky. I'm privileged to be able to afford good insurance. And I'm persistent—which is free.

Heather came with me to the appointment. Once again, not only was it good to have someone with me for moral support, but having someone as knowledgeable and calm as Heather was doubly helpful. I didn't know what to expect, and I was anxious about getting the PET scan done, getting a preliminary or "wet" read of the scan, and racing to meet the UCSF doctors who were squeezing me in. I did not influence the timeline, and even though we arrived at the scheduled time, I had to wait in the lobby until they were ready for me.

I was finally called in but had to wait while they prepared the nuclear medicine. The nuclear medicine technician explained that first, they'd administer the radioactive sugar through an injection, then I'd spend an hour in isolation while my body metabolized the sugar. Tumors would glow on the PET scan due to the radioactivity of the tracers in the sugar. After an hour, they'd do the whole-body PET scan. The radioactive sugar would be eliminated naturally by my body within the following hour, and I'd be safe to be around people after the PET scan. I was intimidated by the lead-lined sheath for the tube of radioactive sugar. My mind raced with questions about what was being put into my body and what damage it might cause. Honestly, the nuclear medicine technologist was terrific and explained the difference between her constant work with radioactive material (Marie Curie did not die well) and my one-time exposure to radioisotopes with short half-lives (they decay quickly) that would be excreted efficiently within hours. I guess Neal wouldn't notice me glowing in the middle of the night.

After the injection, there was more waiting. I was isolated in a room. That was when my Michigan buddy, Dr. Jordan Shavit, happened to call, and we laughed when he called me "hot." That's scientific slang for being radioactive. Sometime during the call, the nuclear medicine technologist came to check on me and was horrified to find that I was talking. The movement of your jaw can cause radioactive sugar to hang out there, falsely impersonating a metastasis. Neither Jordan nor I knew that. I lost my safe companion for the hour-long hot room wait.

After an hour that felt like a swift thirty minutes and a second thirty that seemed to last three hours, I had my PET scan. As I left the procedure area, I asked about the wet read. The technician answered, "Sure, but making the CD will take twenty minutes." I was stunned, silent. I was already forty-five minutes late for the team at UCSF. And the team wanted the wet read. *Will they be able to develop my treatment plan without it? Should I ask them to wait even longer? What if they can't?* Without experience or meaningful information, I had to make a judgment call. We left without the wet read. I'd have to sit in the batter's box longer.

I was nervous when I walked in for my first meeting with my UCSF team. My pathology and earlier scan results were spread before them on the computer. They didn't have the PET scan results because I'd abandoned the wet read CD. My team was extraordinary, but their plan was filled with caveats.

They had an initial plan that would be confirmed based on the results of the PET scan and the UCSF pathology tests after UCSF Pathology performed a confirmation analysis on my biopsy slides.

There are multiple types of breast cancer. The most common are ductal carcinoma in situ (DCIS, Stage 0, non-invasive, in the milk ducts), invasive ductal carcinoma (IDC, the most common, originates in the milk ducts, and what most of us think of as breast cancer), invasive lobular carcinoma (ILC, breast cancer that originates in the milk-producing lobules), inflammatory carcinoma (invasive breast cancer that blocks lymph vessels on the skin of the breast, causing swelling and redness of the entire breast), and a few rarer ones. (See www.survivingbreastcancer.org for more information.)

Along with the type of cancer, pathologists determine the hormone receptivity of the tumor. For instance, with invasive ductal breast cancer, there are multiple types depending on what hormones the tumor reacts to. The types are HER+/HR+, HER-/HR+, HER+/HR-, and triple negative. These hormone receptors, along with the growth rate and other characteristics of the tumor, guide the oncologists to the optimal treatment protocol, which determines your individual treatment plan and the potential pitches you will see and hit. DCIS may require active surveillance, which means getting biannual scans to see if the tumor has grown. Invasive HER+ tumors are candidates for Herceptin (trastuzumab) from Genentech, a low-side-effect, highly effective treatment.

Each combination of pathology and stage, therefore, has different treatment protocols. One of the hardest things about talking with other breast cancer patients is that the treatment, with its side effects and challenges, is very distinct for each cancer. I wanted to know what my treatment was going to look like, as my most vital impulse under stress was to take control. I knew I was not in control, which was very unsettling.

Although there was less than a 5 percent chance the PET scan would show cancer beyond the primary tumor, we needed to know. The tumor was aggressive, and there was no sign of it in June. Since June it had developed and invaded a lymph node. *Spry fucker.*

After hearing the 5 percent probability, my rational mind argued in circles with my emotional mind. *Rationally*, 5 percent was a very low probability. *Rationally*, there was no cancer detected in the biopsies done on the tissue removed in October during my breast reduction. *Rationally*, there was nothing to worry about. But *emotionally*, rational thinking was thrown out the window. This tumor was very aggressive and grew so fast that the doctors thought it was "cool." What if it took off through my body, and the PET scan revealed we had a bigger problem? What if I was riddled with cancer? What if my metabolically active tumor didn't have an appetite for chemo, and it didn't work? What if my body could not withstand the onslaught, and we had to stop or pause cycles? Would this very aggressive tumor gain a permanent foothold? Luckily, my rational brain knows how to kick ass. *Seriously, Joelle, five percent is nothing. Keep a realistic perspective.*

This is hard to do when you are in the box waiting for the pitch.

I didn't have to wait too long. The PET scan results were in that evening, and Dr. Esserman's office called to let me know my PET scan was all clear except for the one tumor and cancerous lymph node that had already been identified. There were no signs of cancer outside of those spots.

To say I was relieved would be an understatement.

This was the best possible answer. And the rhythm of the treatment became clear. The plan was weekly low-dose carboplatin-Taxol for twelve cycles. If my tumor didn't react with a clinical complete response (cCR), I would then receive a mix of Adriamycin (doxorubicin hydrochloride) and cyclophosphamide, two chemotherapy drugs often used in combination to treat localized breast cancer and known as the AC regimen. Treatment would be every two weeks for four cycles. At that point, irrespective of the cCR, surgery would follow.

Because I carried the BRCA1 gene, the only recommended surgical option was a bilateral mastectomy. For those with the same pathology but no genetic marker, a lumpectomy is an option. Having already decided to have a bilateral mastectomy before I had cancer, I was not saddened by the surgical direction. But that's because I had already grieved the loss of my breasts. From a surgical perspective, I was back to where I started.

More waiting followed. This wasn't a carefree time. Waiting gave my mind free rein. It was very, very hard to focus on anything other than *I have cancer, and it is still growing inside me.*

Two weeks passed. A second pathology review was done during this time, and a port was installed. A port is a small medical appliance implanted beneath the skin, connecting to a vein via a catheter, and a needle is inserted through the skin into the port to inject fluids into the body or draw blood. It's used for many medical treatments, including chemotherapy treatments. My doctors also secured me a seat with a DigniCap Scalp Cooling System, designed to reduce hair loss during chemotherapy treatment. My weekly infusions would occur in the UCSF Infusion Center—on the same days as my oncologist Dr. Chien's clinic, preventing additional trips to the hospital. That was Dr. Chien's idea, and it was excellent. I preferred to box cancer into one day a week.

It was hard to wait for the first infusion. I wasn't looking forward to the hellish parts of chemo, but I wanted the cancer out of me, and the wait was torture. Although tremendous strides have been made to reduce the side effects of chemotherapy with pre-treatments, no one knows how a body will respond to the poison of chemo until the first cycle of receiving the stuff. I knew the side effects of chemo could be disabling because I lived through it with my sister. And I knew there was a class of drugs that dramatically reduced the nausea and vomiting. I asked Dr. Chien if Emend (aprepitant) could be part of my pre-treatment. Emend works by blocking neurokinin, a natural substance in the brain that causes nausea and vomiting. She recommended a cousin of Emend, Cinvanti, suggesting it might be more effective. My insurance covered it, so we made it part of every infusion. Knowing I had a way of reducing the nausea and vomiting induced by chemo made me much less anxious about the first infusion.

I used this time to prepare. Again, my stress response is to take control. My self-soothing is through action. Action gives me both pride of accomplishment and a feeling of power. Here are ten things I did while waiting for the first infusion:

1. Received and tried on my sister-in-law's chemo tops with zippers to access the port. She also sent her wigs in case I lost my hair.
2. Ordered the DigniCap kit with enough time for it to be delivered.
3. Ordered new slippers for the infusion center.
4. Ordered an aromatherapy pendant necklace that diffuses essential oils. I thought this would help me relax without disturbing my fellow chemo patients.
5. Ordered ice socks and mittens and froze the ice packs.
6. Borrowed my sister's Yeti cooler to bring the ice packs to the infusion center.
7. Organized my Cancer Obliteration Project binder, which would come to every infusion and doctor's appointment.
8. Picked up prescriptions.
9. Found and downloaded a pill reminder app to alert me when it was time to take medications.
10. Practiced patience. I was as organized as I could be for my treatment to start. All I could do was wait.

LESSONS LEARNED

- [ ] It takes a team of professionals to tackle breast cancer, but you, the cancer patient, should play a lead role.

- [ ] Be professional, polite, and persistent when booking medical appointments and procedures. Pleasantries, flexibility, and creativity go a long way.

- [ ] Find an oncologist you trust. Breast cancer is stressful enough without being uncomfortable with your doctor or medical team. Research and talk to more than one oncologist, if possible. Follow your gut.

- [ ] PET scans are full-body scans meant to detect tumors. Although they can be arduous, they save lives. A positive result means the cancer hasn't spread, and a negative result allows doctors to create the best treatment plan.

- [ ] Waiting might be the most challenging part of organizing a treatment plan after a breast cancer diagnosis. You desperately want the cancer gone. Unfortunately, there is no magic bullet. Stay calm and do your best to carry on.

Alysia's Journey

I wasn't the only breast cancer patient with a story to tell.

Four times over five years, Alysia was told not to worry about a shadow on her mammogram and round lymph nodes. The doctors at three different clinics said she was "fine." The doctors told her these symptoms were perimenopause. The doctors told her she had dense breast tissue. The doctors told her that her lymph nodes were round and inflamed because of the flu or the COVID-19 vaccine recently administered. Her doctor said the sore spot on her breast didn't feel like cancer.

Her doctors resisted an "unnecessary" biopsy because biopsies are invasive.

After years of being falsely reassured and denied a biopsy, Alysia was diagnosed with invasive lobular breast cancer (ILC). This slow-growing cancer had likely been present in her body for ten years, and when excised, it had infiltrated thirteen lymph nodes and was Stage IIIA or IIIC disease (depending on the institution's grading).

ILC is nearly impossible to detect or diagnose with mammograms, ultrasounds, or MRIs. It comprises 10 to 15 percent of total breast cancers, and the only way to confirm it is through a biopsy.

"I wish women knew what I know now: follow your gut and push hard for what you need."

The care coordinator in the mammography center led Alysia to a room with an outdated book about cancer and introduced Alysia to the local cancer center. And then she told Alysia what to expect, except that no one knew the stage of Alysia's cancer yet. The care coordinator started talking about lumpectomies and the cancer being curable. That was the worst thing anyone ever said to Alysia.

"Okay, so breast cancer. I'd had colorectal cancer, which turned out fine. And wow, with all the money put into breast cancer, all breast cancer research, I couldn't be luckier. What a cancer to get! I was very positive about it until I discovered there wasn't a unique or proven standard of care for lobular cancer. The standard of care is for ductile cancer."

Unlike my children, who were teenagers when I was diagnosed with breast cancer, Alysia's kids were young, and she is a solo parent. They were frightened when she told them the news. They'd been through cancer hell with their mother before, and they worried they were going to lose the only parent they had. But Alysia told them about her doctors' appointments and encouraged them to ask questions. "People say don't talk with your kids about death," said Alysia, "but I disagree. Even little kids get it, and they are resilient." Alysia interviewed a teenager whose mother, a close friend of Alysia's, had gone through breast cancer when he was small. He reassured her that her kids needed to know as much as possible. Alysia also found a family therapist who helped her children express their fears.

A long-time friend and work colleague introduced Alysia to a Los Angeles–based breast reconstructive surgeon, Dr. Dhivya Srinivasa, who offered to talk to Alysia early on Saturday morning. Alysia didn't understand why talking with a reconstructive surgeon first would be ideal, but it was exactly what she needed to do. Dr. Srinivasa knew Alysia's options for surgery, given her extensive lymph involvement. Initially, other surgeons recommended a lumpectomy because studies indicated the same outcomes as mastectomies. However, Dr. Srinivasa advocated for a mastectomy given the large number of lymph nodes involved and since many of her patients returned with cancer in the other breast. Alysia pushed for a bilateral mastectomy with DIEP flap reconstruction based on that input. The reconstructive surgeon assembled a team and booked surgery two weeks after their first meeting—almost impossible since it was just after COVID-19 and surgery rooms were backlogged.

"Immediately, I contacted a friend who had had cancer years before to learn about her experience," Alysia said. "She dropped everything and came over to my house. She said, 'Alright, we are going to work on a plan.'" She started going through Alysia's daily activities with the kids and her job—details Alysia had taken for granted. She wrote everything down, set up a meal and service train for Alysia and her kids, and invited school parents to participate. "I needed someone to get my kids to and from school," Alysia said. "I wanted them to continue their activities to stay healthy and mentally challenged. And we needed groceries for the house."

Unlike the network of friends who helped in my time of need, some people Alysia thought were her closest friends didn't help. Some didn't even call. But it wasn't all bad. "I had people come out of the woodwork to make my family full meals and pick up my kids. People I didn't even know would call to help. It was phenomenal."

Alysia flew to Los Angeles from Montana, where she met her brother from Wyoming. Her days were filled with appointments, scans, and tests to prepare for her upcoming surgery. She made sure her brother attended every doctor's appointment with her to catch details that Alysia didn't catch.

Alysia became more mindful of the good things the doctors told her. For example, later in treatments, her MD Anderson Cancer Center oncologist mentioned that women with young children often have better outcomes. Alysia's mother encouraged her to set goals—milestones she could look forward to in the coming years.

The surgery was supposed to be six to eight hours in duration. Still, it was more complicated than originally thought. It took fifteen hours and a team of four surgeons to remove the cancer and lymph nodes, reconstruct the lymph vessels (LYMPHA procedure), and complete the DIEP flap reconstruction. Afterward, Alysia's breast cancer surgeon, Dr. Kristi Funk, encouraged Alysia to think positively and believed Alysia would be okay. Alysia took that advice. She didn't spend time wondering what caused her cancer. She knew she lived a healthy life and that sometimes cells go awry.

Of the sixteen lymph nodes removed, thirteen were positive for cancer. An oncologist at Cedars-Sinai Medical Center told Alysia she had a 40 to 60 percent chance of recurrence, and if it recurred, Alysia would die in three to four years. This was Alysia's lowest point, a sobering reality check.

Chemotherapy and radiation followed surgery, and Dr. Srinivasa recommended a private oncology nurse practitioner, Paige Woodward, to help Alysia navigate these final treatments. Paige and Alysia met often during chemotherapy. Paige allowed Alysia to vent her concerns and ask questions, essentially transforming Alysia into an educated cancer patient.

There are no completely effective scans for ILC metastasis. Dr. Funk prescribed a blood DNA test to monitor for residual cancer cells. This has not been proven and is still in early development, but Alysia agreed to participate. Early CT scans showed two unusual spots on Alysia's liver and lungs, and these would be monitored every six months for only two years. Besides that, Alysia would have to be hyper-vigilant about her body.

As expected, Alysia worried about the future. *Who will take care of my kids if I die?* Once she had a guardianship plan for her children in a known, stable home, Alysia's anxiety went from sky-high to ground level.

She found herself accepting the inevitability of eventual death, if not from cancer, then from an accident or old age. Her cancer experiences changed how she thought about mortality. Once she accepted her mortality, she found she felt more positive and alive day to day. She stays present and aware of her life, kids, and family.

Her mental health improved even further after she outlined an estate plan.

"A lot of people get cancer," said Alysia. "The gift of cancer is a lifelong filter to what and who is essential. I live life more deliberately now."

These are wise words. If you or someone you love is facing a cancer diagnosis, help them live in the here and now.

LESSONS LEARNED

- ☐ Even though we have modern screening and testing tools, 20 percent of breast cancers go undetected. Equipment can only detect so much, and medical professionals are human beings with flaws, biases, and incompetencies. If you suspect breast cancer, step up to bat. Ensure your voice is heard.

- ☐ Empower your children to express their emotions regarding your breast cancer diagnosis. Encourage them to ask questions and answer with honesty. Seek professional therapy to provide your children with an outlet when needed.

- ☐ Sometimes, the best medical practitioners for your specific cancer situation are not available or local. Be prepared to travel for the best care possible or create a team of local and distant doctors. They're often happy to work together.

- ☐ Create a plan to organize your home life. If you have children, their routines are important for their physical and mental well-being. Keep them in school, at home, and among friends and family while you focus on your health. Put your plan in writing and allow friends to contribute.

- ☐ Some people are helpful when confronted with a friend's cancer diagnosis. Some are not. Be open to those who help and move beyond the ones who disappoint. The people who show up will blow your mind. Let them help.

Josie's Journey

Josie[5] was awaiting biopsy results. She'd asked the radiologist to call after a major client presentation so she wouldn't be distracted. Before the presentation, Josie's phone buzzed. It was her OB-GYN. With an apprehensive breath, she answered.

"I don't have the results yet," said her doctor, "but if you have cancer, and if it's HER2-positive, that's a good thing. HER2-positive breast cancer is now known to respond well to targeted therapies, so don't worry." While this was great to hear, Josie wasn't surprised. Her mother was a breast cancer survivor. Her father had survived prostate cancer. Her uncle had four different cancers, survived them all, and ultimately died of something else. In Josie's family, people got cancer, were treated for cancer, and survived cancer.

After Josie's presentation, the radiologist called. "You have HER2-positive invasive ductal carcinoma," she said, pausing to let the words sink in.

Thanks to the call from Josie's OB-GYN, Josie wasn't afraid. "At this point," said Josie, "I didn't think it would be serious. I assumed I wouldn't need chemotherapy. I figured the only thing I would have to focus on was my health choices."

In the wake of her diagnosis, Josie dedicated herself to rigorous research, combing through many scientific studies and leaning into the vast expanse of online information. Equipped with questions, she sought consultations from different oncologists, ensuring she understood the nuances of potential therapies. Her discussions with fellow survivors were invaluable, providing not only moral support but practical advice on navigating treatment side effects and the mental challenges that lay ahead. Her determination to be well-informed and proactive empowered her to make educated decisions about her health, feeling a sense of control amidst the uncertainty. "I focused on avoiding over-treatment or under-treatment," said Josie. "I wanted just enough to take care of the problem."

When I was introduced to Josie through a mutual friend, she was particularly concerned about protecting her body from the damaging effects of chemo and radiation and figuring out if those treatments were necessary, given doctors had mixed opinions. She was also concerned about keeping her thick, dark hair. She was worried about chemotherapy side effects—including nausea and hair loss. The very thought of radiation therapy filled her with a sense of dread. Josie shared her concerns with her oncologist. He suggested waiting on radiology until after chemotherapy and surgery. "Joelle was such a can-do, experienced voice during these times," Josie said. "Her voice in my head lifted me to the possibility of getting through cancer and being happy." I was pleased to build Josie's self-confidence during and after cancer.

For weeks, the weight of the biopsy results loomed large, threatening to disrupt any semblance of normalcy Josie and her family had managed to maintain. Josie's three daughters struggled with their emotions, even though Josie was confident she would survive. They didn't understand. They were nervous. It rocked their foundation to have their mom face such a severe disease. "One of my daughters suffered at school and started seeing a therapist," Josie said.

As I had found, the journey through breast cancer often takes unexpected twists, and Josie's path was no exception. Josie chose a medical team, but her breast surgeon and reconstructive surgeon did not have privileges at the same hospitals and could not operate together. Josie broke down in tears. Her breast surgeon recommended separating her surgery into two distinct surgeries. The lumpectomy would come first to remove the cancer, followed by a period of healing, potential radiation, and observation. The reconstructive surgery would be several months later, offering Josie's body the time to recover. This two-stage approach would also provide an added layer of precaution, ensuring that all cancerous tissue could be identified and addressed before the final reconstruction. Though this plan stretched the timeline of her treatment, it was a tailored response to Josie's health status and personal concerns, underscoring the adaptable, patient-centric approach to battling breast cancer.

Amidst medical hurdles, life continued to unfurl. Only weeks after the cancer diagnosis, Josie received news of her layoff. "It was a blow," Josie said. Yet, in its wake, an opportunity emerged to focus solely on her health. Josie committed to taking control of her situation despite the upheaval around her. The anticipated nausea never materialized, yet Josie's hair, which she hoped to preserve through cold capping, thinned. Most strikingly, her hair loss peaked not after the dreaded second round, as was expected, but after her final treatment. These unforeseen effects served as stark reminders of cancer's unpredictable nature.

Josie was not alone in navigating these challenges. By witnessing their mother's resilience, all three girls gained a profound respect for her strength in adversity. The vulnerability shared between them during this time fostered a unique closeness. Josie's daughters, as constant companions, infused dark days with love, support, and moments of joy. This shared experience deepened their bond, transforming what could have been solely a time of struggle into one of meaningful connection. Josie's athletic spirit also played a crucial role, with daily walks becoming a source of physical rejuvenation and emotional release. Walking became her social exercise routine. Each walk deepened her appreciation for friends and family.

During her journey, Josie continued to read research papers and studies. She shared her concerns with her doctors, which led to reduced rounds and dosages of chemo and an innovative two-part surgical plan versus the conventional, larger, more aggressive single surgery.

Through her battle with cancer, Josie undertook a comprehensive audit of her life—evaluating sleep patterns, nutrition, relationships, and exercise. Cancer, in its unwelcome way, prompted a recalibration of her priorities, illuminating paths to a more balanced life. "Cancer gave me the chance to think about what was important before it was too late," said Josie.

LESSONS LEARNED

☐ Communication with your doctor can relieve a lot of stress before, during, and after a breast cancer diagnosis. Take your findings/research/concerns back to your doctors. Ask for what you want or need. Keep the lines of communication open and encourage your doctors to do the same.

☐ Do your research. Oncologists provide printouts about your pathology and treatment. Understand your breast cancer diagnosis, and don't be afraid to ask questions when you need to know more. Your medical team is there to guide you.

☐ Reach out to other cancer patients and cancer survivors. They've been where you are—wherever in the process you may be. They can relate, provide moral support, and offer practical, experienced advice.

☐ Your breast cancer journey is bound to take unexpected twists and turns. Try to roll with the punches. You can get through.

☐ Cancer is bound to push you to your physical and mental limits. You can, however, build strength in adversity. Focus on your bonds with family and friends. Take the opportunity to self-reflect. Evaluate your sleep patterns, eating habits, exercise routines, career choices, and social connections. Where can you make improvements? Cancer can be an opportunity to live a more balanced life if you choose.

Heather A.'s Journey

I met Heather A. through the Peloton Breast Cancer Survivors group ("the Tribe"). She had been gaining momentum as a financial coach and ran a successful housecleaning business when she felt a lump in her breast. At thirty-eight, she had no family history of cancer and was a healthy, active non-smoker, so she wasn't too worried. It wasn't her first lump, and Heather confidently attended the mammogram exam solo.

Heather knew this time it was different when the radiologist asked to talk with her. The radiologist recommended a biopsy and warned Heather the lump was probably malignant. "It's going to be a difficult six months," the radiologist said.

Only six months? Heather thought. "After the doctor told me the news, I was surprised I was supposed to drive home," she recalled. "I sat in the car and my mind raced.

I couldn't believe I had cancer. I couldn't go home because my husband and kids were there. *What would I say? How would they react?* My kids were thirteen and fifteen, and I didn't want to worry them until I knew more." *What the hell do I do now?* she repeated in her head. Heather eventually put the car in drive and found her way to her mother-in-law's house. Sadly, her husband's mother was very experienced with cancer.

While Heather's radiology team was compassionate, their compassion led them to downplay the odds, the risks, and how uncomfortable things would be. While they didn't know what type of breast cancer Heather had or how it would be treated, Heather knew she was headed for difficult times. Heather contacted her therapist to let her know she may need more support soon. She also contacted her friend and business coach for help processing the news. "Good morning," she began. "I could use some coaching on compartmentalizing. I had a mammogram that did not go well. I have a meeting with a new client tomorrow, but I'm not going long without crying or swearing."

Her coach replied, "Just let yourself feel whatever you need. Be selfish. Put yourself first." Typically, Heather cared for her family before caring for herself. "Please keep me posted," the coach added. "Not knowing is the worst."

"I have a lot in my head right now," said Heather. While there was never a good time for cancer, the timing sucked. Her housecleaning business had struggled through the COVID-19 pandemic closures and was starting to bounce back. "My brain is a messy place. I don't think there's enough paper to get it all down and clear it out."

Over the weekend, between her mammogram and biopsy, Heather accepted that she very likely had cancer and would be going through treatment. She talked to her husband, and they decided to wait until the biopsy results came back to tell the children. Her husband held out hope the test results would present good news. She was determined to reframe her focus and learn from the experience.

Cancer immediately started disrupting Heather's life. She had been waiting two and a half months for an appointment with her OB-GYN, which she had to cancel because the appointment overlapped with the biopsy. That issue wasn't related to the cancer, so it went onto the back burner. She'd have to wait another month for an MRI and even longer to see an oncologist. "It seemed crazy there was such a long waiting period," Heather said. "I tried to turn that around in my head. I figured I should be more worried if it were faster. I released any expectations about what treatment would be like. Whatever cancer would throw at me, I'd face. I prepared to do whatever I had to. I wasn't going to challenge the doctors or second-guess their recommendations. I didn't think there would be many decisions for me to make. I thought the doctors would just tell me what to do."

Ultimately, Heather was diagnosed with multiple tumors, with the largest being several centimeters in size. One lymph node was involved. The oncology protocol was six cycles of chemotherapy every three weeks. She would have to take Herceptin and Perjeta (pertuzumab) for an entire year. The surgeon offered Heather an array of surgical options, from a lumpectomy to a mastectomy, with different reconstruction alternatives. "I had small breasts, barely an A-cup," Heather said. "And when I thought about having three sections removed, a lumpectomy just seemed like an awful outcome visually for one tiny little boob."

Heather began discounting the reassurances from her doctors and tuning into what her body was feeling each day. For example, the medical team told her she could return to cleaning houses after her biopsy and port placement. But she had bruises, and the pain from her procedures restricted her range of motion; there was no way she could go back to work. Luckily, her clients were understanding and supportive.

No one spoke to her about the gynecological and sexual side effects of chemotherapy, or how she'd be catapulted into early menopause just from the chemo. In addition to the expected side effects such as nausea, diarrhea, hair loss, and bone pain, she had hot flashes, night sweats, difficulty sleeping, and joint pain—all from menopause. And with triple-positive tumors, she couldn't address the menopause side effects. Fortunately, her husband was supportive throughout her experience.

Heather took control of her mental health by using the extensive tool kit of resources she had from her mental breakdown several years before and what she had learned in becoming a coach. She learned more about her brain and self-care then, and that experience helped her through her cancer.

"Everyone expected me to be super depressed," said Heather. "Friends and family expected me to be sad and feel like shit and never have a good day." But Heather was committed to practicing mindfulness. She practiced tried-and-true breathing techniques, meditated, and stayed calm. She wrote in a journal, noting her feelings.

When she found herself spiraling into a rabbit hole of catastrophic thinking, she did a body scan meditation to reconnect with how her body felt. She took notes on how she felt each day, what side effects she was experiencing, and set micro-goals. "I refused to be a depressed, sad mess for the foreseeable future," Heather added. "When things were bad, I took care of myself. When things were good, I enjoyed the happiness."

Heather elected to keep working. She cleaned houses, and when her coaching clients attempted to diminish their issues in comparison to her cancer, Heather reminded them there was no contest. Their problems weren't minor just because her problems were more extreme. They were worthy of attention.

"Cancer was personal growth on steroids," said Heather, laughing. "Everything I had learned while becoming a coach helped me to look outside myself and observe how I was feeling and what was going through my head." Heather learned not to feel bad about receiving help. "The community I'm surrounded by is more substantial than I ever thought it could be." And she also learned to let go of those who wouldn't or couldn't help. "People have strong reactions to cancer. I see a lot of hurt in Facebook groups when breast cancer patients note how some friends and family react to their diagnosis or disappear from their lives. How people react and behave has nothing to do with you. It has much more to do with them, their insecurities, their life experiences, and their feelings." Heather focused on the positive and didn't let the negative affect her. When she woke every morning, she would check in on her body and see if she felt rested and energized. She'd ask herself what her body needed and listen to it.

Heather said, "Before I was sick, I remember wishing away my days, waiting for things to improve. After the breast cancer diagnosis, I realized that kind of thinking was just ridiculous. I was wishing away years, weeks, and days of my life. Instead, I had to embrace the here and now and realize there is good in every experience—a lesson to be learned. Cancer taught me a lot about myself."

LESSONS LEARNED

- ☐ Cancer is serious, and no one should feel pressure to be upbeat and happy in a severe situation. It's all right to share when you are sad, scared, or frustrated. If possible, try to distinguish between reactions and actions. Recognize your emotional reactions and continuously work to be levelheaded.

- ☐ When stressed, focus on your breathing with box breathing: four beats to inhale, four beats to hold, four to exhale, and four before the next inhale. Fighter pilots learn the technique because three or four box-breathing cycles demonstrably lower blood pressure.

- ☐ Journaling can be an efficient and effective way to reduce anxiety. So, when you find your mind racing through unlikely but possible scenarios, grab a pen and paper. Write how you feel. Ask why you feel that way and what you are most worried about. Only you will see what you write, so be honest with yourself.

- ☐ Find the silver linings to enjoy your life. Have fun. Stay grounded in the present as much as possible. Don't let yourself get so depressed and anxious that you aren't living anymore. Acknowledge the good moments by pausing, noticing, and absorbing them. Stash them into your memory bank to take out during the inevitable crappy moments. Most of all, *live*.

- ☐ Cancer can be a powerful reset button. It forces you to look at life's choices in entirely new ways. Perhaps your cancer diagnosis will ignite positive changes in your self-worth, thought processes, career, and personal relationships. Welcome the new and improved view.

BATTER UP

There ain't no sugarcoating it; a breast cancer diagnosis sucks—big time. Even if you're swimming in a genetic cesspool that requires vigilant screening and testing, a breast cancer diagnosis will throw you a nasty curveball. No one can prepare for cancer.

A cancer diagnosis doesn't just affect your health—it can have a significant impact on your finances as well. Studies show that three out of four people with cancer worry about how they will pay for cancer treatment and keep up with their day-to-day costs. This statistic underscores the widespread financial stress that accompanies a cancer diagnosis. It's essential to recognize that the first few weeks after diagnosis, before treatment begins, are often overwhelming and chaotic for most people. During this time, few think about the financial implications of the cancer curveball they've been thrown. Taking the time to assess and plan for the financial impact can significantly reduce stress and prevent long-term economic hardship.

If you've been recently diagnosed, let yourself grieve. Cry, scream, or hurl small objects ... then let those emotions go. Wipe the tears away, dust yourself off, and stand proud and strong. You've got this. There are currently more than four million breast cancer survivors in the United States of America. This includes women still being treated and those who have completed treatment. Cancer *can* be defeated.

Some people even kick cancer's ass more than once.

As I wrote this book and fought my cancer battle, my sister, Tracey, received her second breast cancer bombshell. She'd had chemo twenty years ago and a prophylactic mastectomy a few years after, yet here she was, once again diagnosed with breast cancer.

This can't be! How is this possible? It was a new cancer, not a recurrence. Doctors said there was only a 2 to 3 percent chance of this happening, but it did, shocking the entire family. "Enough is enough!" my family cried.

But the lump in Tracey's breast was small. It was caught early, and the prognosis was good. And because Tracey was a breast cancer pro, she faced this setback head-on. She knew the odds were in her favor. And she wasn't fighting alone.

Cancer has impacted our family in several ways, but it has also brought us closer. We are there for each other through all the ups and downs. Our children have become aware of their genetic history and the fragility of life and have learned that cancer isn't always a death sentence. They have tools should they ever face cancer. We've become pillars of strength that can buffer any storm.

Please stand with us.

If doctors have given you a breast cancer diagnosis, and you are in the throes of tests and uncertainty, you might fear death—*who wouldn't?* But this fear does not define you. Wading through medical tests and procedures isn't easy, and the time in between and the waiting will be difficult. Yet you don't have to go it alone.

Gather a medical team that understands that your mental health is just as important as your physical health. Share your worries and hopes with your partner, kids, parents, siblings, friends, and colleagues. Consider therapy or find hubs of like-minded people online or in person. Surround yourself with loved ones who can help you through the rough moments. Cancer is, in fact, a team sport.

Play ball.

Part III:
Treatment

12. Beanball

No one welcomes cancer. It sucks the air from the room. It's unwelcome and scary. My psycho-oncologist shared that many cancer patients initially respond with denial. People avoid tests that confirm a diagnosis. Some experience intense feelings of guilt or shame, as if they caused their cancer, which they didn't. Many are paralyzed by the number of doctors' appointments, tests, and new vocabulary they suddenly need to manage or master. The paralyzing anxiety can be exhausting at the very moment when energy preservation is required. Denial and avoidance are dangerous strategies to succumb to for any extended period.

Resistance is futile.

Only after accepting I had breast cancer, which happened very quickly for me, could I assess my situation, evaluate options, and launch into decisive action. For me, acceptance was a state. I had to get my mind to focus on the important stuff, which included my career. Cancer is not just a battle against a disease; it is a fight that encompasses various aspects of a patient's life, including their job and, in turn, their financial well-being. For many cancer patients, the economic impact of treatment can be overwhelming, leading to unexpected struggles and hardships. While Neal and I were positioned to weather the storm, not everyone had the same experience. My friend Sarah, for example, struggled immensely with the financial burdens of cancer.

Sarah's breast cancer diagnosis came as a shock, and as she embarked on her treatment journey, she soon realized that the costs associated with cancer care were more than she had anticipated. Despite having health insurance, Sarah discovered that her plan had limitations, leaving her with significant out-of-pocket expenses. The mounting medical bills, coupled with the everyday cost of living, put a strain on her finances. She faced additional expenses such as transportation to and from appointments, parking fees, and specialized dietary needs. These seemingly small costs added up, further exacerbating her financial burden.

At the same time, Sarah experienced a decrease in income because she had to reduce her working hours due to the physical and emotional toll of cancer. This loss of income made it even more challenging for her to manage the mounting medical bills and everyday expenses. Sarah had to make difficult choices, often sacrificing her well-being for the sake of affording treatment.

Sarah sought support from financial counselors and navigators who helped her understand her medical bills, explore financial assistance programs, and find resources to alleviate the financial strain. Sarah also contacted local community organizations and support groups that aided with transportation, lodging, and other practical needs.

Sarah's story was not unique. Many cancer patients face similar financial struggles, and it is crucial to address these challenges head-on. The economic difficulties faced by cancer patients are diverse and often overwhelming. The top eight most common financial issues include:

High treatment costs. Cancer treatments, including surgeries, chemotherapy, radiation therapy, targeted therapies, and immunotherapy, are expensive. The cost of medications, hospital stays, and follow-up care can add up quickly, and treatment availability and fees may differ dramatically for people outside the United States.

Insurance coverage limitations. Many US insurance plans have limitations, such as high deductibles, co-payments, and out-of-pocket annual maximums. Some treatments or medications may not be fully covered, leading to a significant financial burden.

Loss of income and reduced productivity. With 75 percent of cancer patients requiring extended time off or a reduction in work, the loss of income can create substantial financial strain, especially if there are no disability benefits or sufficient savings. Cancer and its treatments can cause fatigue, physical limitations, and cognitive changes, further impacting a patient's ability to work at their previous capacity.

Additional expenses. Cancer treatment often involves expenses beyond medical costs, such as transportation to appointments, lodging for out-of-town treatments, childcare, home care, medical supplies, parking fees, and specialized dietary needs.

Emotional and psychological impact. Dealing with a cancer diagnosis and the treatment that follows can lead to emotional distress, anxiety, and depression. These mental health challenges may require additional support and resources, which can come with financial costs.

Impact on caregivers. Cancer affects patients *and* their caregivers, who may need to reduce working hours, resulting in financial strain for the entire family.

Debt and financial toxicity. Some patients may accumulate debt due to medical bills, loans, or credit card expenses, leading to long-term financial burdens and distress.

Limited access to resources. Some populations may face additional barriers in accessing financial resources and support.

Given these challenges, I knew it was crucial to anticipate and prepare for the financial impact of cancer treatment. Neal and I pored over our insurance policies. I organized my work schedule so I could focus on my health. We didn't need to access financial assistance. We would crush cancer's curveball without breaking the bank, and I only had the next stage, treatment, to worry about.

After I met my oncologist, I felt better. My oncologist, Dr. Chien, was unassuming but confident. She was compassionate and straightforward. She could observe my swing's metrics (my labs and side effects) and recalibrate my approach because she had countless other batters in the box, facing the same pitch. I realized that I could not interpret the pathology, labs, and radiology reports, so I shouldn't be anxious about things I imagined I saw when I looked at the reports. That's what Dr. Chien was for, and she was part of a breast cancer–focused practice and would work alongside doctors who collaborated on my case when needed.

Dr. Chien explained that multiple treatment protocols could work for me, but she recommended the carboplatin-Taxol plus Keytruda (pembrolizumab, an immunotherapy drug) option for my first treatment protocol. She noted how all treatment plans depend on the patient's health and medical history, as well as the stage and pathology of the cancer. Her willingness to explain the other options and educate me on why this protocol best suited me conveyed respect. I felt I had a tighter grip on the plan. The current standard of care for my breast cancer was chemotherapy before surgery. The UCSF breast cancer team had the best response to my questions about the lymph node—it didn't matter. What mattered was how the cancer responded to the treatment. Based on tumor response, my time in the batter's box would be longer or shorter.

Since I'd planned to have my breasts removed before being diagnosed with breast cancer, I already knew I wanted a bilateral mastectomy and DIEP flap once the chemo treatment was complete. Chemotherapy is a long, drawn-out series of pitches to throw the hitter off the plate. It is a train derailment of your life. But other than refusing treatment, I didn't have a choice about stepping up to the plate to swing the bat. When diagnosed with breast cancer, treatment is the only option.

My doctor recommended a weekly high-density dosing of Taxol and carboplatin for twelve cycles. This protocol, concurrent with immunotherapy—pembrolizumab (called pembro by my team)—every three weeks for a year, shows the best long-term results. Then, I'd have an MRI to see how the tumor was responding. Based on the response, the next step was four cycles of Adriamycin and cyclophosphamide. I was hoping to avoid the AC. Both my mother and sister were treated with AC, and the side effects were brutal.

UCSF had technology and recommendations to help me manage side effects. Their Mission Bay Infusion Center had the DigniCap Scalp Cooling System—a head cap I would wear during chemotherapy to keep my scalp cold and reduce hair loss. The system was like an oversized air conditioner and known to be effective with Taxol and carboplatin. I was told Taxol has neuropathy potential, which would feel like pins and needles in my hands and feet. Ice mittens and socks were known to reduce that side effect, so I'd be wrapped in a warm blanket while freezing my head, hands, and feet. I expected to be quite the sight.

Based on the doctor's guidance, I expected fatigue to be the worst side effect. I would need to listen to my body and rest as needed. Oh, the nausea—they were going to give me lots and lots of drugs for that, including Cinvanti, which was the same type of drug that eased Tracey's nausea. Mouth sores were another side effect to watch for. So, apparently, I would be eating bland, cooked food and using something called "magic mouthwash." That was not the THC type, although there was a chance I would need that, too.

"I'm happy to start today," I told Dr. Chien when she walked me through the plan. The sooner I started, the quicker the whole ordeal would be over.

She chuckled. "There are a few steps before chemo can begin," she said. She had a list of at least five things that needed to be done before treatment could start:

She needed to see the PET scan results.

The pathology slides had to be retrieved from Mills Hospital (the parent organization of the Mills-Peninsula Women's Center) and sent to UCSF for review.

Blood tests needed to be scheduled and completed.

An echocardiogram would need to be booked in case I needed AC treatment, which has significant cardiac toxicity.

An interventional radiologist would have to place my port (described in Chapter 11: On-Deck Circle). It would be used to intravenously feed medication or fluids into a large vein leading to my heart.

"It's unlikely chemo will start next week," said Dr. Chien, "but we should be ready the following week."

I would have to be patient. "I'll talk with the oncology nurse as soon as she's available," I said. "I want to learn more about the protocol and create a schedule." I knew to use the time to get organized, ask people to drive me to and from chemotherapy, hang with me, and switch out the ice packs in the mittens and socks every twenty minutes.

"Patients often use a cooler with ice for the mittens and socks," said Dr. Chien. "We'll be watching your platelets, and your white cell counts. Infusions of Procrit—for a low red blood count—or Neulasta—for a low white blood count—might be needed." She went on to tell me that on the days when I would get three-way infusions—three drugs on the same day—with the DigniCap Scalp Cooling System fitted, the entire process would likely be about five hours. Treatments of just Taxol and carboplatin would be about thirty minutes shorter. Once I finished chemotherapy, the immunotherapy (pembrolizumab) would continue every three weeks for twelve months, but that infusion would be thirty minutes after labs.

I was encouraged to exercise and eat normally, and I was allowed to travel, provided I felt up to it. I was pleased to hear this since I was looking forward to our trip to Florida to see our son Taylor play baseball.

"You should be ready for surgery by the end of May or June," added Dr. Chien. *Several months to go,* I thought. I crossed my fingers, hoping my red and white blood cells would sustain the dense dosing and I wouldn't need the very tough AC treatment, bringing the surgery forward.

It was a lot to absorb. Having Neal and Heather in the room was very comforting. Being allowed to use Otter.ai to record and transcribe the discussion was also extremely helpful. Transcribing the doctor's words into written text would allow me to review the doctor's instructions more clearly.

I was relieved to have a treatment plan. Unlike when my mother and sister were treated, the prevailing protocol now was to do chemo and immunotherapy before surgery so the medical team could monitor the response of the cancer to the treatment and adapt the regimen based on the reaction. My surgery would be scheduled for three to four weeks after the last chemo cycle, pending my body's strength.

The goal was a pathological complete response (pCR), the term used when there is no evidence of cancer in the post-surgical pathology analysis. This means that the therapy worked to eliminate the cancer cells. Although my tumor was aggressive, BRCA1 gene-oriented triple-negative tumors are known to consume chemotherapy and immunotherapy ravenously. So the medical team was optimistic that they could achieve a cure.

The word "cure" wasn't used when my mother went through chemotherapy in the eighties. *At her thirty-seventh year of survival, I think she's cured.* Since my mother's initial cancer forty years ago, the science of healthcare has come a long way, and I always knew there was a strong probability that I would face this disease with a positive outcome. Plus, my mother's and sister's cancer experiences prepared me well for this moment. I felt confident I would survive breast cancer.

LESSONS LEARNED

- [ ] Accept your cancer diagnosis as a fact of life as soon as possible. Then, actively engage in planning your approach to treatment.

- [ ] Bring someone, take notes, and use an AI transcriber like Otter.ai for all your appointments. There will be many details, and it's easy to be overwhelmed.

- [ ] Advocate for proactive side effect management, ask for what you need, and inquire about outcomes. It helps to see the potential light at the end of the tunnel.

- [ ] Even if you want to go as fast as possible, there are preliminary steps before treatment. Very few cancers require next-day chemotherapy or surgery. Ask your team to share all the steps, dependencies, and the likely start date.

- [ ] Know that cancer treatment can be a burden on your career and finances. Discuss your treatment schedule with your employer. Look at your insurance policy to better understand its coverage and limitations. Don't hesitate to call your insurance provider to discuss policy details you're unsure of and seek financial assistance *before* you find the cost of living overwhelming. When your finances are in order, you can better focus on your health.

13. The Mental Game

All I wanted was to feel normal. I wanted a break from the thoughts spiraling in my mind. *What will the treatment feel like? Will I experience side effects? What if chemotherapy doesn't work?*

There was a limit to how much TV I could watch without feeling like a mound of mush. I was eager to seek out other forms of distraction, especially those that kept me close to my family. My kids were all athletes with varying levels of commitment and competitiveness, so I focused on being able to attend their games and watch them play.

Our youngest, Ariel, loved lacrosse and was a (somewhat) rare left-handed attacker. Watching her being aggressive while supporting her teammates made me happy. Long before my cancer diagnosis, she joined a travel lacrosse team, and they were scheduled to play at the Sand Storm Lacrosse Festival. My niece, a collegiate lacrosse goalie and the New England Small College Athletic Conference (NESCAC) 2023 Goalie of the Year (we're not a little proud), said Sand Storm was her favorite, so we had planned for Ariel and Neal to go. I was planning a quiet weekend at home recovering from my surgery, which was now off the cards. Unfortunately, I was diagnosed the Monday before Sand Storm.

I was fortunate and privileged to be able to distract myself with a trip. My older children were away at college, and I didn't want to be at home alone with my thoughts for the entire weekend. While I was sure if I stayed home, my friends would have rallied to keep me distracted during the day, my nights would still have been alone, and nights were when my mind raced. It helped to have my husband nearby. It also helped me to be physically exhausted. We had rented an Airbnb property, which meant there was sufficient accommodation. I was so excited to watch my daughter play lacrosse at the Sand Storm Lacrosse Festival. I met them in Palm Springs, where they had arrived by car the night prior.

Since Neal and Ariel were already at the venue with our car, I took a ride from the airport to the polo fields that had been transformed into fifty lacrosse fields and was dropped off at the main entrance. Unfortunately, they were about a mile away and moving, according to the Life 360 app our family uses to digitally track one another, especially when trying to find each other on trips or hikes. As I was walking towards the fields, I got an automated Walgreens update on my cell phone. Like an idiot, I looked at the notifications.

Damn ... there were a lot of things in my Rx that I did not recognize. My mind was off to the races. *Do I need all these medications? How will I keep track of them all? Will these medications interact with each other? How will I determine which medications work for me?*

Standing in the parking lot of the massive polo complex, I started to cry. I hated feeling out of control, but my emotions were limited. I was well prepared and informed about what would come, but these medications were unfamiliar. I didn't recognize any of the names and that made me feel vulnerable and weak. I felt incompetent, which then made me feel bad about myself.

I went from zero to a hundred instantly, suddenly feeling like I was on a collision course with my health.

This entire journey was an exercise in tolerating being out of control and learning how to reset those feelings into something more productive than self-critique. But standing in the parking lot with more than ten Walgreens alerts on my phone, having no idea how I would find my family, and dragging my overnight suitcase, I felt overwhelmed. I didn't know how to reset and find my equilibrium again.

I cried big time.

I felt stupid for crying and silly for feeling overwhelmed. Yet the self-criticism wasn't helping me solve any problems. I was arguing about pulling myself together and dealing with the issue versus allowing myself to feel bad that this was happening. My emotions were beating up my mind. Although I knew I was a world-class problem solver, I was paralyzed. The Walgreens alerts had unleashed my pent-up emotions.

An idea popped into my head. *Call Heather. She's a doctor. She's a survivor. She's offered to help anytime. And, since she's family, she probably won't be rattled by me being irrational and emotional.*

Heather answered the phone, and I blurted out, "Lots of weird prescriptions are getting filled. Starting is the only way to finish, making it more real."

"It is a lot to take in," said Heather. "Do you want to talk?"

I read the medication names to her, and she told me the brand names that my *Chemo Teach* chemotherapy education Zoom call earlier that week had covered, mapping the two together. "You won't likely need them all," Heather said, "but it is good to have them." She explained which ones were escalation pathways if an initial medication didn't make me feel better.

I was so relieved. I was fortunate to have a hotline to someone knowledgeable who could explain the generic names of medications to me on a Saturday as I wandered the polo grounds crying and trying to find my husband and daughter. I could have called the Nurse Advice Line, researched the drugs online, or researched the links on MyChart or a cancer site, such as the American Cancer Society, Breastcancer.org, or Sharsheret. But I was lucky to have a sister-in-law who worked in oncology.

With exasperation, I finally found the correct welcome tent—there were three! Neal and Ariel embraced me, noticing how red my face was.

After I settled into a chair and had something to eat, I called Heather again. "I'm feeling better," I said, "thanks for listening."

"I am here for you anytime," she said. "Do you want me to call Walgreens to see if they can turn off the notifications about your medication pick-up? Then you don't need to be reminded about it this weekend. If so, send me the pharmacy info."

That sounded like a good idea. I also sent her my list of drugs.

"Those are the exact drugs I used for nausea," said Heather. She'd swung and crushed the cancer curveball herself. "I asked my nurse when I could start the Zofran [ondansetron] after the Emend wore off and took it no matter how I was feeling, and then took it religiously every eight hours after that for four days. I would add in the Compazine [prochlorperazine] for breakthrough nausea."

"Ya," I replied, "I need to avoid the nausea."

"I will also send you information from my dietitian about things to eat to help with nausea."

The memory of my sister's first chemo treatment frightened me. There was no escaping how sick it made her, and her reaction lasted for two to three days after each infusion. In that moment, I felt really dumb for not having done the surgery a year earlier. Perhaps I could have avoided this mess.

"Thank you," I said. Heather was a lifesaver, or at least a mind-saver, at that moment. "So you took the Compazine when you were treated for cancer?"

"Yes, I did use the Compazine quite a bit. I didn't use the meds for the first cycle, but I learned my lesson! I was better with them going forward. My third, fourth, and fifth cycles were the worst, symptom-wise, maybe because the side effects were somewhat cumulative. Cycles six through eight weren't as bad, although I still had side effects. For some cycles, I did start the Compazine proactively, like the Zofran."

"I'm nervous," I admitted.

"You will probably meet with nurses, nurse practitioners, or physician assistants before you start the chemo, so try not to worry. You will also see Dr. Chien along the way. They will be excellent partners for you through this process. They are very knowledgeable about the side effects, will take excellent care of you, and will have great tips and tricks for how to get through it."

The call was over in about ten minutes. After, I felt a bit moody and perhaps silly but relieved. My husband felt terrible that I was so upset about the medications and that I had trouble finding him. I have a strong sense of direction, so this was unfamiliar ground for us both. He's not a physician and wouldn't have been helpful regarding the medications. If I hadn't had Heather, I would have called the Nurse Advice Line for my hospital or the American Cancer Society. Both are free services, and the American Cancer Society's hotline is open twenty-four seven. For people who don't have a partner, open yourself to being supported by friends or family members. People surprise you and rise to the occasion. My husband and I tried to focus on my daughter and the games.

The lacrosse was fun to watch. Ariel played great and had the "lax tatts" to show for it. Lax tatts are bruises that form where the opposing players' lacrosse sticks hit the upper arm. Players wear them with pride.

As the games ended for the day, my husband asked if there was anything I wanted to do to enjoy my last few days before chemo started. I wanted to eat sashimi. One of the things I had to avoid once I began chemo was raw food—raw veggies and raw fish. I like sashimi, so we found the best sushi place in Palm Springs, and I enjoyed a sashimi platter that was gorgeous and delicious. It was a small reward for getting through the day and finding opportunities to be happy while allowing myself to feel sad, out of control, and overwhelmed.

Mentally, preparing for cancer treatment is no easy task, but I found a way.

LESSONS LEARNED

- [ ] When waiting for treatment to start, find some form of distraction—religious observance, family togetherness, enjoying something in nature—anything to keep your mind from racing.

- [ ] Cancer is an exercise in tolerating being out of control and learning to reset those feelings into something more productive than self-critique. That skill is helpful after cancer, too!

- [ ] When you see unfamiliar prescriptions, take a breath. Many doctors prescribe in advance, so you have what you need when needed. Ask a doctor or nurse to explain everything.

- [ ] Doctors often prescribe generic versions of drugs. When you get medications, the label will tell you whether the medication is generic or a brand name, so you won't get confused.

- [ ] Phone a friend when the information is overwhelming, or the emotions are intense. Even if that friend is a stranger on the other end of the American Cancer Society helpline. If you are outside the USA, ask your oncologist what services might be available for support if you need it after hours.

14. First Inning

Cancer is a real drag. At its best, it was a significant interruption to whatever I had planned. It was an unwelcome curveball interfering with my otherwise great life. At its worst, cancer put my mortality front and center, with all the accompanying questions about whether I'd lived a worthwhile and meaningful life. *I wonder how many philosophers were born of trauma.* I read Viktor Frankl's *Man's Search for Meaning* and concurred with his assertion that suffering can be a source of meaning. Most of the time, though, cancer was just a downer.

When the first infusion day arrived, I was nervous but excited to get the process started. My mother came with me since I knew I would need support. What I didn't expect was more waiting.

I checked in for the lab draw and then waited.

A nurse checked my vitals. "Your blood pressure is elevated," she said.

They don't see this all the time? "I'm anxious," I said. *Breathe. Be mindful.* My blood pressure lowered. The nurse drew my blood. I'd have to wait for the results.

I checked in for my oncology appointment, and then we sat in the waiting room.

The test results arrived on MyChart, the electronic health record (EHR) used by my hospital. MyChart had my appointments, messaging with my healthcare team, lab and radiology reports and results, billing, and even the EZ Check In app to expedite my appointments. I had yet to learn what all the lab results meant, but it looked like green meant good.

The medical assistant brought me back to the doctor's clinic. She rechecked vitals and asked about any new allergies or other new developments. She was charming. She suggested I change into a gown and wait for the doctor.

The nurse practitioner reviewed the chart, checked everything, and examined me.

Then I waited longer. I was happy I'd brought Stego. Stego was a small, stuffed dinosaur—probably six inches from nose to tail. He was the perfect size to wear my ID bracelet as a collar. When I had my port placed, Neal came to the recovery room, having picked Stego from the gift shop. It was a blue-green Stegosaurus. "It spoke to me," Neal said.

"Let's name him Stego," I said, then smiled. Stego snuggled beside me until I could leave the interventional radiology department with my new port, which we named Voldeport. And Stego became my chemo mascot.

The doctor finally arrived. She checked my chart, described what would happen next, and examined me. I felt better because the labs were good and she was encouraging.

I could get dressed and check in for my first infusion.

The anticipatory stress for my first infusion was disappearing; somehow, I was sleepy already. After checking in with the nurse, we had to wait again.

When I got called back into the infusion center, the medical assistant gave us a quick tour. My first chemo infusion was on Floor 3—future ones would use Floors 4 and 5. Immediately after being buzzed into the infusion center on Floor 3, you see a room on the left with multiple phlebotomy stations. This is where I'd already been for my lab draws. Just beyond that room is a chair and computer setup. The chair doubled as a scale, and the medical assistant took my vitals there before the lab draw. My mother and I walked past both stations and into the unfamiliar. On the left was a massive door with a caution sign, ensuring we knew it would swing outwards. That was the bathroom. Straight ahead were two private rooms with hospital beds.

"What are those for?" I asked the medical assistant.

"Those are for patients who need infusion to specific parts of their bodies or are too ill to be in the recliners."

I hoped I would never need the private chemo rooms.

As we turned the corner, the nurses and medical assistants had a bullpen in the center of the large room where they were engaging with computers to confirm orders and monitor the release of medications. Around the perimeter were recliners in pairs, with their backs to the windows, and chairs for guests. The recliners had IV stands, and a computer and supplies station was positioned between each pair. I noticed the signs saying cell phones were not to be used and the use of face masks was encouraged.

We were headed to Seat 12, the furthest nook in the infusion center. With my chemo bag in tow, I looked like a pack donkey heading to my seat.

"Here's your seat and the DigniCap machine," the medical assistant told me. "Can I get you a warm blanket and anything to eat or drink?"

"A warm blanket would be nice," I said. The recliners and chairs were comfortable. My mom sat across from me with the Yeti cooler as her footrest. I stared either at my mother or the wall and wondered why my recliner wasn't facing the campus window. The recliner had a button for heat, which I liked, and for vibration, which I did not. Because my legs are so short, I immediately lifted the footrest and put a pillow behind my back. I imagined that I was boarding an airplane for a five-hour flight and wanted to feel comfortable. I also remembered from my mom's and sister's experiences that I wouldn't feel queasy or sick while in the infusion center. That would happen later, if at all.

There's a chorus of random beeps in an infusion center. The infusion machines beep when they complete an infusion. They beep if their battery is low. They beep if something isn't quite right. Every patient has a different regimen, and it starts at a different time, so something is constantly beeping. The DigniCap machine also beeps when it's reached its proper cooling temperature and when you are disconnected for too long because you went to the bathroom. There are only three of those, so they don't beep as much as the infusion machines. The nurses and medical assistants needed to hear all those beeps, but I did not. Suffice it to say, I appreciated my headphones.

The infusion center smells faintly of antiseptic because everyone is immunosuppressed. My aromatherapy pendant was designed to replace that scent with lavender or bergamot, but only for me. The floors are linoleum, and I had to wear shoes or slippers whenever I walked to the bathroom. The hardest part of entering the infusion center is seeing the other cancer patients. Many of them look frail. Many have thinning or no hair. Some look hale and hearty. Some look old. No one appeared to be in pain, but no one looked happy either. There is much waiting, even after being seated in the infusion center. I had prayers, letters, movies, and books to enjoy, and my mom for conversation. I needed them all. I also felt a lot more cheerful than the people I saw around me because I was finally taking action to obliterate this cancer, and that felt like retaking my power. I was upbeat and happy with the nurses and thanked them for educating and caring for me. My philosophy was to spread light, hoping it would reflect on me. Additionally, I don't like being morose.

As we waited, we flipped through magazines. I hated the wait. I don't idle well. I had to work hard to still my mind and divert my focus from the disaster prophesying. A slow-moving, four-foot-high robot rolled along the passageway between the bullpen and the infusion stations. I asked the medical assistant what it was and found out that on Floor 3, the robot delivers the chemotherapy drugs. UCSF did not use that system on Floors 4 to 6, but I'd learn about their systems later.

Eventually, once the infusion center knew the pharmacy was mixing the chemo medicines, the pre-treatment began. The pre-treatment was timed to help with reactions to the chemo as it was infused. For example, some patients have an allergic reaction to carboplatin, and the doctor prescribes Benadryl to counteract it. But the Benadryl must be in full force when the carboplatin is infused. Benadryl is infused no more than fifteen minutes prior to starting the carboplatin infusion. For me, the Benadryl-prompted nap started immediately after Benadryl was infused. The other drugs counter nausea, bolster the immune system, and settle the stomach, but they are only infused within thirty minutes of starting the chemotherapy. The cold cap must be on before the infusion begins, so at one point, I had two medical assistants wetting and combing my hair to place the cap while the nurse was infusing different pre-treatments into my IV. Sometimes the pharmacy has a lot of orders and is slow. The pharmacy will not mix the chemotherapy drugs until the labs are released and reviewed; at this point, the oncologist approves the day's infusion. The idea that my infusion could be delayed because my body was too weak to handle it was terrifying. I resolved to do everything I could to stay as healthy as possible. For me, that included exercising, hydrating, and eating well.

Because I had a port already placed, the nurse who drew the labs before chemo did the "port access" using a small medical device with a long needle that penetrated my chest and inserted into the port's access point. One of my prescriptions was for lidocaine, a local anesthetic, which I placed on my skin over the port one hour before my labs. If I timed that right, I would barely feel the port needle being inserted. After accessing the port, the nurse collected the lab samples and attached an IV Octopus. These tubes allow the nurse to infuse medication, including pre-treatments, chemotherapy, and immunotherapy. They have clamps to stop the flow, and they connect to the infusion machines. The nurse placed a sterile adhesive bandage over the port access point, preventing the tubing from being yanked when I moved. Unfortunately, I discovered after a few infusions that if my skin wasn't completely dry from the nurse's antiseptic wash before accessing the port, my skin reacted to the bandage and was itchy. Benadryl helps a little with that, but mostly, I had to tell the nurses to go slowly and ensure all the alcohol had evaporated off my skin before sealing everything.

Once the port is accessed, everything goes through the port. The port is connected to a large vein above the right side of the heart called the superior vena cava, a circulation superhighway. When the Cinvanti was administered, I immediately tasted rubber in my mouth. When the Benadryl was administered, I had five minutes before I nodded off. My pre-treatment began once my nurse had confirmation from the pharmacy that the chemotherapy drugs were en route. The infusion nurse cheerfully announced that we could start, and using a syringe, the nurse slowly squeezed the pre-treatment drugs into my IV line. My psycho-oncologist had recommended I request extra IV fluids, so I had a liter of saline dripping into my IV Octopus, and the pre-treatments would mix into that stream. The nurses control that stream's speed and the speed of the pre-treatment's administration. I was curious and asked which drug they were administering and what to expect. The nurses were patient educators. They told me to put on the ice mittens and socks fifteen minutes before they started the carboplatin. My hands, feet, and head all had to be near freezing to prevent the chemotherapy side effects of neuropathy and hair loss. To maximize the benefit, I had to wear the DigniCap for the entire infusion and two hours after the Taxol. Ice mittens and socks were required only for one hour of carboplatin infusion.

After all the pre-treatments, the nurse brought the first bag of chemotherapy, my carboplatin. It would be infused over one hour. The nurse robed herself in an extra blue gown because of the toxicity of the drugs. She held the bag before me to confirm my name and date of birth. Then she scanned my ID band (on me this time but would move to Stego's neck for future infusions). Another nurse joined her and read the code on my ID band. My nurse confirmed the code in the computer and named the drug I was to receive. The second nurse confirmed that the bag of medication is that drug. All these steps are in place to prevent dangerous errors. Once all was confirmed, the bag was hung and connected to the IV Octopus, and the cancer-killing poison began to slowly drip into my veins. My mom helped me be comfortable and assured me I would get through this. I was genuinely relieved to be starting. I was anxious about the unknown reaction I might have later that night or the next couple of days, but I had my prescriptions and my comfort food. And I had my mom to take care of me if I needed her. I was as comfortable as one could be while toxic poison was infused into my veins.

This exact procedure of confirming my identity and the drugs would happen twice more for the Taxol and Keytruda. Checking my ID band required the nurses to wake me from my Benadryl nap, and it was hard to fall back to sleep, making the day longer. I talked with my mom. I read a book. I watched episodes of *Firefly Lane*, which my sister-in-law Heather recommended. I tried to sleep. I sent my mom on a quest for lunch, and we both enjoyed a chicken parmigiana sandwich. I had blocked the day from work, so I didn't send emails or use Slack. Heather, during her chemo, worked and attended Zoom meetings off-camera. Queen!

After one hour of carboplatin, thirty minutes of Taxol, and thirty minutes of Keytruda, I had two hours of extra cooling. Only then could I be disconnected from the DigniCap and the IV Octopus. The last step was removing and replacing the port access device with a Band-Aid. Six hours after arriving at the infusion center, we were done. Unlike my sister, I didn't have a protocol that called for a device to be attached to my arm to inject Neulasta twenty-four hours after infusion. I was free to leave Cancerland for the next six days. The nurses wanted to hear if I experienced any side effects or allergic reactions, but otherwise, they'd see me next time. They gave me a $5 coupon for parking. I left feeling like a superhero. The toxic chemo had taken its first shot at me, and I was walking out of the hospital feeling strong and focused on getting to the next milestone, which was the following week's chemo, only six days later, with labs that would propel me towards complete cancer obliteration.

One down, eleven to go.

LESSONS LEARNED

☐ Request extra IV fluids to keep the medication flowing out of your body. It's more comfortable. I drank 24 oz of water from my bottle and got a liter of infused saline.

☐ Ask questions if you are curious. The nurses are excellent educators.

☐ Ask for the day's timeline to prepare you for the schedule.

☐ Bring whatever distracts you, like books, music, and movies. You are unlikely to have privacy, so conversations with friends or family who join you will be minimal, and cell phones are discouraged. Other patients are resting, so aim for quiet.

☐ Choose your mindset. You can fear and dread chemotherapy or view it as your weaponry in the battle against cancer. Some patients imagine it as a video game, with the drugs seeking and gobbling up cancer cells like Pac-Man. Pick a mindset that works for you and focus on it.

15. Batting Rituals

One of my tactics to control my reaction to the speed and shape of cancer's curveballs was to have a set of regular rituals and routines that I call *happiness tripwires*™. I used these happiness tripwires to transform the weekly cancer treatments into experiences with positive associations. For what it's worth, I also called them *Cancer Obliteration Days* since that's what was happening—or what we hoped would happen. The treatments were meant to get rid of cancer. Chemo days were five and a half hours long, not including travel time. I knew it was going to be a long, repetitive, and sometimes lonely haul, but I was determined to face chemotherapy head-on.

Every chemo day started with washing my hair. As part of the cold-capping protocol provided by DigniCap, I could only wash my hair once a week. I enjoyed the feeling of water running over my head and the scalp massage from washing and conditioning my hair. I needed these self-care moments to set the tone for the day. After showering, I picked comfy, loose-fitting clothing and packed slippers to wear while sitting in the infusion center recliner. My go-bag had my binder, iPad, slippers, headphones, Stego, aromatherapy pendant and oils, and a wooden cylinder holding twelve wooden hearts given to me by my college best friend, Shira, who lived across the country, sharing twelve things she loves about me. Everything in the bag improved my comfort.

With permission from my oncology team, I religiously drank Athletic Greens to provide my body with vegetable nutrients and probiotics. I exercised five out of seven days by lifting weights, doing metabolic conditioning three times a week with my bestie, Jessica, and walking the other two or three days. Jessica and I had been working out together for at least fifteen years, and while she shifted to coming to my home gym (thanks to COVID) instead of alternating between our homes or going to a public gym, we didn't break stride. Aware of my treatment schedule, our trainer, who worked for my sister and her husband, programmed exercises appropriately. These routines were a regular part of my training for the infusion days.

To me, food is fuel, and my breakfast is pastured eggs with spinach, onion, and sometimes peppers. I don't drink coffee, and my sister taught me that orange juice is a sugar jolt, so I drink water with my eggs. I make steel-cut oats with brown sugar and butter if I need variety. After breakfast, my ride arrived, and I had a twenty-minute visit with a friend. It was great to hear about my friends' lives and spend time together while driving to the infusion center. I liked arriving early so the nurses could do the port draws and labs on time. The sooner my labs came back, the sooner the infusion started. The sooner the infusion started, the sooner it was over and the closer I was to obliteration.

After the port draw for labs, I had an hour-long wait. I'd read a letter from my son Taylor—a happiness tripwire. At college, he was more than three thousand miles away, and I had asked him to write me weekly letters describing his school days and baseball games. I desperately needed my children to live their lives to the fullest, even if I couldn't be there to watch them. I cherished these letters during my weekly treatments. They added joy to a possibly bleak experience. The letters served a dual purpose. It was challenging for Taylor to focus on school and baseball when I was undergoing treatment for cancer. Although his days were hectic, I knew he worried about me. The letters he wrote served as an outlet for the anxiety manifested during those days, allowing him to feel more connected to me. And every week, Taylor's letters were an elixir for my soul.

After reading Taylor's letters, I'd usually open my binder to read my prayers and start my iPad to listen to a few online prayers I enjoyed. My rabbi, Rebecca Schatz, compiled prayers and songs I could say and play, all on YouTube, and I conveniently made a playlist—another happiness tripwire.

Often, I'd get a text from Julian, my friend from high school and college. Julian inevitably and intentionally texted me every chemo day, and our playful banter helped distract me—a happiness tripwire. I looked forward to his emoji-laden notes.

My sister-in-law Heather recommended downloading TV shows, which I tried, but I preferred banter, music, letters, and my Benadryl nap. An essential element of my routine was humor. I'd find things to laugh at with the check-in clerks, medical assistants, and nurses. The robot that delivered the chemotherapy medicine was fodder for my funny bone. I enlisted friends to help keep the funny coming. The daily dose of laughter from a friend's email library of "you have the wrong jxxxx@gmail.com," the antics of another friend's dog captured in photos, something my kids shared, or something humorous from Neal always served to lighten the day, break up a moment, and give me the space to focus—lots of happiness tripwires.

I had someone with me for every chemo session, which allowed me to get to know a couple of people better (Julie and Molly) and share time with people I already knew and loved. They were all part of distracting me during treatments. All the distractions made me happy, and I decided it was good to let myself feel satisfied, loved, and supported as I faced my chemo days.

After my labs came back all clear (and I was fortunate they did every week for all twelve weeks), my friend and I would go to my recliner in the infusion center. I'd kick off my shoes and wear the fluffy slippers I only wore on chemo day—happiness tripwire. Then I'd start the playlist from Ben—his choice of music, another connection of sorts. I'd share all this with my friend and chat some more.

I'd remove my aromatherapy locket, dab a little lavender or bergamot, then put it over my head to rest on my chest. I'd take out the small wooden cylinder from Shira that held the twelve hearts presenting the reasons she loved me and place it on my side table. I'd place Stego, the dinosaur, on the side table next to the cylinder—three happiness tripwires in quick succession. My water bottle sat next to

Stego. My laptop or iPad was on the other side of the table for when I wanted it.

Once everything was in order, I would sit back in the recliner, elevate my feet, ask for some heated blankets, tea, and saltine crackers, and settle in for the day, as a fast infusion comprised one hour for labs and four and a half hours of infusion and cooling. A normal infusion session was five and a half hours after labs. An empty stomach was more likely to make me feel queasy, so I always had a lunch plan for infusion days. My friends offered to arrange lunch for each infusion, either packed in my cooler or to-go from a nearby restaurant. I chatted with my friend, the medical assistant, and the infusion nurse. I was happy to see them because this was a day when we were all actively trying to obliterate the cancer. My obliteration mindset made the infusion days positive.

After the medical assistants affixed my DigniCap, I'd be given Benadryl. I was grateful that Benadryl knocked me out. I slept very deeply, except when the nurses needed to confirm my identity before starting a chemo infusion, when my hands were too cold in the ice mittens, or when my feet were uncomfortable in the ice socks I used to stave off the neuropathy side effect. I didn't want pins and needles in my hands and feet as a constant reminder of cancer.

My hands and feet were uncomfortably cold in the ice gear. I would fidget. I needed to pull my hands out of the mittens even when I wore liners on my hands. My hands and feet were on ice while my head was just above freezing. The nurses nestled the rest of my body in multiple warm blankets. Stego sat on top of the blankets or right next to me. I'd slip my bracelet off my wrist and onto Stego after the pre-treatments and before the ice mittens, and the nurses would scan him for identity confirmation. It was a great system that kept me safe and asleep. Two nurses were required to match my ID bracelet to the information on the IV bag.

It seemed silly to suggest a stuffed animal improved my cancer treatment, but Stego materially enhanced my experience. I didn't want to dread chemo days, and I knew that the prospect of feeling ill, losing my hair, being fatigued, and experiencing chemo fog were all part of the cure. I felt like I needed to counter those genuine impacts to quiet my anxiety, so I found small ways to help me look forward to chemo. They helped, even though I knew it was a psychological game I was playing with myself.

These were my top ten chemo day rituals—or happiness tripwires—besides Stego:

1. Washing my hair as a once-a-week treat at the start of chemo day. I love my shower, and the self-care ritual made me feel indulged and normal.
2. While I waited for my labs, I read a letter from my son, focusing on his life and feelings of love and support.
3. Putting on my aromatherapy pendant. The lavender or bergamot essential oil eliminated the hospital antiseptic smell without bothering my fellow infusion patients. It was a touch of luxury in a sterile environment.
4. I listened quietly and sang along with my treatment day prayer list (thank you, Rabbi Rebecca Schatz), followed by my son's chemo playlist.
5. Texts from Julian with virtual hugs.

6. I wore my UCSF fleece sweatshirt on chemo day. It had the right pockets and fit, making everyone wonder if I worked at UCSF. I also wore a fleece and comfy pants with a top that made port access easy.
7. Switching into my chemo-day-only, fuzzy-foam, slip-free slippers.
8. Hugs, handholds, and calls from my chemo buddy, family, and husband.
9. A lunch treat—chicken parmesan sub? Grilled cheese and tomato soup? Chinese soup dumplings? I did not deny myself things I enjoyed for lunch on chemo day.
10. Warm blankets ... lots and lots of warm blankets. The medical assistants and nurses would swap out my blankets whenever I wanted a warmer one. Whenever I detached the tubes from the DigniCap and walked to the bathroom, the team changed all the blankets.

Even knowing the rituals were a game I played with my mind, it felt a lot better than wondering if the labs would be good or if I would feel sick or tired after chemo. Whatever makes you feel better in the batter's box is worth taking up to the plate.

Once I had an idea of the type and speed of the pitches I'd see during my treatment, I started to think about when and how I would add milestones beyond the therapeutic ones. Therapeutic milestones included the MRI after week twelve of carboplatin-Taxol to see if I was going on to surgery or AC infusion. Surgery was another milestone.

I wanted micro-milestones and awards for reaching them.

There was something to celebrate every couple of weeks. They were small celebrations, but they made the months of treatment go faster. There was always something to look forward to or someone to see. These drug-free uppers slowed the pitches and, at times, even made swinging fun; they were happiness tripwires.

My son's baseball team has an iconic spring baseball trip to Florida, where they play many games in a short period. Before cancer, my husband and I planned to go to Orlando, cheer for our son, and get to know the other baseball families, as this was his first year at college. With Wednesdays as cancer days *and* our daughter's birthday in the middle of the second week of the planned trip, we identified one long weekend when we could head across the country, stay in an Airbnb property, and enjoy early-season baseball. Being healthy enough to travel from California to Orlando in mid-March was a micro-objective. Knowing that I could see my son and he could see I was okay was another primary motivator and reward.

There were visits from Shira (Chicago, college best friend), Julie (New York, business school friend), Heather (Boston, sister-in-law), and Michele (Park City, sister-in-law). We planned a "halfway-through-chemo" dessert quest with Jessica, Ariel, Sivana (Jessica's youngest, who is the same age as Ariel), and me. We found Japanese desserts!

My daughter organized a Play for Pink fundraiser with the support of her Menlo School boys' and girls' lacrosse teams, their competing teams, and the parents in the Menlo lacrosse community. Her efforts raised $5,000 for Sharsheret.org to deliver cancer support.

Jessica's older daughter designed team T-shirts everyone could wear in photos for a chemo completion celebration.

I planned to have a "chemo's over" champagne toast with my girlfriends—it would be my first sip of alcohol in four months! And we wanted another crack at the Bye-Bye Boobies party before the surgery that would remove my breasts.

After an infusion, I needed to relax while settling in at home. Chemo days were not easy. My mental game included a plan for creature comforts at home. I chose where I wanted to sleep or rest, ensuring other people in the house could respect my space. I would focus on the present, letting go of the past, and trust that the future would be all right. No one is well-served dwelling for very long in their mind's petrified and worried space, so I created a routine to reset myself from worried to balanced. This routine put me in a mental state that enabled me to perform at my best. The mental game in baseball is to create a routine and do something consistently: visualize, breathe, count, sing, or anything else that helps get you in a calm frame of mind to perform.

Chemotherapy isn't particularly fun, and cancer isn't a game. In fact, during a cancer at-bat, a strike-out can be deadly. Treatments take a long time, and some of the treatment makes you feel sick or at least uncomfortable. Yet, during my chemotherapy regimen, hundreds of people held me virtually and physically, and their support, comments, humor, prayers, news, and love gave me strength. I felt happy on my chemo days, and that happiness was buoyed by having minimal side effects. My nurses and doctors wondered if my minimal side effects resulted from the enjoyment of the people and the memories I wove into those days. We'll never know.

LESSONS LEARNED

- [ ] Uplift yourself with humor. Most people have a funny friend. If not, there are online apps you can sign up for to get a daily joke, limerick, or puzzle. Whatever pauses your racing mind and gives you a moment of relief is good.
- [ ] Embed happiness tripwires into your infusion-day routine to bring you joy.
- [ ] Prepare your home for your return after infusions and have rituals to settle your mind and body.
- [ ] Create meaningful mini-milestones focused on reaching a critical point and being rewarded for your progress.
- [ ] Welcome people to visit and support you.

16. The Fans

Off-speed pitches are unavoidable. During cancer treatment, they are frequent and have unique curves and speeds. That said, you are in the batter's box whether you like it or not, so asking for help to give you a better mental game and stronger swing is a good idea. We all need to eat. We don't live in infusion, radiation, or surgery centers, so we must travel to them and home again. There are other needs for batters with children. And even more needs for people whose pitches fling them far from home.

Friends and family—the fans—are vital during cancer treatment.

I leveraged the lessons of my mother's and sister's cancers to specify the support I needed from my friends and family. Knowing what was either essential or trivial to me was crucial. For example, I am not a foodie. Food is fuel to me, although I appreciate people who are excellent cooks. So when I asked for people to provide meals, I was open to whatever people wanted to cook, with some guidelines about ingredients we don't eat and guidance from my oncologist regarding spicy, undercooked, or raw food. I did not expect anyone to do anything specific, and I cast my net reasonably wide. I trusted that people genuinely wanted to help and would participate however it suited them. Seeing what people chose to do and who I would spend time with each week was fun.

I didn't wait until I had cancer to build a community and discover what roles different people in my life would play best. There's considerable evidence that multiple close relationships benefit life expectancy and mental health. Common sense is that life is more enjoyable when you share it with people, and different people bring different things. I'm also an extrovert and genuinely enjoy being around people. That said, I don't usually affiliate with social groups or cliques. Instead, I have close friendships with individuals from different parts of my life.

Jonathan, who cared deeply about my health, especially when I traveled during chemotherapy, is the grandson of my grandfather's best friend, the son of my father's closest childhood friend, and my friend since birth. Julian, the texter, is my closest friend from high school. Shira, who came to stay with me during part of my chemotherapy, is my best friend from college. Neal and I met in business school as section mates. My sister, Tracey, and I have cultivated a close relationship and live nearby. Neal's sister, Heather, became a dear friend when Neal and I started dating. Jessica and I met when we were both six months pregnant with our firstborn children, and our friendship blurred the lines between friend and family as we raised all six of our children (three and three) together. Over the past ten years, and significantly reinforced during COVID, five women from my business school class texted, enjoyed quarterly dinners, and had weekly calls during the lockdown. We've supported each other through professional and personal challenges—my cancer was another one on a robust list.

If you want a friend, you must first be a friend. These people, and the many others who bring color to my life, were important to me. Reaching out and staying in touch with people always made me happy. I endeavored to show up and be there for my friends. When I needed them, they showed up for me.

The different people in my life have different strengths. Neal is a resilient optimist who is an endless source of ideas. Tracey is an intuitive, natural communicator with cutting-edge best practices to live a healthy and robust life. Jessica is an incredible and committed organizer who likes structure and invests heavily in community building. Heather is calm, compassionate, and fantastic at translating medical-speak into plain English. Knowing which skills, talents, and interests aligned with roles on the team made it much easier for me to ask the right person for the proper support.

I asked Heather to fly to California to support Neal during my prophylactic surgery, and she was pivotal when we were processing the cancer diagnosis. Jessica knew my quirks and helped me understand what I needed and from whom. She and Tracey quickly allied to support me and each other, while Tracey helped me keep our parents informed and comforted. Neal's job was to make life as easy as possible for the kids and me while being the person who was always available for a hug. Julie, who became a very close friend during my cancer journey, was an advocate and thought partner and was always ready with something to make me smile—often a photo of her crazy dog.

I invited more people to be part of my journey through writing on CaringBridge, where I also shared the ever-changing timeline. Fortunately, Jessica is a logistics quarterback who I knew would care more than I would about the details of my support. Through years of experience with births, parties, fundraisers, sicknesses, b'nai mitzvahs, and shivas, I knew that Jessica was a detail-oriented planner who would believe me when I said I didn't care about something. I was confident that my community would engage with the sign-up lists that she was sending out. Jessica knew what to ask because she knew me very well. She knew I wouldn't give specifics about food because I'm not particular, so she provided prompts that generated some parameters regarding meals, visits, and driving.

I was lucky to have two National Cancer Centers within fifteen miles of my house. That gave me a level of choice, convenience, and care many people do not get. Some people need specialized treatments that aren't available near their homes. My mother was able to centralize her care at Stanford but have her infusions near her home in Florida, making her batter's box much more comfortable. I tried to control the calendar in a wrestling match with UCSF as they scheduled infusions, and I would persuade and charm them to attempt to minimize extra visits to the hospital. Jessica facilitated asking people to drive me to and from treatment, to stay for the treatment—until I realized I slept for most of it—then revised the request to keep me company for the delay between labs and pre-treatment. I think the people who drove me and kept me company found the experience surprisingly enjoyable because I was happy to see them, and I created a routine that made chemo day a good one.

Don't be a hero or a martyr unless you have no choice. Be a human and embrace whatever community you have around you. These universal supports made the experience easier—more comfortable and less stressful. I asked for all these universal supports except Door Dash at lunch—that idea came to me around infusion eleven or twelve:

Dinners on chemo day, plus on one or two more. This is often called a meal train. I chose deliveries on Mondays, Wednesdays, and Fridays because we had too many leftovers if people brought food every day of the week. When my sister, Tracey, was undergoing chemo, she preferred meals on chemo day, plus on one and two days after chemo. Design the schedule that works best for you and your family.

Door Dash/Uber Eats for lunch on chemo day. Some infusion centers have a lunch cart (way to go, Mass General!), but mine did not. Everyone needs to eat, and there are delivery services such as Door Dash, Uber Eats, and Deliveroo (UK) that deliver almost anywhere. Some people bring a packed lunch from home, like frozen soup or a sandwich. Most infusion nurses will gladly heat food up for you.

Drivers to and from the infusion center or doctors' appointments. If you are getting medications that make you sleepy (IV-Benadryl, Ativan) or if your stomach is very sensitive, you do not need a car accident on top of treatment, so don't be a hero—let your good driving friends help you.

Ask for a daily giggle. Laughter is excellent medicine. My friend Justin had been responding to people who accidentally emailed him (he has a common Irish last name) with humorous responses since 2012. "You got the wrong jxxxx@gmail.com." It was a riot, and he had enough such emails to send me one daily. Julie has a crazy dog, and she sent me photos of the funny things Cybill Shepherd would do. They were my designated laugh medicine providers.

Walk with me. I am an extrovert, and I enjoy talking with people. I didn't want to sit in my house alone, feeling lousy, and I needed to move to get fresh air and live life. Since I'm an early-morning walker, I asked people to walk with me. I knew how long I could walk and where I wanted to meet. Be transparent; it helps everyone. This way, you don't need texts or calls asking where, when, and so on.

Play cards/board games/mah-jongg with me. Even if I felt lousy, there was a limit to how much I could binge-watch TV or read books. You likely will want to be social, too. I reminded people that I was immunosuppressed and that anyone spending time with me (in a house, in a car, or on a walk) must be healthy. Otherwise, they need to cancel. The patient (or batter) must come first in the batter's box.

Chemo day company. I recommend choosing who you want with you for your first treatment. Most people are nervous, scared, and even disoriented that first day. There are many people and many steps. I needed to check in three times—once for the oncologist, once for the lab, and once for the infusion—all at the same place. Confusing! My mom came with me for my first treatment, and that was a comfort. I was the first person for my sister. My dad was the first person for my mom. After the first chemo day, I felt more oriented and was able to think about the other people who would be comforting companions during my infusion. Ultimately, it became a question of who would self-entertain while I slept!

Visits. Perhaps you prefer to avoid doing any activities but want to talk. It's okay to switch any walk or activity to sitting and talking. And it's okay to say you are getting tired and end the visit early.

Although my children were largely independent when I was diagnosed and treated for breast cancer, kids, young and old, need to keep their lives as normal as possible. I was aware of cancer patients with younger kids. These people needed extra help, and some used apps like Signup Genius to organize friends and family who could make their lives a bit easier during trying times. For most cancer patients with children, the following can be very helpful:

1. **Pick-up and drop-off for school or daycare.**
   Sometimes, infusions will start at 7:30 a.m., and some cancer patients must drive for hours to the closest infusion center. These hours don't always jibe with school hours. Friends with children who go to the same school or friends who live in the neighborhood are great for ensuring kids get to and from school on time. School staff or daycare providers sometimes connect with parents in need. Some parents schedule chemo on Fridays so their partner can work from home or take the day off to ferry the kids.

2. **Babysitting after school**. Infusions often run long, and the pressure to be done in time to watch kids after school can be overwhelming. Friends with children who go to the same school or live in your neighborhood are invaluable.

3. **Driving kids to or from activities.** Most parents don't want to disrupt their children's lives with cancer any more than necessary. This goes for young kids and teenagers, too. Asking the parents of children in the same activity for carpool assistance—at least on chemo day—can be very helpful. While partners carry the load when cancer hits, even parents need a break sometimes. Asking for help is important for everyone.

4. **Playdates.** One survivor I spoke with shared that she wanted her children to have cancer-free weekends, so she asked volunteers to host each of her kids on Saturdays and Sundays. Most weekends were filled.

There are other needs if you must travel long distances for treatment. If your treatment diverts to a clinical trial, you may need to travel to the trial site to participate. Many people are ashamed that they cannot afford all the costs associated with cancer. Some even refuse to ask for help. There's no shame in conveying that you are stressing your resources to access the best care for your cancer. Most US cancer patients report that the financial strain is more stressful than the disease and treatment. There are financial support foundations that can help. Sharsheret has a good list of support links, and many treatment centers have financial assistance. Some things to ask for from your community include:

1. **Hotel points.** Hotel points or points plans can be gifted so cancer patients have a place to stay during treatment without prohibitive costs.
2. **Airfare points.** As with hotel points, airline points or plans can be gifted, and there are airline-specific programs for patients who need to fly to receive treatment.
3. **Rooms at friends' homes.** People often open their homes to help if asked.
4. **Banked vacation days.** One of my friends is a nurse, and her peers gifted her sick and vacation days to supplement her disability income and help minimize the financial stress of cancer.
5. **Food delivery gift cards.** When struggling with cancer, feeding yourself or your family can be difficult. Gift cards for take-out food from Door Dash, Caviar, Uber Eats, or Instacart, to name a few, can help cancer patients and their families.
6. **Donations and crowdfunding.** Online crowdfunding platforms like GoFundMe and Fundly gather donations or contributions that can help a cancer patient cover the high costs of cancer-related travel, medical care outside of what is covered by insurance, and general living when work is disrupted. Don't wait until you are at risk of foreclosure or racking up credit card debt to ask for help. In the United States, a considerable percentage of cancer patients will need significant time off from work and lose income during treatment. Depending on your financial reserves, deductibles, annual limits, lifetime

coverage limits, and expenses associated with treatment, you can experience financial stress. Ask for help early to minimize those problems.

Asking for help relieves your stress and the helplessness your friends and family feel as they watch you endeavor to smash the curveballs. Guiding your friends and family to your sign-up sheet will minimize your stress.

A note for well-intentioned friends and family: Ask before you send something. Flowers are beautiful, but scents can nauseate a chemo patient. There are only so many stuffed animals anyone can have. Unexpected food might not have a place in the fridge or freezer. If your friend doesn't have a sign-up list, offer to be the person who organizes it for them—the most significant gift of all.

Not every fan should be called upon. I was determined to ensure my daughter didn't have to be a caretaker, cook, or counselor during my cancer treatment. My heart breaks that I couldn't insulate my daughter from my cancer experience entirely. She's a compassionate, emotionally connected, thoughtful, and intelligent young woman. She leveraged support, but she doesn't remember much of the second half of her sophomore year of high school because I was being treated for cancer. The enormity of that reality was an eclipse that darkened the rest of the spring for her and weighed heavily on my mind.

But we worked around cancer. Ariel got her driver's license during my chemotherapy, with me at the DMV to cheer her on. We made many good memories during my cancer year, after I completed treatment: We went to Disneyland and Broadway. We saw Taylor Swift, Billy Joel, and P!nk in concert. We went to Ann Arbor to visit my alma mater and cheered for the Wolverines in the Big

House. My band performed during treatment, and Ariel performed during our breaks. I hoped her memories of my cancer years were primarily positive, and I prayed that she would never have to tell her fifteen-and-a-half-year-old daughter she had breast cancer. In the next twenty years, scientific breakthroughs in preventative treatment will likely stop this cycle.

Until then, gather your friends and family around you in your time of need. Fans will cheer you on.

LESSONS LEARNED

- [ ] Be specific about the support you need and how it will be implemented. When do you want meals? What type of food do you like? Be clear so those around you know how to help.

- [ ] Make a budget and test the impact of reducing your work hours during treatment. Ask for and apply for financial assistance early.

- [ ] If you must travel for treatment, ask for help with hotels, flights, and transportation.

- [ ] If you have young children, ask people to help with activities, playdates, and carpools. Don't worry if you aren't doing your share right now; you can catch up later.

- [ ] Laughter is good medicine. Ask funny friends to supply giggles or sign up for Joke of the Day. Tickle your funny bone.

17. The Batting Helmet

Until I experienced chemo myself, I didn't know how my body would react. Hollywood, books, and personal history combined to make me worried about what would happen if I exposed my body to chemotherapy, the helpful poison.

I was scared, anxious, and nervous. I didn't feel like a warrior or fighter; I felt resigned. *I must do this, and I have to endure what comes with it. I will have to make the best of it.* Several side effects had me worried. The waiting increased my anxiety. There was nothing I could do to make the wheels of the healthcare party van spin faster.

Chemo medicines are cumulative in the body. The most apparent indication of the accumulation is hair loss, which starts between infusions two and three. While cold capping can help, it's an extra cost that most insurance companies are unwilling to cover in the USA, even though they'll cover wigs. Although cold capping is now FDA-approved in the USA to reduce hair loss, it wasn't available for my sister or mother. I anticipated that chemotherapy would cost me my hair because that's what happened to my mother and my sister. In preparation, I bought hats, my sister and sister-in-law loaned me their wigs, and my dear friend Steve did a photo shoot to capture my hair pre-treatment. I was resigned to the experience that my mother and sister endured. If I were prepared, I wouldn't be as traumatized by losing my hair as they were. Preparation equaled paid avoidance.

I knew my hair would grow back—perhaps with strange characteristics. My sister's curly hair came back straight, and my mother's straight hair came back curly. But I was sad thinking about shaving my head, wearing wigs and hats, and looking like a patient. And the thought of growing my hair back out was daunting. Maybe I would permanently shift to short hair to avoid the ugly phase that lasts a few years.

Dr. Chien mentioned that I could elect to cold cap if I did infusions at UCSF Mission Bay, which has DigniCap machines. One of my friends succeeded with Penguin Cold Caps, where someone changes the frozen cap every twenty-five minutes when they thaw. Cold capping cools the scalp to near freezing during chemotherapy infusion, so the hair follicles absorb less chemo. Maybe I could get through chemo without looking like a chemo patient. Dr. Chien said cold capping was very successful for the first chemo cocktail I would be getting. However, it was less likely to work if I needed the second cocktail.

While I asked for the necessary details to consider my options, I wasn't sure how I felt about it. I mentioned my worries to Heather, my sister-in-law. "Maybe it's vanity," I said. "Perhaps I should carry on as if nothing is happening rather than face the reality of being a cancer patient." I was usually proactive about addressing issues and conflicts. And I was pretty comfortable with my lack of fashion sense. "I guess losing my hair is something I could endure," I said. "But I feel a little silly about wanting to avoid it."

"You are not vain," Heather said. "It is perfectly reasonable to want to look like yourself when you look in the mirror, interact with other people, or take a picture during the treatment period."

Heather was right. Despite feeling a little vain, I wanted to keep my hair—if possible. I proceeded with the DigniCap protocol.

The pre-treatments were infused relatively slowly, and some resulted in side effects that were immediately detectable. Cinvanti, the antiemetic I mentioned in Chapter 14: First Inning, tasted like rubber—not that I'd tasted rubber frequently, but I was sure I'd held something rubber in my mouth at some point because that taste was familiar for the five to ten seconds it lasted. I received Pepcid to head off indigestion, and a steroid to buck up my immune system. Benadryl became my best friend because I was sleepy within five minutes of that drug being infused.

Getting me into the DigniCap became comical. There are three DigniCap seats on each floor of UCSF Mission Bay's three DigniCap-enabled infusion centers. The medical assistant must wet your scalp entirely after ensuring the cap connects and cools with the machine. For my first infusion on January 26, my mother and I were in a corner of the third floor of the infusion center, and the medical assistant walked over with a stool and a spray bottle to wet my hair. I have a massive amount of hair. It's dense and dries quickly. My hair stylist has been cutting and styling my hair for fifteen or more years and, every time, comments on how much hair I have. Before starting treatment, I asked a friend who is a talented professional photographer if he would photograph my hair. I wanted the DigniCap to work. I looked at the spray bottle and the medical assistant. I said, "With my hair, you need a bucket."

I became a two-person hair-dampening patient for the rest of my infusions. A chemo glam squad! I was a fashion disaster with my DigniCap. I didn't mind being photographed because I thought it was funny and I'm not vain. Once dampened, the cold cap was tightly affixed to my head and tightened up using Velcro (on top, not touching my body or my hair). At this point, I had a branching IV coming out of my port and two large tubes coming out of the back of my head. I belonged in a science fiction movie.

Moving around was complicated, and I'd only do it to use the bathroom. I could only be disconnected from the DigniCap machine for seven minutes; otherwise, my head might start to defrost. I wouldn't say I liked how it looked and didn't post selfies on social media. I was also worried about getting a terrible headache from a brain freeze, but somehow I kept forgetting to take ibuprofen before I got to the hospital. I'm unsure if I was experiencing chemo-brain spaciness or some passive-aggressive resistance to the experience. In any case, the infusion nurses would inevitably get the nurse practitioner to prescribe a dose of ibuprofen.

The Benadryl and warm blankets assured me I would settle into a comfortable, dreamless nap. As mentioned, my psycho-oncologist, Sadie, had recommended I get an extra liter of hydration during chemo, as it would flush my system and make me more comfortable, and it was a generally good idea. Dr. Chien ordered the extra hydration. That guaranteed I would have to do the DigniCap disconnect and sprint to the bathroom at least twice during my infusion.

What chemo alumni know is that the side effects usually come hours or a day after the infusion. Anticipatory anxiety left me a bit peckish before every infusion, so I asked for saltine crackers or ginger ale at the start. One time, I asked for Tums. Fatigue attacks the body systemically, which is good because that's how it finds roaming cancer cells and destroys them, but it results in anemia. That's why the labs test red blood count, and my oncologist could prescribe Procrit or another red cell stimulator if I needed it. Immunotherapy drugs can affect thyroid function, making me even more tired. My labs included thyroid function tests so my doctors could supplement my thyroid if necessary. Thyroid damage from immunotherapy is permanent, and I was glad that I didn't have that side effect. When I needed help, many knowledgeable people were available at the infusion center.

When my sister started her treatments in 2003, she was positively flattened by nausea and vomiting the first night of her infusion and throughout the entire weekend that followed. Two and a half days of vomiting, nausea, and discomfort were traumatizing for her, her husband, and me. Our mom felt terrible that she couldn't hold Tracey's head through the dry heaving. My biggest fear was having the same type of reaction as my sister, and to make treatment less nauseating, I had to stay ahead of the nausea.

It's counterintuitive to treat yourself for symptoms you don't have, but it's too late by the time you have them. Whenever I had to rehab from an injury, my physical therapist and doctors advised me to stay ahead of the pain and inflammation by taking anti-inflammatories on a schedule. When my children were babies, I mostly avoided the tears by putting them to sleep before they were fussy. It's the same idea with chemo.

With chemo, I was performing a chemistry test on myself. *Will Zofran minimize nausea?* Zofran didn't make me sleepy; I could take it every six hours. If that didn't work (and it didn't), or if there was any sense of discomfort, I took Compazine. Compazine made me sleepy, and I could take it every eight hours, but I had to wait three hours after the Zofran to try it or Ativan. Ativan reduced anxiety as well as nausea. I also took Claritin every twenty-four hours after my infusion to minimize bone pain—a surprising side effect of Claritin.

On days I took them all, I took Zofran at 5 p.m., and if I didn't feel great, I was supposed to take Compazine or Ativan at 8 p.m. Then, if I were still awake at 11:00 p.m., I'd take a Zofran. I'd pop a Compazine at 4 a.m. or an Ativan at 2 a.m. Then Zofran at 5 a.m. Then Ativan at 8 a.m. or Compazine at noon, with a Zofran at 11 a.m. Frankly, it was enough to make one crazy. But sleep is essential, and I needed to sleep as much as possible *and* stay ahead of the nausea.

My head was already spinning with how to keep track of all this when I wasn't dealing with the side effects themselves. I hate being a bother to my family, and I wouldn't say I like complaining. I'd seen what my mother, grandmother, sister, father-in-law, and friends had endured, and frankly, I wanted something different. Gratitude is a known anxiety reliever and a natural upper, so I focused on appreciating what wasn't happening. But sometimes I missed the memo about the benefits of asking for help—especially from my medical team. The companion memo states that not asking for help or sharing information creates stress for your healthcare team.

My brother-in-law kept a detailed journal of the meds my sister took as they conducted their chemistry test to manage her chemotherapy in 2003. My dad did it for my mother in 2014 when she battled bladder cancer. Both my brother-in-law and my dad became the medication alarm clocks. I didn't want Neal to be logging my vomiting and scheduling my meds. After the first infusion, I found an app to track my medications and remind me when each was needed. This allowed me to stay ahead of the nausea. For the first few infusions, I was religious about the Zofran. Still, I didn't need anything else except delta-9-tetrahydrocannabinol (THC), one of the cannabinoids found in cannabis and which is the plant's main psychoactive component. Another component of marijuana is cannabidiol (CBD), which is rumored to be an anti-inflammatory. I had never used marijuana before—something that shocked my kids and my friends. I needed it because the steroid given during my chemotherapy pre-treatment to bolster my immune system kicked in around 4 p.m. and made me jittery and unable to sleep at night. THC knocked me out—but that was another chemistry test as I was a novice regarding the amount, strain, and delivery mechanism that worked best for me. Until Dr. Chien and I adjusted the steroid dosage, I found that a five-milligram THC/CBD gummy with a small dropper of olive oil infused with THC was enough to make me sleepy and keep me asleep all night. Another benefit of THC is that it is an anti-nausea treatment.

The chemo upset my GI tract, and then the Zofran confused it. Suffice it to say, my relationship with my toilet became closer. After week three, Dr. Chien suggested I avoid the Zofran and see how I felt. With some trepidation, I did it, and discovered that, just like my sister, Zofran did nothing for me. After week six, with my labs looking like I wasn't having chemo, Dr. Chien was open to reducing the steroid dose to the bare minimum. From that point forward, I didn't need any help sleeping. And the Cinvanti had eliminated the nausea issue. I didn't need Zofran, Compazine, or Ativan. My app could go on holiday until my surgery, when I would need it to stay ahead of the pain.

This was my treatment process:

Arrive early for the port draw and hope for good lab results.

Get comfortable in the recliner and get my scalp soaked for the DigniCap.

Pre-treatment meds for thirty minutes.

Put on the ice mittens and socks—the worst part. Pre-cool for fifteen minutes.

Ninety minutes of chemo.

Take off the ice mittens and socks to use the bathroom. (Extra hydration has that side effect.)

Start post-treatment cooling (two hours for me). Every three weeks, immunotherapy is performed during post-treatment cooling.

Including the natural waiting time of the process, the end-to-end treatment loop was five hours. When I created my cancer obliteration Google calendar after the first conversation with Dr. Chien, I also blocked my work calendar for my infusion days and the two days afterward. After twenty-five years of working in high technology, building and leading marketing and sales teams, I transitioned in 2021 to consulting and executive coaching. I was still building this new business when I was diagnosed. One of the tools I use for my practice is a self-scheduling link that allows clients, contacts, and prospects to book any open space on my calendar. I had to block out the times when I was recovering from chemo and wasn't available for someone to schedule an appointment. The initial blocks I put in place also limited work (and income) to two days a week. After a few weeks, I realized that I didn't have cancer treatment responsibilities for the other six days, so I stepped out of the batter's box, exercised, worked, traveled, and lived my life—being careful about large indoor spaces because even if my labs were good, I was still immunosuppressed. I removed the blocks on my calendar for the two days after infusion day and, with a little effort, was back to working four days a week with only one day off for cancer treatment.

Not everyone can work. For some, chemo makes professional responsibilities impossible or difficult. I was lucky. Still, there were side effects to contend with.

I grind my teeth when I sleep. And sometimes my tongue gets beaten up in the grinding. Although I slept through every chemo session, I woke up from the Benadryl nap during the fifth round and felt like my tongue was a little off. It felt thick and slightly swollen. It wasn't bothering me much, so I didn't consider it worth mentioning. I didn't want to upset the nurse with something so trivial. But the infusion nurse disconnected me from the IV when I mentioned my tongue felt a little thick.

"Oh no," she said.

I didn't realize a swollen tongue could block my airway. I wasn't having any trouble breathing and wasn't even sure if my tongue was swollen or if I had ground my teeth during my nap and just caught the edge of my tongue.

"You can't keep side effects to yourself," the nurse told me. The nurses want to know everything as it's happening. My nurse was upset that I hadn't mentioned it earlier. I was sure she was having visions of me passing out with a blocked airway and that she'd missed it. She didn't. I didn't. But I realized that I wasn't bothering her (or him—some of my nurses were men) by telling her what I was experiencing. My nurses vastly preferred more information to less.

That night, my tongue still felt off. My husband was out of town, and my friend Julie stayed with me in case I needed something and couldn't drive. We wound up in the ER to have it looked at. That visit resulted in me becoming the proud carrier of an EpiPen and adding more steroids to my medication collection in case I needed fast action at home. I never did. My dentist recommended a mouthguard.

It was a foul ball, but there were many surprises during chemotherapy. Everyone thinks about nausea and hair loss because they're expected, and TV shows and movies about cancer always include those two dramatic side effects. But they're not the only ones. The *Chemo Teach* Zoom session informed me about all the remote possibilities, but it was too much information to consume. I had pages of printouts regarding the different drugs in my regimens and all the side effects. There were too many statistical possibilities to organize.

And everyone is different. A friend of mine developed a massive rash across her entire body; another developed tinnitus. My sister experienced gas and indigestion before she was nauseous and vomiting. If she caught the distress at the indigestion level and quickly administered an antiemetic, she could prevent extended vomiting and discomfort. A lot of people develop brain fog from the chemo. Everyone's experience in the batter's box is unique.

I desperately wanted to make my swing smooth and smash the pitch. I was attentive to my oncology team and took notes to create my approach for the chemo curveballs. I wanted to know the early signs of side effects so early action could stop them. In retrospect, I never looked like a cancer patient, and consequently, I determined who knew that I was being treated. There were some associates in my professional sphere whom I did not tell about my diagnosis and treatment, and it's not clear whether they ever knew. I'm still connecting with people who had no idea I had cancer. That was empowering.

In June 2023, a psychologist wrote an article about how important it was to her practice that her cancer wasn't apparent to her patients or even a topic of discussion. The loss of hair would signal to all *I have cancer.* She raised an excellent question: *Why doesn't insurance automatically cover cold capping, an FDA-approved, chemotherapy-specific treatment?* For many women, losing their hair causes a lot of stress and grief, yet insurance companies don't always cover the necessary treatments to reduce hair loss. I had an eighteen-month battle with my insurance company. They initially told me cold capping was part of my chemotherapy benefit and had even pre-approved it. Even then, after countless hours of research, negotiation, and on-hold music, they told me that while it was part of my chemotherapy benefit, cold capping was excluded from my "durable medical equipment" benefit. They made the claim process very challenging because their online process isn't designed for members to submit claims for medical equipment.

I feel for people in the United States who do not have any savings or insurance. When I spoke to people in Canada and the UK, they had coverage but needed more choices about time and place of treatment.

Some people's insurance requires them to pay a percentage of the covered cost in addition to co-payments. People living in certain countries outside the US are not allowed cold capping as part of their medical insurance benefits. Fortunately, in the US there are grants available to help. DigniCap has a list of available grants, and Sharsheret has a tremendous financial kit, guidance, and some grants. Many people are financially and emotionally devastated by cancer, so ask for help when needed.

In the end, I lost about one-third of my hair. Keeping my hair and continuing to look like myself was a source of strength when I stood in the batter's box and faced cancer's pitches. It gave me control over who knew and who did not know I was being treated for cancer. It made me feel like myself when I looked at my kids and husband in a mirror. I was lucky I could minimize what I lost to breast cancer.

LESSONS LEARNED

- [ ] Explore options to retain your hair and create a budget, as insurance will not cover any of it.

- [ ] Purchase or borrow scarves and hats to feel stylish and in control. When you lose some or all of your hair, it happens quickly and it's helpful to have something on hand to help you look your best.

- [ ] Wigs are usually fitted after hair is lost and can take a few weeks to be delivered.

- [ ] Share every side effect with your medical team and let them decide if it's important.

- [ ] Experiment with side effect management, including, if legal, marijuana products. Tell your medical team about every experiment and record what you tried and what it did.

18. Treatment Teammates

The fourth and fifth floors of the UCSF Mission Bay Infusion Center have a dramatically different layout than the third floor, where I had my first infusion. While Floor 3 had an L-shape, with infusion recliners along the perimeter and wood-paneled dividers between every two recliners, evoking the feeling of a living room, Floors 4 and 5 felt and looked like a hospital. Along the length of the building on these two floors were large windows, like on Floor 3, and there were pods of four recliners, a seat for a guest, infusion equipment, a white cubby for my belongings, and a privacy curtain on a track ten feet above. The ceilings on Floors 4 and 5 of the infusion center were higher. There were no bullpens for the nurses and medical assistants. Adjacent to every pod were cubicles. There were no robots on Floor 4 or 5. The medications arrived through a special-purpose drug elevator. There were three DigniCap stations and a large, body-sized freezer with Penguin Cold Caps, used to prevent hair loss. There were even private rooms with beds for specific infusions—the ones I wanted to avoid.

Amidst the sterile walls of the fourth floor of UCSF's Infusion Center, I noticed the same woman diagonally across the pod space from me, week after week. She was young and had a man with her who appeared to be replacing the frozen cold caps she needed from an enormous cooler on her left. They didn't seem to be friends.

At the second infusion, when I saw her after four or five hours, I passed her seat on my way back from the bathroom, asked how she was doing, and mentioned that I noticed we were here on the same days and for the same duration. I shared that I was being treated for Stage IIA, triple-negative breast cancer, and had started chemo on January 26, 2024. Jacqueline shared that she also had triple-negative breast cancer and had started chemo on the same day. The doctors discovered an unrelated, slow-growing, malignant kidney tumor in the PET scan for her breast cancer.

We were both at the same point in our twelve-week carboplatin-Taxol protocol. Neither of us wanted to experience Adriamycin and cyclophosphamide (AC) or "Red Devil." AC is highly toxic, and our oncologists shared that our hair was unlikely to survive the AC onslaught. My sister's initial chemotherapy protocol was AC, and I vividly recalled her terrible three days post-infusion pre-Emend/Cinvanti and the loss of her stunning curls. We wouldn't have a say if the carboplatin-Taxol didn't eliminate our tumors. Jacqueline elected to use Penguin

Cold Caps because data showed they were slightly more effective in protecting hair from AC.

We bonded instantly.

While my infusion days were mostly joyful and sickness-free, Jacqueline wasn't having as much fun. She was thirty-eight years old, single, with no family history of breast cancer, and otherwise healthy. I couldn't imagine facing this disease alone, and when I saw her, I thought of what my mother might have felt when she was undergoing treatment. People didn't talk about cancer in the eighties. My father was shaken to his core and lacked extensive coping skills and supporters for his trauma, so supporting my mother didn't come easy. Every three weeks, my parents had to drive an hour to the Manhattan hospital and then back home. Jacqueline was driving over an hour each way from Santa Cruz. Not only did the drive remind my parents that Mom was fighting cancer again, but my dad fundamentally disliked Manhattan. Back then, it was dirty, congested, and unsafe. There was nothing good about these infusions. Mom was exhausted and queasy when they came home, so she would disappear into their room for the next thirty-six hours. Perhaps many people would have supported our family, but my parents didn't feel they could ask. Jacqueline seemed like my mom in this way.

Reaching out to Jacqueline started with me putting something good into the universe because no one did that for my mother. Jacqueline didn't ask for my friendship. And I didn't realize how much I would appreciate having a teammate in precisely the same place for these innings. We were a support group of two.

I avoided formal support groups because I didn't feel I needed support from other cancer patients and didn't want to be obligated to give it. In my previous conversations with cancer patients and their families (I'd been having them for forty years), I found myself often more informed and with more perspective because of my lifetime of exposure to breast cancer, treatments, surgeries, and complications. I didn't feel particularly lonely in my therapy because not only could I talk with my mother and sister, but I also had a network of other women who were survivors and available upon request.

Jacqueline and I exchanged numbers after that first introduction, and I texted her that night or the next day to ask how she was doing. That started a series of texts and calls where we became confidants and shared the challenges of navigating the treatment process. We compared cold capping, side effect management, UCSF delights, and frustrations.

> Joelle: *Hi, Jacqueline. How are you doing? I'm feeling queasier than previously. Sending you love.*
>
> Jacqueline: *Hi! I am just getting back to text. I am feeling good overall but dreading having to drive up to UCSF again tomorrow for a quick injection. It was so nice talking to you today. Do you take meds for the nausea? I am fasting, and that helps with day-one side effects.*
>
> Joelle: *Are you getting Cinvanti infused? Miracle stuff. I take Prilosec because I feel more indigestion. I also took a 5mg THC/CBD gummy on Wednesday night (about 15 minutes ago) to tamp down the steroid jitters so I could sleep. I don't fast ... keeping my tummy filled with some food works better for me.*
>
> Jacqueline: *I should take some cannabis right now, LOL.*
>
> Joelle: *Better living through chemistry.*

Jacqueline's tumor was larger than mine; it grew considerably in the time between initial detection and the start of treatment—about two months. She was an OB-GYN charge nurse who managed the night shift in a Santa Cruz hospital. She was single, with no kids, no partner, and a dog she loved. Like mine, Jacqueline's tumor had not metastasized, and she was expected to make a full recovery. She was headed toward a lumpectomy, in contrast to my bilateral mastectomy and DIEP flap reconstruction—primarily because for people without the BRCA mutation, the outcomes are the same. Both of us were mentally preparing ourselves for AC. My oncologist thought it was highly likely that I would need it.

> Jacqueline: *Dr. Esserman suggested that you avoid the AC if you get to pCR.*
>
> Joelle: *Right.*
>
> Jacqueline: *Are you getting scanned in week eleven, too?*

Although we met at week eight, Jacqueline's MRI was already set up. My doctor put in the order for the MRI a few days after my week nine appointment because she couldn't feel any tumor. Jacqueline's was scheduled for April 5, and mine for April 19. Jacqueline noted that if we needed AC, that was the day for the first infusion. AC can only be infused four times in a lifetime because it is highly cardiotoxic and will do irreparable damage to your heart above a specific, low lifetime or cumulative dosage.

> Joelle: *Jo [Chien] is sure I'll need AC. I can do anything four times.* [This became my strength mantra because with a firm end date, I can

> endure anything four times.] I'll get scanned after week twelve—and UCSF didn't have timely room for me [to get my MRI at UCSF]—so I'm doing it at Sutter!

Hours later, I texted Jacqueline again.

> **Joelle:** *UCSF freed up an appointment for me to have my MRI in week eleven at UCSF.*
>
> **Jacqueline:** *Mine [my oncologist] is giving me the AC vibes, too. I get scared about losing my hair despite my efforts. It's so dumb in the grand scheme of things, but my hair has always been ingrained in my life.*

My mother lost her hair, although I don't remember ever seeing her bald. She usually wore wigs, turbans, and scarves to present herself. To bolster her immune system, she had to take steroids, which made her oval face round and puffy. She didn't look or feel like herself. I shared my sister's story with Jacqueline, including her "wigs-optional" wedding. I also shared photos of my sister's fabulous hair today so that Jacqueline might find some hope.

> **Jacqueline:** *I have been struggling because I can't pinpoint the reasons for my cancer. [Less than 10 percent of breast cancers have a genetic origin. Most people are like Jacqueline and are surprised by the diagnosis.] I'm like, is it something I wear, use, night shift, etc.? It fills my cup to hear about a triple negative survivor... All my terrible fears may never happen.*

Like most women with breast cancer, Jacqueline was searching for the reason she developed this tumor. Having BRCA1 is fortunate in many ways: I knew my probability of breast and ovarian cancer. I was screened regularly—and at a much younger age than Jacqueline. I was conscious but not crazy about my diet, alcohol consumption, and exercise. I had my children before I was forty and nursed each for a year. I never smoked. There was nothing more I could do to prevent breast cancer, and questions of "why" it happened didn't torture me. Jacqueline was dealing with the disorientation of being diagnosed with a disease she was too young to have.

> Joelle: *Everybody's got something. Our family's got cancer genes. Other families have other genes. None of us leave this world alive, so I choose our genes. It's now your thing, too—so fuck it and let's beat it, obliterate it, and move on. That's how I think, but I have those two role models.*
>
> Jacqueline: *That's a great mindset. I never thought I would have a first diagnosis of an aggressive cancer and a second primary after my 38th birthday. Life is interesting. I like to look at this and make it my bitch. That's what my neighbor tells me every time he sees me.*
>
> Joelle: *You were blindsided.*
>
> Jacqueline: *It felt that way, for sure. My best friend is my ob-gyn, and she was a blessing because she was able to give me the news so gently and lovingly before I had to schedule an appointment to be told by this sterile radiologist. You have excellent people supporting and surrounding you; that's all you can hope for.*

Jacqueline and I compared notes about the various medications we took to manage the side effects. We talked about our different cold caps. She was told she could shampoo two to three times per week, while I was told once weekly. I was told I could exercise, and she was told not to get her head too warm. We started talking about her job and mine—as well as the crossroads she was at because of the cancer. She went on disability for the duration of her treatment, while I ramped down the number of clients I would advise and coach. We talked about my trips to see my boys and her love life.

That entire conversation (and more) transpired on the day we met. Cancer makes fast friends and cancer teammates even faster.

Jacqueline, with her long, strawberry-blonde hair, and me, with my shoulder-length salt-and-pepper hair, were thrown together as if fate had conspired to make us teammates on this journey. As we sat across the room from each other, connected to IV lines titrating the lifesaving poison into our bloodstreams, our bond was forged through the shared experience of treatment. I was shocked that Jacqueline was driving herself to and from therapy from Santa Cruz once a week. She didn't want to inconvenience her friends and family. Both of us tolerated carboplatin-Taxol well. Jacqueline was having more anemia, while my body was handling the initial chemo attack in surprising stride. It crossed my mind that this friendship might be stressed if one of us needed AC and the other didn't, but I liked Jacqueline and enjoyed our conversations. We'd deal with that situation if it transpired.

The risk with my skipping AC was that if the pathology after my bilateral and DIEP showed any cancer, I would have to do it afterward, and doctors could not monitor the response. I would skip AC if they could not detect anything through scanning anyway. I was going to ask if they'd consider a liquid biopsy (blood-based, and I knew two providers) because that pretty much rules out any other evidence of cancer. I've since learned that liquid biopsies, today, only detect later-stage cancers. My oncologist didn't feel it would be helpful.

> Jacqueline: *The liquid biopsy sounds promising. I was optimistic about skipping AC, but part of me feels it's the standard of care and safest option. But then another part of me wants to avoid that poison at all costs. They have a thorough process for ruling out evidence of a tumor to move forward without AC, so that's positive. Your tumor is small, so it's a good possibility that you can avoid it. I'm sorry you must have a biopsy. Those suck.*
>
> Joelle: *Right now, I'm hoping that since Jo [Chien] couldn't palpate it, it bodes well. I want a pCR, and if that means AC, then AC it is!*

We both had anticipatory anxiety on chemo days, and both expressed gratitude for science and the care we received on infusion days. We were both excited that our tumors were responding to the chemo. We shared notes on scheduling the MRIs to confirm the obliteration of the cancer. My MRI moved up, and Jacqueline celebrated with me.

Jacqueline got her MRI results—clinically cancer-free—before I did, right after our eleventh infusion. Because she didn't have the genetic markers, the oncologist recommended that she skip the twelfth infusion and start strengthening herself for her outpatient surgery. I had the MRI and needed a fine-needle aspiration (FNA) of the tumor site and the lymph nodes to confirm I was cancer-free.

> Joelle: *Just left her [Dr. Esserman]. I think I was one patient ahead of you. You were right; they are going to skip AC for me. She's trying to organize surgery. How about you?*

Jacqueline: *Mine is gone! Surgery is at the end of April. I'm not even doing Taxol this Wednesday. Is that the same for you?*

Joelle: *OMG. That's awesome. That's great news!*

Jacqueline: *What did your MRI say?*

Joelle: *Tumor gone. Lymph nodes look good, but I want an ultrasound to confirm. I need to meet with the plastic surgeon, too. Laura met with me—Jo in Japan.*

Jacqueline: *Tumor is gone! Yay! That's amazing!*

As treatment teammates, Jacqueline and I shared the same treatment schedule and tackled the various pitches thrown our way together—chemotherapy, immunotherapy, surgeries, and other medical procedures. Our conversations transcended the clinical aspects of our journey, delving into the nuances of our distinctive experiences. In each other, we found understanding and a source of strength that extended beyond the medications pumping through our veins.

Jacqueline and I supported each other outside the infusion center, texting and discussing doctor appointments, providing shoulders to lean on during tough days, and celebrating small victories. Jacqueline shared her concerns about being single and the fear that cancer might hinder her dreams of having a family. My heart broke for her, and I encouraged her to assume that she would live a long life and could have a family if she wanted. Even in the face of varied challenges, a teammate makes the journey beyond bearable and even enjoyable.

LESSONS LEARNED

- [ ] Be respectful but approachable and friendly in the infusion center. Even sharing a smile brightens someone's day, and you might make a lifelong friend.

- [ ] Whether through luck, an in-person support group, or an online forum, it is helpful to talk with someone who is at the same stage in the journey as you.

- [ ] Celebrate the small wins, even if they aren't yours. I was thrilled when a fellow cancer patient could skip the twelfth cycle, and she was delighted when I got my pCR after the fine-needle aspiration biopsy.

- [ ] Even people with the same pathology and same protocol have different pitches. Everyone's body responds differently. Support. Explore. Don't compare.

19. Home Run

I was batting smoothly against the chemotherapy/immunotherapy pitches. I was fortunate that my side effects were managed and minimal. For my first two or three treatments, I worried a lot that something in my labs would cause a delay. I saw my oncologist for the first treatment, then every three weeks. I didn't realize how anxious I was before my first post-chemo meeting with her, but I was uncomfortably constipated. When I saw her, I asked what the exclamation points in some of my lab tests meant for my treatment.

Cue *A Chorus Line*—they meant nothing. Absolutely nothing. My labs were fantastic.

Suddenly, my intestines released all the stress they'd held for me (in a bathroom—nothing gross). My labs stayed great throughout treatment. *I'm stubborn down to my bone marrow.* Not only were my labs tremendous and my symptoms minimal, but my tumor gorged itself on chemo, and the MRI showed no more cancer. I was ecstatic.

To be conservative, my oncologist wanted me to finish the twelve-week course and validate the eradication of the chemo through a fine-needle aspiration (FNA) biopsy of the lymph nodes. Of all the curveballs I'd experienced with cancer, the core needle biopsy that led to the initial diagnosis was by far the most painful, and it bruised my right breast for more than four weeks. The biopsy felt like someone wearing brass knuckles drove a fist into the side of my breast. When Dr. Chien asked for a final FNA, my visceral response was fear. *How much does that hurt?*

Turns out—it doesn't. UCSF doesn't do core needle biopsies anymore. If you are reading this and heading into a biopsy, ask for fine-needle aspiration. It's much less painful.

I was downright peppy for my last chemo appointment. The Cancer Obliteration Project was right on track. My schedule was a little busy, and the universe kept sending me medical assistants who shared my first name. The first Joelle (this was Joelle W.) was the medical assistant who called me in for a port draw, took my vitals, and took a photo with me. She'd seen my name on multiple days but had never met me. She helped me secure a quiet infusion spot—an angel.

Then I checked in for my surgical consult, and the medical assistant who called me into my appointment was *also* named Joelle. Joelle T. knew about Joelle W. but had yet to meet her. A *third* Joelle in the cancer center was working on the fourth floor as a nurse practitioner. I got photos of the first two, and Joelle T. tried orchestrating a picture of all the Joelles with me. Joelle's Joelles. Our name is sufficiently unusual that running into one person with it is extraordinary—but four in one place? The universe was strangely aligning for my last chemotherapy infusion.

My last-day-of-chemo schedule was a bit insane because we were trying to finalize the next step, and that entailed making our best effort to ensure that in addition to the breast, the lymph nodes had no cancer cells. This was the schedule created for me:

8:30: Port draw

9:00: Surgical nurse practitioner consult

9:15: Ultrasound

9:15: Oncology office visit

10:30: Infusion—a four-hour, fifteen-minute block from the minute we start the pre-treatment

3:00: Ultrasound fine-needle aspiration (biopsy)

No—there are no typos in that list. I did not create this schedule. I explained the scheduling problems to the team: at 9 a.m. I couldn't be in three places concurrently.

My infusions required thirty minutes of pre-treatment and pre-cooling, plus an hour and a half of infusion, then two hours of post-treatment cooling, and fifteen minutes to defrost my head. From the first thirty minutes through the two hours of post-treatment cooling, I was plugged into a machine cabled to the wall. I got unplugged for seven minutes to use the bathroom and had to move fast. That wasn't a problem, but it restricted my movement around the hospital. But this was round twelve—I knew the drill! It was not possible to do the post-treatment cooling in the ultrasound room.

Suppose you've done the math and looked at the schedule. In that case, you've realized that it only works if you skip something *and* the infusion process starts at 10:30 a.m. Infusions can only begin once the oncology team has reviewed the labs and released the medications, so changes were needed. We cut the in-person oncology visit—although my oncologist did call me while in infusion, and we talked. I think I was deep in the thrall of Benadryl, but I was told it happened.

I was about to have a batting slump. Briefly.

The ultrasound showed normal lymph nodes. Excellent! We could proceed to biopsy ... after the infusion.

Suffice it to say that my last infusion started late, and ultrasound FNA biopsies require the pathologist in the room to ensure the sample collected is sufficient to make a pathology diagnosis. The biopsy was supposed to happen after the infusion was done, and it could not be done while I was plugged into the DigniCap Scalp Cooling System. Long story short, my last day of chemo ended with a foul ball.

The breast imaging team called to tell me that I needed to be rescheduled for the next day because I was forty-five minutes late, and they only did fine-needle aspirations within a specific timeframe. I wanted to get the biopsy and be done with cancer. I felt judged for being late, wronged for the delays I couldn't control, and frustrated that no one helped me when I raised the issue days earlier and again that morning. I was mad. I was where MyChart said I would be, and the UCSF patient tracker I wore indicated I was getting infused. *How could they not know where I was or why I was late? Why was I at fault for being late when I couldn't leave the chair?*

It felt like there was no one keeping an eye on my treatment end to end. Suddenly we had an issue that threatened to kibosh my exhilarating finish.

When Neal and I met with the nurse manager of the breast imaging clinic, I wasn't my best self. The surgical nurse practitioner had assured me the schedule would be okay. In retrospect, I don't think she did the calendar math and didn't realize the schedule was impossible. That nurse practitioner wasn't fully listening to me, and I chose to believe she could reshape time. She had no idea that FNAs are only performed between 1 and 3 p.m. and that the team would not wait for me. The nurse manager explained the situation a few times and then realized I needed an apology because my approach and swing were both on track, but somehow, the pitches went wild, and I got hit by it. I was shocked and disappointed.

I celebrated anyway. One can never have too many celebrations when one has vanquished cancer. About eight girlfriends came over to my house, and we popped the cork on my favorite Italian sparkling wine—Banfi Rosa Regale Brachetto—and toasted the end of the chemotherapy treatment. I wasn't allowed to drink during chemotherapy, and that toast was my first alcoholic drink in months, and it was sweet despite the minor snag.

I had the ultrasound FNA the next day. Everyone was welcoming, supportive, and wonderful. The lymph node was so tiny it was tough to find. When the radiologists found it, its neighbor node was more prominent, and they wondered aloud if they should biopsy the bigger one rather than the clipped one. I chimed in, "Do them both. We're here. Let's get the most definitive answer and try to leave nothing to chance." Everyone agreed, and so we did.

If the FNA was clear, I was on track for surgery.

My last day of chemo was a bummer at first, but I chose to focus on the big win: chemo was over. With a bit of rest, an apology from the breast imaging nurse manager for the mix-up, and a few minutes of perspective, I realized I was still done with chemo, and my cancer had, most likely, been thoroughly obliterated. When we got the results, they were negative. I had smashed the chemo curveball and hit a home run.

LESSONS LEARNED

- [ ] Treatment involves multiple specialties, and they don't know one another's timing. Ask questions if something on the schedule doesn't look right.

- [ ] Delays will happen, and it's okay to be disappointed. Then, find a solution. Don't take rescheduling personally. It's not you—it's the system.

- [ ] If you have a question or suggestion regarding your treatment or a test, express it. You are a part of the treatment team.

- [ ] Celebrate small victories and invite your community to celebrate with you.

Jacqueline's Journey

Jacqueline was a vibrant OB-GYN night charge nurse. In the quiet seaside town of Santa Cruz, she shared a home with her dog, Lalo, under skies painted with the hues of countless sunsets and sunrises. Life had its rhythm, defined by the tides and Jacqueline's night shifts—until one day, the rhythm skipped a beat.

"When I felt pain in my chest, I shrugged it off," Jacqueline recalls. "Since when did breast cancer signal its arrival with an autograph of pain?" She wasn't the only one who thought this way. Her cousin, a primary care provider, suggested it could be a muscle tear.

Within mere weeks, what started as an innocuous ache grew into an unmistakable lump—an invader that wasn't there at her last self-exam. Jacqueline's instincts led her to a mammogram. Her fears were echoed in the grim faces of the technician and the radiologist. The ultrasound biopsy the following day confirmed what her heart had anticipated. Just one day after her thirty-eighth birthday, Jacqueline was diagnosed with triple-negative breast cancer. "My world halted," Jacqueline said. "The person I was ceased to exist in that instant. The nurse, the friend—that version of me was a memory." This invasive ductal carcinoma didn't care about her lack of family history or her clean genetic slate.

The first days after the diagnosis were a blur. "You catapult from your life into an alternate universe where time is simultaneously too fast and dreadfully slow," said Jacqueline. As a single, spirited woman known for her fitness and fiery locks, Jacqueline feared the erosion of her physical identity beneath the waves of cancer tests, treatments, and surgeries. *Will I recognize myself when my hair cascades down the shower drain? When my complexion grows weary and my eyebrows vanish, will I look like me?* She researched the efficacy of different cold-capping alternatives. She determined that Penguin capping would provide the highest probability of retaining her hair. She felt moments of bitterness—she was only thirty-eight, single, and didn't have kids. Cancer felt like another barrier keeping her from what society deemed "normal."

Amidst the chaos, Jacqueline found her guiding star: an oncologist whose wisdom shone through her compassion—a beacon of trust. The initial weeks were all business, filled with hospital visits for testing, leaving little room for introspection. She pondered a clinical trial, only to stumble upon another shadow: an unrelated renal tumor. It was slow-growing yet life-threatening. This additional tumor excluded her from the trial. Hope flickered but didn't extinguish, thanks to a dedicated medical team and their arsenal of state-of-the-art protocols. But around the eighth or ninth week, Jacqueline found herself in the throes of an emotional meltdown in her oncologist's office. He assured her that many cancer patients experience an emotional breaking point.

Jacqueline found solace and hope in the stories of others who were a few steps ahead in their cancer battles. She would look at them and say, "I'm going to be okay." These interactions—the little hopes, tips, and tricks she picked up from them—became a lifeline. Jacqueline and I met in the infusion center and became fast friends. We cheered for each other, celebrated progress, and had each other's backs during challenging moments. With time and perspective, Jacqueline began to see her journey as a gift. She realized that her life, as it was before the diagnosis, wasn't what she had envisioned for herself. Yes, the cancer diagnosis was a harsh blow, and the process was far from ideal, but there were numerous silver linings to her ordeal. She got off the night shift, landed a better job, and discovered who her real friends were. She felt accepted within the cancer community. She felt that certain people were placed in her life at the right moments, almost as if by design. These people became her most cherished companions throughout her cancer ordeal. It all seemed meant to be.

Despite undergoing cancer and its treatments, Jacqueline maintained her bubbly personality and long hair, which often surprised people. In her new job at a surgical center, she met women early in their breast cancer journey. They would see her and find it hard to believe that she was still undergoing treatment. Jacqueline would reassure them that chemo wasn't always as bad as they thought—at least it wasn't for her. The first time she underwent radiation, Jacqueline broke down in tears on the table. The staff was incredibly kind, wiping her tears away as she lay immobilized on the table, strapped down for precision. It was an intimidating experience, both physically and emotionally, yet the treatment caused only a slight discoloration of her skin, akin to a mild sunburn. Everyone's experience differs, but she didn't suffer many side effects.

For Jacqueline, the emotional roller coaster was the hardest part. When she was deep in the throes of grief, she'd spend time with her dog, who always managed to make her feel better, or visit a friend who had recently undergone the same process. This friend helped her anticipate and normalize the emotional waves, reassuring her that she was exactly where she needed to be on her journey. Her friend's support reminded Jacqueline that her feelings were expected and that she wasn't alone in her struggle.

No one must go it alone.

Jacqueline discovered a sense of purpose and control in guiding others on their cancer journeys. Drawing from her experiences, she began mentoring others who had recently received a cancer diagnosis. Her advice included practical tips, such as cold capping to preserve hair during chemo, eyebrow microblading, and wearing ice mittens to combat neuropathy. For Jacqueline, this mentor role provided a sense of control in an otherwise uncontrollable situation. Being able to help others navigate through their cancer journey became a source of strength for her. "Everyone should have access to resources and support when facing such an enormous challenge as cancer," said Jacqueline.

She turned her hardship into hope for others, and paying it forward became a significant part of Jacqueline's story.

I feel the same about this book. I hope you do, too.

LESSONS LEARNED

- [ ] While rare, breast cancer can present as pain in the breasts. If you experience chest pain and it doesn't subside, conduct self-exams and consult your doctor. Ideally, your medical practitioner will schedule a mammogram.

- [ ] After being diagnosed with breast cancer, you might experience moments of bitterness, anger, or resentment. It may feel like cancer has stripped you of happiness. While these are common feelings, talk to others to gain perspective. And know these emotions will pass.

- [ ] Gather a solid medical team. Find an oncologist who fights for your life as fiercely as you do.

- [ ] Seek support from other cancer patients and survivors and find a therapist you feel comfortable talking to. Having a safe space to express feelings and thoughts will help you navigate the internal conflicts that come with a cancer diagnosis. In many ways, the emotional toll is more significant than the physical one, so don't trap your emotions inside.

- [ ] Many breast cancer patients break down emotionally at some point in the process. If you find yourself crying, let the tears flow. Rest assured; you are not alone in feeling this way. Cancer is a tough pill to swallow.

Tracey's Journey

Amidst the rolling Pacific's backdrop and the highway's calming hum, my sister, Tracey, and her husband, Thom, marked two decades of marriage with a road trip along the scenic California coast. Their celebration was more than a milestone—it was a triumph of love over life's hurdles. Tracey, having just successfully obliterated her second Stage I invasive breast cancer tumor in 2023, echoed the same defiant spirit she clung to in 2003, years before, when the first tumor sought to unravel their just-begun forever. Here they were, love deepened with scars, proving they could navigate any storm together.

As their car hugged the twists and turns of the coastline, it was hard to miss the symbolism in their journey. You see, twenty years ago, when they were just lovebirds itching to say "I do," cancer came knocking, uninvited.

The diagnosis hit like a coastal fog—dense, disorienting, and threatening to obscure their vision of a shared future. When Tracey said yes to Thom's proposal on Valentine's Day 2003, she hadn't imagined wig shopping would be a part of her wedding preparations. The couple had a list of plans and dreams for their big day, but life threw them a cancer curveball. A small lump, initially dismissed by her doctors, was diagnosed as Stage I, triple-negative, highly aggressive, invasive breast cancer after it was surgically removed at Tracey's insistence. The surgeon whom Tracey saw to remove the lump was dismissive about the lump being cancer and thought Tracey was having an unnecessary surgery. He did it anyway. After the pathology report came back, he had to tell her she needed additional surgery because he didn't ensure clear margins.

Given the dismissiveness of the surgeon, she and Thom sought a medical team in whom they could place their trust. They wanted professionals who would partner with them, educate them, and provide comprehensive answers to their queries, enabling them to make informed decisions.

Tracey told me, "I remember how one surgeon described the difference between invasive and in situ [Stage 0] cancer. He drew a picture on a piece of paper and said, 'In situ are juvenile delinquents, and invasive cancer is a career criminal.'"

Given the nature of her diagnosis, her Stanford medical team prescribed chemotherapy. Tracey, hoping to retain some semblance of normalcy amidst the chaos, asked if chemotherapy could wait until after their wedding, three months away. The swift and unequivocal rejection of this request by her doctors brought home the gravity of her diagnosis. It was a chilling realization that underscored the immediacy and severity of her condition.

"It got real, real fast," Tracey said.

To better understand the speed and trajectory of Tracey's cancer curveball, her treatment team wanted genetic testing to confirm the gene. The results were that she was BRCA1 positive. The pathology of her tumor was triple negative. (As mentioned earlier, there are many types of breast cancer. See Chapter 11: On-Deck Circle for more details.) This meant that my sister's cancer was negative for estrogen and progesterone and didn't produce much or any of the HER2 protein. For the science- or business-oriented, Genentech developed a miracle drug, Herceptin, with little to no side effects, as a highly effective treatment for HER2-positive tumors. My sister's tumor, just like my mother's and mine, was HER2-negative and hormone-negative. It also was a fast-growing tumor, meaning it was aggressive. Thankfully, my sister had detected her tumor when it was tiny and was insistent that the surgeon remove it. Her original surgeon had recommended against the surgery because "it's nothing." My sister saved her own life through self-advocacy.

In the initial whirlwind of medical appointments with surgeons, oncologists, fertility specialists, genetic counselors, and the tumor board at Stanford, Tracey and Thom stumbled upon a clinical trial. This trial aimed to safeguard Tracey's ovaries by inducing temporary menopause throughout her course of chemotherapy, using a drug called Lupron. Fast-forward two decades and this once experimental treatment has become the standard of care for pre-menopausal women diagnosed with breast cancer, like Jacqueline at age thirty-eight. In this sense, Tracey was a trailblazer.

In addition to the Lupron trial, the couple participated in a pioneering Stanford fertility program designed specifically for cancer patients. This program sought to make embryo preservation more affordable for patients should their fertility be compromised by chemotherapy, providing them with a safety net for their future family planning.

"The period between diagnosis and the start of treatment is as bad as it gets," Tracey said.

A few months prior, Tracey and Thom had completed an Ironman triathlon together. She was at the peak of her physical prowess, feeling invincible. They were deeply in love, their shared business was gaining traction, and they were excitedly planning their idyllic destination wedding. Abruptly, their conversations shifted from wedding invitations and seating charts to discussions about fertility treatments and the handling of unused embryos.

As they began to understand all the components of Tracey's treatment and decided to proceed with their wedding as planned, the timing of the interventions became critical. Tracey needed additional surgery to ensure clear margins. The fertility treatments and harvesting of ova (eggs) would occur while she recovered from surgery before starting chemo. Tracey, Thom, and their medical team meticulously coordinated to ensure their wedding date would be on the off-weekend between treatments. However, the Friday before her second surgery, the cornerstone of their carefully constructed schedule, Tracey received an alarming call from the hospital, canceling her surgery. In a state of panic, they reached out to every doctor on their team but found no answer at 4 p.m. on a Friday, with most doctors attending a conference in San Antonio.

Undeterred, Thom managed to locate Tracey's surgeon, Dr. Jeffries, in her room at the conference's host hotel. He fervently implored her to help keep their plans intact. Dr. Jeffries reassured them, to their relief, that everything would proceed as scheduled.

"I found that at times during those early stages of diagnosis, I had somewhat of an out-of-body experience," Tracey recalls. "These doctors were talking to me about me, and I remember feeling bad for the woman sitting there getting this information. It was a total disconnect. I was like, 'God, it sucks for her. She's, you know, so young and healthy, excited about her upcoming wedding, and now she must deal with this. Poor thing.'"

Tracey and Thom took an active role in her treatment and survival journey, seeking answers, collecting data, and making informed decisions about surgery, radiation, birth control, prophylactic options, and, ultimately, hormone replacement. In addition to the physical aspect, Tracey concentrated on maintaining a positive mindset and regulating her emotions.

With guidance from the tumor board, Tracey and Thom opted to proceed with dose-dense chemotherapy using Adriamycin and cyclophosphamide (AC) every two weeks for eight weeks, followed by Taxol every two weeks for another eight weeks. Tracey and Thom had their "wigs-optional" wedding at the halfway mark in treatment after completing AC and before starting Taxol. It was initially difficult for them to manage her side effects. After her first AC infusion, I recall Thom calling me, asking if I could come to their home immediately. Tracey had been violently ill all night, and Thom needed help. I had just fed my newborn son, so I changed him, dressed, and told Neal I had to go to Tracey's. He asked when I would return, and I said I had no idea. Neal had our toddler, and I had the baby.

I entered the couple's two-bedroom garden apartment and hugged Thom. We put Taylor, asleep in his car seat, on the floor of their master bedroom, and then Thom led me to their bathroom. My sister was lying on the floor with her head of wild curls splayed out next to the commode. There were couch pillows around her, but she was lying on the tiles in exhausted agony. Thom told me that she couldn't keep down water, so he couldn't get the antiemetic pills into her. I wonder who thought that the best option for someone vomiting was to ask them to swallow and keep down a pill. She couldn't. There was little I could do but pull back her hair, rub her back, and slowly try to sit her up. I told Thom to take a break and go out to exercise or sleep. I'd help Tracey. She had been vomiting for twelve hours and wouldn't leave the bathroom floor. She was weak, dehydrated, disoriented, uncomfortable, angry, sad, and exhausted. After an hour or so with no vomiting, I was able to move her slowly to her bed with a garbage pail at the ready. My weak, sick, and miserable sister bore little resemblance to the woman who'd confidently trained and completed that grueling Ironman triathlon only four months prior.

I felt terrible for my sister. I was sad that she was so sick. I desperately wanted to help but lacked the knowledge and mechanism to do anything more than console and comfort her. I was glad I could relieve Thom for a few hours, but sitting by while someone you love is in anguish is miserable. I felt impotent against these side effects. And I was angry at her oncology team for being unavailable to help her on the weekend. I thought they'd set her up, unintentionally but thoughtlessly, to be tortured for forty-eight hours.

Doctors eventually recommended Tracey take some of the anti-nausea pills she had been prescribed, but she couldn't keep water down. The only non-oral antiemetic was marijuana, and our very conservative parents had offered to bring the pipe and weed from Florida (before it was legal to have it), when they flew out to see her before treatment started. She was able to buy marijuana locally and did get a little relief from it. But she was thoroughly depleted by the daunting possibility of three more rounds of this chemo regimen and four more of another one after that, with the understanding that the side effects were cumulative.

My mother's chemo probably looked like Tracey's, but we were kids then, and we didn't see her on the bathroom floor. Thom and Tracey were in the batter's box for this curveball, and I was helping from the dugout. Thom asked me to be the team manager temporarily and take control the following Monday when Tracey returned to the infusion center for IV fluids. Thom has an incredible way with people; he's warm and genuinely cares about others' well-being. I'm better described as a bull in a china shop. There was no doubt that Thom would not be comfortable with how much pressure I would apply to *make the doctors or nurses make her feel better.*

My sister was in no shape to advocate for herself at that moment. My future brother-in-law was traumatized and exhausted by watching his beloved in such pain. I was the problem solver then; I had the energy and access to the pertinent information. A solo batter hits curveballs, but many people help the batter prepare, train, and persevere. Tracey and Thom needed another person to buffer some of the worst initial moments of assessing the curveball. In many ways, the cancer diagnosis is the first curveball, and each nugget of information, treatment, and conversation brings new ones—the "side-effect sinker" of disabling nausea, for example. Everyone needs a team to help assess, prepare, and cheer as you determine your approach and how you will hit the pitch.

Once Tracey was stabilized with IV fluids, she was as fixed as possible. Aprepitant (Emend and Cinvanti are the brand names) blocks a chemical in the brain called substance P, which controls your vomiting reflex. It delivers a three-day reprieve from nausea and vomiting induced by chemotherapy. After three days, most patients have little to no nausea. IV Emend made the chemo tolerable for my sister. It's a blessing she has no memory of that time. Thom and I will never forget it and the miracle of Emend.

Due to chemo, my sister lost her stunning curls for a while. She temporarily developed neuropathy tingles in her hands. She lost weight she couldn't afford to lose. She managed the side effects over time, but mostly on her own. At the time, oncologists vastly underestimated the intensity and duration of side effects. For my incredibly fit and healthy sister, those side effects were intense and debilitating—and avoidable. None of us knew what to advocate for in advance, and I wish we had. That's a significant motivator for creating this book.

Tracey's chemo was different from my mother's, even though their tumors were very similar. Tracey was treated with high-dose Adriamycin and cyclophosphamide (AC, aka Red Devil) because, in 2003, oncologists believed that it was the most effective combination of drugs against triple-negative breast cancer. As mentioned, AC is highly cardiotoxic. Twenty years earlier, my mother was infused with a different cocktail called 5FU (fluorouracil) via IV, and she took methotrexate (a steroid), cyclophosphamide (a chemo drug), and prednisone (another steroid) orally every day.

Oncology science continues to evolve. Thankfully, research around the most effective and least toxic treatments continues to receive considerable investment and attention. Part of creating an approach to the curveball is pausing to ask questions about treatment alternatives, efficacy, and side effect management—if your oncology team doesn't proactively offer that information. Even if they do, don't be ashamed to ask again.

Despite their ordeal, Tracey recollects joyful moments: friends coming over for game night the evening of treatment, their wedding, hikes, and runs she could complete on good days.

"Having to be so vulnerable and honest and talk about shit that nobody wants to talk about when they are young and in love made our relationship feel more substantial," she said. "It positively shaped our partnership. Nobody would choose to get married in the middle of chemo, but it was a very love-filled celebration. I've always been grateful for people showing up for us."

Their wedding was a beacon of hope for Tracey, driving her through the challenging AC treatments. However, returning home from the joyous event was difficult, especially with their honeymoon to Fiji postponed and her next round of chemo only days away. The gloomy Bay Area winter only added to their melancholy. To lift their spirits, Thom arranged for a few newlywed days at the local Ritz-Carlton before Tracey's first round of Taxol. Fortunately, Taxol proved more bearable than AC, with fatigue and steroid-induced acne being the most significant side effects.

After enduring the trials of chemotherapy and radiation, Tracey emerged victorious and ready to pick up where they'd left off. They booked their honeymoon and began asking questions about starting a family. The standard medical advice was to wait two to three years after treatment before trying to become pregnant. The waiting period could have been better, with Tracey now thirty and Thom thirty-seven, and the couple needed more clarity on how many children they hoped to have. They learned that the recommendation stemmed from the heightened risk of recurrence in the years immediately following treatment.

Tracey recalls the doctor compassionately explaining, "Simply put, the concern is bringing a child into this world when the mother may not be here to raise it. You guys should talk about this before making any decisions."

When they did so privately, Thom tearfully said, "If, God forbid, anything were to happen to you, I will want any part of you that could still be here."

Six months later, she and Thom joyously discovered they were expecting their first child and, two years after that, their second. A happy side note to this story is that they did not need the embryos they preserved and were ultimately able to donate the unused embryos to the UCLA Broad Stem Cell Research Center. Tracey and Thom hope their genetic material will make a difference in breast cancer research, specifically BRCA1 research.

Tracey and Thom knew that their vows were more than words. They were survival tactics. Two decades later, their bond is the stuff of legend, the kind you tell about when someone needs a little light to guide them through the darkness.

LESSONS LEARNED

- ☐ Meeting different specialists and exploring treatment options can feel like an out-of-body experience. However, it's okay to observe if you take notes, come prepared with questions, and have someone else with you to help you recall what was said.

- ☐ Cancer tests your most intimate relationships. Couples and individual counseling can help fortify your partnership during and after treatment.

- ☐ Cancer treatment does not have to equal infertility. If you haven't had children and are facing breast cancer, explore fertility preservation options with your care team. It may require another specialist from OB/GYN to join the team, but it can preserve your options.

- ☐ Many hospitals have a weekly tumor board that brings together all the physicians working with cancer patients to review a case and assess treatment options. A tumor board can give you the benefit of many minds working together. And if your cancer pathology, stage, and treatment are straightforward, don't be concerned if your case isn't brought to the tumor board.

BATTER UP

Throughout my cancer journey, I was my advocate. I questioned what I was accepting or not accepting as a limitation or constraint, and those questions guided my mindset, actions, and advocacy. There is power in asking if there is a better or faster way to be treated for cancer. Advocate for appointments as soon as possible, and bring all your data, questions, a note-taking mechanism, and another person to doctors' appointments. Ask for help—you don't have to go it alone. You don't have to know everything. You cannot control everything, and the more you trust your medical team, friends, and family, the more freedom and happiness you will experience.

Everyone's curveball is unique. There are fifteen pathologies of breast cancer and eight different hormonal combinations, resulting in a hundred and twenty different combinations of breast cancer diagnoses. Some are rare, while forty combinations are most commonly diagnosed. Additionally, tumors have different growth rates. People bring different health profiles and priorities to their treatment journey. This makes it nearly impossible to compare my visit to the batter's box to someone else's visit, and yet there are lessons to be learned from each batter's approach to create and adapt your own.

Determining your treatment protocol will require more tests, appointments, and waiting. With a hundred and twenty varieties plus your health profile, giving your medical team a complete view of your curveball is worth the time, stress, and confusion.

Curveballs appear to be moving faster than they are. You want the cancer out. You want treatment quickly.

You likely have the time for the tests, appointments, and conversations.

There is a large community of breast cancer patients, survivors, and supporters. Explore as it suits you, recognizing that people with similar recent experience may have discovered gems you can use. Someone in the same situation with the same type of breast cancer can be a unique teammate and comfort—and you can find them through your infusion center nurses or keen observation.

The mindset you develop for your treatment can be transformational, uplifting, and supportive in the ups and downs of all the pitches that come with treatment. My dual focus on finding joy through happiness tripwires, milestone celebrations, and people involved with my treatment, as well as my orientation that this was my personal Cancer Obliteration Project, reduced my stress, opened me to welcome love, humor, and support, and made my treatment team eager to care for me. My mini-milestones celebrated progress, generated gratitude opportunities to thank the community for helping me, and made me feel normal, which lifted my spirits and strengthened my swing in the batter's box. You can allow people to help you in the batter's box in many ways, and people will surprise you with their willingness to help.

By the end of my chemotherapy protocol, my oncologist marveled at my lab results, saying that I didn't have the lab results of a chemotherapy patient. My approach, and a dose of tremendous luck, made my experience more manageable. Many other survivors report that the journey improved once they welcomed care, experienced moments of joy, and advocated for what they needed. Don't wait until the end of your chemotherapy at-bats to make the journey as good as possible. Even if the chemotherapy doesn't obliterate your cancer (and I hope it does), at least you will have had joy along the way.

Advocate for what you need and articulate what's happening in your body to your team. Asking for extra hydration made me more comfortable. Reconfiguring the ordering of pre-medication administration so I could enjoy a Benadryl-induced nap made infusions go by faster. Leveraging Stego's neck to maintain medication safety and stay asleep was terrific. My oncologist realized that my GI issues were likely from prophylactically taking too much Zofran and showed me another path to avoid nausea and constipation. When my tongue felt swollen, the team wanted to ensure I had steroids and an EpiPen on hand to rapidly counteract any threat to my airway. I exercised regularly before treatment, and my medical team encouraged me to continue exercising, making me feel strong, normal, and social. If the schedule doesn't work as you hoped, take a breath, ask for help creating a new schedule, and try to roll with it.

Sometimes, the curveball will hit you like it hit my sister and brother-in-law when, after cancer, they had the double-whammy of needing to protect their future family dreams and a forty-eight-hour post-infusion nausea nightmare. You'll likely brace for the worst before your first at-bat in the infusion center. With pre-treatment, advocacy, and maniacal attention to staying ahead of the nausea, you likely will have an easier time than your nightmare scenario. Plan for the worst but celebrate and adapt if it's better.

Even though it's unpleasant, ensure you understand your insurance and out-of-pocket expenses and build a budget if you need to work less and therefore earn less during treatment. When facing cancer treatment, the financial impact can be substantial. A 2018 study by the American Cancer Society found that cancer patients in the United States spend an average of $5,000 out-of-pocket in the first year after diagnosis, even with health insurance. For some, the costs can be much higher. Minimizing the financial stress of cancer treatment is crucial. Here are ten important actions you can take:

Learn about the costs. Discuss the potential expenses of cancer treatment with your cancer care team. Ask for estimates and explore less expensive options if available. This step is crucial in helping you prepare for what lies ahead and making informed decisions about your care.

Review your health insurance policy. Ensure your health insurance coverage is active, up-to-date, and comprehensive. Understand your policy's coverage, including deductibles, co-payments, and out-of-pocket limits. This knowledge will help you anticipate your financial responsibilities and avoid unexpected bills.

Seek financial counseling. Consult a financial counselor or navigator who can help you understand your medical bills, insurance claims, and available financial assistance programs. Many hospitals and cancer centers offer these services for free.

Explore financial assistance programs. Research and apply for financial assistance programs, such as co-pay foundations, manufacturer assistance programs, and disease-specific organizations that offer financial support. These can significantly reduce your out-of-pocket costs. They'll also help you understand alternative funding sources you can explore, such as if you have a 401(k) plan and whether it permits penalty-free withdrawals due to a health crisis. Many options are less stressful and less expensive than credit card debt. There is no shame in asking for help.

Communicate with your healthcare providers. Discuss your financial concerns with your healthcare team. They can suggest cost-saving measures or connect you with resources for financial support. Remember, your healthcare team is there to help you in all aspects of your treatment, including managing costs. Additionally, if your healthcare team isn't located close to home, it is often possible to receive chemotherapy, immunotherapy, and even radiation at another location directed by your team. This reduces travel costs and stress.

Plan for time off work. Anticipate the impact of cancer treatment on your ability to work and plan accordingly. Explore short-term disability or family medical leave to ensure financial stability during treatment. Review your employer's policies around sick leave and discuss possible flexible work arrangements. You will know more about what you will likely need after your first course of treatment.

Create a budget. Develop a budget that accounts for medical expenses, daily living costs, and potential income changes. Prioritize essential expenses and seek ways to reduce non-essential spending. This will help you manage your finances more effectively during treatment. I've posted a simple, free tool at www.joellekaufman.com.

Seek community resources. Contact local community organizations, charities, and support groups that help with transportation, lodging, meals, and other practical needs. These resources can help reduce your overall expenses.

Research clinical trials. Consider participating in clinical trials, as they often provide access to cutting-edge treatments at reduced or no cost. Discuss this option with your healthcare team. Clinical trials can offer both potential health benefits and financial relief.

Stay organized. Keep track of medical bills, insurance statements, and correspondence related to your treatment. It can be very confusing, with the amount billed substantially higher than the covered and contracted amount. If possible, stay in-network, as it will reduce your burden and your costs. Reviewing the bills will help you identify errors, track expenses, and ensure accurate billing. Don't be afraid to call and ask questions. Good organization can save you money and reduce stress in the long run.

Too many cancer patients report that finances were the most stressful part of treatment in the United States. It's criminal, but it's a fact that medical expenses, along with the associated loss of income and extraneous expenses, can mount quickly in the US. Be prepared so you can focus on your health and not your wallet.

Your journeys to the batter's box before and during treatment can unlock more profound love, sweeter connections, and gratitude. There will be moments that suck, and those need to be acknowledged and felt, too. But overall, you can create an approach that generates more joy and less suck so that you crush the cancer curveballs.

Part IV:
Surgery

20. Batting Practice

My fine-needle biopsy was negative, and my lymph nodes were clear. Chemotherapy had worked. Neal and I elected to attempt a late-season ski day at Alpine Meadows to celebrate. The day was beautiful, and it was funny to watch locals in costumes playing ski golf—an Alpine Meadows tradition we didn't know existed. I decided to take it easy, do a couple of runs, and enjoy Tahoe's blue sky and beautiful scenery. But I forgot to factor in the altitude.

I managed one run. I was sad and frustrated as I sat on the slope, catching my breath. For one of the only times in my cancer experience, I felt physically weak, and it made me feel bad. I relish feeling like a powerhouse, and for the most part, I thought chemo hadn't knocked me too far backward. That December, two weeks before diagnosis, I was quickly skiing the most expert runs of Revelstoke.

Having trouble carving turns in the snow and catching my breath were definite reminders that my body was weaker than ever. Logically, I thought my strength would rebuild. Emotionally, I was crying with frustration and disappointment. My husband loves to ski, and I was disappointing him, too.

I'd been skiing since I was five or six, and this was the first time in my life I could only do one run, so it was not pretty. The altitude and accompanying oxygen levels were exhausting. My feet were screaming from the lack of circulation. My legs tired quickly from carving the heavy, melting snow. I'm not a slow skier, so the celebration was a bummer.

Neal was great. He was supportive and even skied slowly with me. He waited patiently while I rested. He filmed my skiing to show our kids that I did it. Instead of skiing alone, Neal preferred to keep me company when I sat at the base picnic tables. There wasn't a moment that day when he was concerned about his own enjoyment other than being with me. Again, I am grateful for being loved and supported on my journey.

We enjoyed a delightful lunch in Truckee, and the next day, my friend Majid and his adorable two-and-a-half-year-old daughter visited us at the lake. Nothing is more life-affirming than piloting our boat around the lake with an enthusiastic toddler helping me drive! Being patient with my body was hard as I wanted to jump back into all the fun things in my life.

I felt well enough to travel twice to see Taylor play baseball, once at his college and once for spring break. I made it to almost every soccer and lacrosse game for Ariel, plus her musical performances. I was super bummed that I wouldn't be able to see any of the NESCAC baseball tournaments in person because it would be right after my surgery, but thankfully, the games would be streamed. I felt like me, but my body reminded me it was not close to being fully healed yet.

Thanks to Jessica, Tracey, and James—our remote trainer—I'd exercised through my entire treatment and maintained much of my muscle strength while losing considerable endurance. My Oura Ring reminded me that my resting heart rate was elevated, with my HRV Balance metric (which captures how my autonomic nervous system is trending over time) and Recovery Index (the amount of time I've slept after my resting heart rate stabilizes during the night) both in the red. The surgery was going to set me back even further for a while, but after the recovery period, I planned to be laser-focused on rebuilding my endurance and strength. I planned to enjoy the summer while I rebuilt. Our annual Big Sky trip was already booked, and I focused on ensuring I could play with my family in the snow within six months, without being impacted like I was at Alpine Meadows.

Now, I had to focus on surgery. I would have a bilateral mastectomy with DIEP flap reconstruction in a few weeks. Briefly, in layperson's terms, the surgery would start with a breast surgeon, Dr. Laura Esserman, removing both of my breasts—while preserving my nipples—as well as any lymph nodes considered a risk. Then, my plastic surgeon, Dr. Merisa Piper, and her team would simultaneously prepare chest capsules, harvest body fat from my abdomen with the veins and arteries intact, form new breasts from the body fat, place them within the capsules, and connect the veins and arteries to the blood supply.

The result is a reconstruction without any foreign bodies and statistically fewer complications. The risks are a long ten-to-fourteen-hour surgery, and the potential for skin necrosis if there is insufficient blood supply to the new breasts. The skin graft and the abdominal fat are considered the "flap" of the DIEP flap procedure.

Unlike most cancer patients, I had years to think about my mastectomies and reconstructions. I remembered my mother's expanders from her unilateral mastectomy in 1983 and how much happier she was when she had the prophylactic mastectomy and DIEP flap reconstruction. My sister had complications after her prophylactic mastectomies that required additional hospitalization and IV antibiotics, and which generated scar tissue. There was nothing rushed or panicked about my decision-making or preparation. Additionally, my in-house support group of my sister, mother, and Jessica helped me think through what I should do to prepare myself logistically. My sister and mother were honest and helpful about the emotional ramifications of removing my breasts when I was considering the prophylactic surgery throughout 2022.

I was booked for a short visit to the nuclear medicine department for an injection that would show my breast surgeon, Dr. Laura Esserman, the sentinel lymph nodes. The National Cancer Institute defines a sentinel lymph node as "the first lymph node to which cancer cells are most likely to spread from a primary tumor. Sometimes, there can be more than one sentinel lymph node."[6] All the lymph nodes up to and including that spot would be removed; I wouldn't have a choice. I was hoping to keep all or most of my lymph nodes because I didn't want the risk of lymphedema—permanent swelling due to lack of drainage. Only after the surgeon removed my breasts and lymph nodes and pathology analyzed them thoroughly for an absence of cancer, could I be sure that I was cancer-free.

My surgery was expected to run from 8:30 a.m. to 6:30 p.m. Since a very long surgery was anticipated, three surgeons plus three residents or fellows were involved—in addition to everyone else in the operating room. I had a surgical team with the chops, experience, and bedside manner to knock it out of the park. I considered what was most important to me as I put together my surgical team before my cancer diagnosis and treatment. And, while I ultimately liked my surgeons, my priority was their skill over their bedside manner. I actively participated in sharing my lifestyle, priorities, and worries. I told them about my kids, hobbies, and career dreams, especially those on hold during cancer.

I needed to know they *got* me.

My breast surgeon, Dr. Esserman, exuded confidence and personality. She had tremendous experience and strong opinions. She was passionate and fun. She was fierce in palpating the tumor and lymph nodes at my initial consult and was sure that my surgery would be successful. She called after hours and gave me her mobile number if needed.

Dr. Esserman recommended Dr. Piper for my DIEP flap breast reconstruction surgery. Dr. Piper's warm demeanor and candidness reinforced that I'd chosen the right team. I asked my doctors endless questions about private matters I'd ask no one else. *Will I have sensation after reconstruction? How do you minimize scarring? Will I ever feel perky without an implant?* Dr. Piper answered each curious query, helping me visualize reasonable expectations.

When Dr. Piper explained the surgery, she was comprehensive but not confusing. She asked me about my priorities and let me know what was possible and what was not. It also helped me to learn about her special sauce. Dr. Piper shared that she uses surgical glue instead of sutures to reduce scarring. She contours for natural results without creases. Little innovative touches proved this wasn't just another routine play, but an artisan dedicated to her craft. For Dr. Piper, breast reconstruction is her World Series and the procedure she relishes most. This passion showed in her meticulous revision process to craft the most natural, proportional result.

After recovery, I'd be in the UCSF Mission Bay ICU for two days. Pain management was a real issue with this surgery, and I planned to be both compliant and proactive. I knew from my family's experiences that it was critical to stay ahead of the pain. The team would check me hourly for forty-eight hours, explicitly monitoring the blood supply to the flaps that would construct the lower half of my new breasts by checking them for a pulse every hour for the first twenty-four hours, and then every two hours until I left the hospital. There would be many incisions and six drains. I was told I would spend another day or two in the hospital until I could walk and shower. I would be hunched over because my belly would be very tight.

The DIEP flap revision surgery would be done six to twelve months later to resolve any issues. My body would take about twelve months to settle into its new normal. I couldn't lift more than ten pounds for three months and I'd likely be napping or groggy for a few weeks.

While I had come to accept that I'd lose my breasts, the remorse was ever-present. I was twelve when my body matured, and the Bodacious Ta-Ta girls joined me on my journey through life. At that age, they certainly attracted some attention—primarily welcome, but not all. They made gymnastics quite a bit harder since my center of gravity shifted, and when I started running track, I sincerely appreciated high-impact sports bras. And while I had no illusions that I would ever have Rockette legs, having T & A served me well.

Of course, when I was thirteen, my mother had her first bout with breast cancer, and the Ta-Tas became a potential liability. It was impossible to go through that experience without wondering if the same destiny lay ahead of me. We didn't have any other incidence of breast or ovarian cancer in the family, and the BRCA genes hadn't been discovered yet. Still, I figured if cancer could happen to my incredibly happy and fit mother, it could happen to me.

Life continued, and my Ta-Tas filled out my prom dresses and formal dresses at Michigan. They were instrumental in holding up my wedding dress in 1998. Most importantly, when the time came for them to do their actual job, they were highly effective milk factories for all three of our children, granting them a robust immune system and allowing me to share that intimacy for each of their first years. And after three pregnancies and three years of nursing, they still had pep and were the same size.

I was thankful for the forty years I had spent with them. Yes, they were double trouble, and indeed, the nine-millimeter tumor that the right one developed was a detour I'd rather not have taken. But all told, they had done well.

I had to say farewell.

It was time for the long-delayed Bye-Bye Boobies celebration. I felt I should have prepared with a T-shirt emblazoned with *Troublemakers* or *Double Trouble* across my chest. Although my left breast couldn't be accused along with the right, both would be fired from their lifelong post. Going out to dinner with friends who had been incredible during my journey was fun. We laughed. We talked. We ate. Some people drank—not me; I was prohibited from drinking for seven days before surgery, but that was okay. I was willing to make sacrifices. The surgery would add a layer of confidence and security. The goal was to be cancer-free for the rest of my life.

LESSONS LEARNED

☐ If you can meet multiple surgical teams, cast your net widely. Ask other patients about their experiences and vet online reviews to construct your prospective roster based on your priorities. Ask your oncologist. Then, in-person consultations will be used to vet the surgeons. I was pleasantly surprised that each surgeon I met was patient, kind, and generous with their time. I noticed how they explained complex procedures simply while considering my whole life.

☐ Confirm locations so you don't have to drive too far. My mother's first mastectomy was an hour away in Manhattan, and for her second, she and my dad flew to Houston to work with the experts at MD Anderson. Try to find a location that best suits you and your family. Financial resources are also vital if you must travel far from home for surgery. There are resources available to help if needed. Ask the destination hospital if that's what you need to do.

☐ Aim for a cohesive squad that operates together frequently. As you vet surgeons, ask how often they perform procedures with their plastic surgery partner—high volume matters, as you want a well-oiled machine. At a minimum, your surgery duo should collaborate weekly, if not daily. Miscommunications can happen when teams don't have clear signals, leading to subpar results.

- ☐ Equally important is picking surgeons who specialize in your cancer type and surgical approach. Ask point-blank how many identical or similar procedures they conduct annually. The larger the number, the better. For example, my surgical team performed three to six bilateral mastectomies with DIEP flap reconstructions per week. Fielding routine curveballs builds expertise. You want surgical sluggers, not bench players. The surgeons with the best outcomes are the surgeons who perform your exact surgery the most frequently. If you can access a surgeon specializing in the reconstruction you want, do it.

- ☐ The best teams clearly explain their surgical philosophy and listen thoughtfully to your preferences, hopes, and concerns. Probe them on why they favor specific incision approaches, implant types, and pain management plans. Compare perspectives, but don't be shy about speaking up about ideal outcomes for your body and lifestyle. Beyond medical credentials, consider who you want by your side during the grueling emotional and physical journey. Kindness and compassion count, too, when you're feeling vulnerable.

- ☐ Be prepared that plastic surgeons often consult separately after you've begun plotting treatment with your breast surgeon. My fantastically frank plastic surgeon, Dr. Piper, met me months after my initial diagnosis, once I was clinically cancer-free and ready to schedule my bilateral mastectomy and reconstruction. This sequential system worked, albeit awkwardly. Build rapport with each vital player individually.

- ☐ Beyond checking boxes for frequency, specialization, and bedside manner, you want surgeons who welcome questions and exude confidence tempered with care. When surgical enthusiasm meets surgical excellence, you've secured Most Valuable Player team members poised to help you reclaim normalcy after cancer's nasty curveball. Please put your trust in them and keep your eye on triumph.
- ☐ When organizing your team, consider my surgical team checklist:
  - ☐ Works together regularly
  - ☐ Performs your surgery together frequently
  - ☐ Specializes in your cancer
  - ☐ Explains choices and recommendations clearly
  - ☐ Encourages your questions
  - ☐ Has strong references from other survivors and physicians
  - ☐ Available when the surgery should be scheduled
  - ☐ Trusted and respected
- ☐ Have faith in your hand-selected crew. With an all-star surgical squad batting for you, you've got this!

21. Game Time

My surgery date was moved around a lot. Eventually, the schedulers slipped me in for a long, major surgery before Dr. Esserman went on sabbatical and Dr. Piper left for her Brazilian holiday. I took what I could get. Otherwise, I'd have to wait much longer and not have Dr. Esserman as my breast surgeon. I wanted to stay healthy, so the date was attainable.

We lived in a two-story home, and the DIEP flap was a major abdominal surgery that required me to remain hunched over for about two weeks after the procedure. It was unlikely that I would want to climb stairs in that position right after I came home, so I planned on staying in one of my sons' empty rooms. I set up the room in advance with some loose clothing in the closet to change into on arriving home. A friend offered a collection of wedge cushions to make myself comfortable when I couldn't lie flat. The wedges also created space for the six drains I would always be wearing.

Jessica recalled that one of her friends used a recliner to be comfortable while sitting after her mastectomy. I didn't own a recliner, but Jessica's mother had one she was willing to lend to me for my recovery. TaskRabbit helped us identify people who could move the recliner two miles from her apartment into my family room. It would prove very helpful before I was comfortable getting on and off the couch. I ordered a donut cushion for the recliner and sofa to avoid hurting my coccyx. I bought a lap desk to rest my tablet or laptop on my knees or lap to read in bed, on the recliner, or on the couch. Sharon, Jessica's mom, also lent me a walker to use post-surgery when I had to remain hunched over.

The biggest postsurgical hassles were expected to be drains and pain management.

My surgeons were going to place six drains—two on each side of each breast and two at my abdominal surgical site. I had to secure the drains whenever I moved, and the drains had to be emptied and their contents measured multiple times a day. The only path to drain removal is reaching a low daily output from the drain. Premature drain removal can lead to hematomas or seromas, fluid buildup, and infections. Any of those issues could lead to more procedures and surgeries—which I was desperate to avoid.

My Sharsheret contact, Aimee Sax, offered to send me their mastectomy kit, and I received it before my surgery. It included a bolster pillow, seat belt pad, and multiple styles of surgical drain holders. The hospital would give me blue tubing clamps to attach the drains to my clothing. They work, but they would be awkward. The hospital would also provide a drainage bulb holder and an adjustable belt for the Jackson-Pratt (JP) drains—thin, flexible tubes with a bulb that removes fluid from a wound after surgery. The drainage bulb belt would work better than clamps, but it was nowhere as discreet as the belt from Sharsheret. Sharsheret's drain holders were perfect. The shower holder kept the drains comfortably neutral and in place while I washed them. The belt was easier to use than the clamps. I would ultimately need my abdominal drains for four weeks and would be able to go out and be social without anyone noticing the drains tucked into their little black pocket.

I exercised some agency and control over the surgery by planning my home comfort and return to everyday life. It gave me satisfaction to identify and set these tools up. One of my biggest worries about the DIEP flap was that I'd be in abdominal pain due to constipation from the anesthesia and pain medications, in addition to the surgical incisions. I wanted to avoid that discomfort as much as possible. I knew that narcotics weren't very effective for me when I had my breast reduction. One of the lessons from my mother and sister was that I had to manage pain before I felt pain, and the only way to do that was to take the pain medication on a schedule with escalation options. I wanted the opioids to be the escalation option, to be used only if needed, so I had to be precise with the acetaminophen and ibuprofen schedule, including the evenings.

As mentioned earlier, my father was the medication manager for my mother, and my brother-in-law did it for my sister. My husband is lovely and supportive, but I didn't think tracking my pain meds and ensuring I took them at precise times played to his strengths. My knee-jerk reaction was that lots of people have this need to take medication on a schedule, so there must be an app for it.

There were many apps.

After working twenty-five years in tech, I knew how to identify my user requirements for the app I wanted. I needed an app that would calculate four and six hours from when I noted that I had taken medication. I wanted alerts to take the medication. I wanted to set up multiple medications and pause them if I wasn't continuing to take them. I wanted the app to be free. I found one for Apple iOS called Max Pill Reminder by Artify Inc. I was confident I had the means to keep the pain at bay.

Several nurses and anesthesiologists called with instructions on preparing for the surgery. I had to wash the night before and the morning of surgery using Hibiclens, a specific antimicrobial and antiseptic soap. *Dove has nothing to worry about!* The soap was gross.

Once I arrived at the hospital's pre-op, I was asked to remove all my clothing and use warmed antiseptic wipes all over my body except my face. The wipes started warm, but during the wipe-down they cooled quickly, and I soon found myself slightly damp in a cold pre-op room. I changed into the garments and socks provided by the hospital and packed all my belongings into a bright yellow bag with my name on a sticker.

Then, I waited.

The room was semi-private, so I didn't want to make phone calls and bother a roommate. Neal sat with me. The nurses confirmed my medical history and placed the IV. I would have preferred they use Voldeport, my chest port, but my port was in the surgical field. The anesthesiologist preferred a hand IV placement.

My surgeons visited quickly to answer any last-minute questions and assure us that the surgery would go well. UCSF had a texting system so Neal would get regular updates to share with family and friends. Just as they were getting ready to wheel me out, the anesthesiologist pushed a sedative through the IV to calm my nerves. I wasn't particularly nervous. I was focused on getting through the surgery and with as little pain as possible.

My breast surgeon liked to sing her patients into anesthesia, and she asked me what song I wanted. I wanted to know if we could duet. We agreed to *Don't Stop* by Fleetwood Mac. The lyrics for that song always made me feel positive and focused on what was next rather than what was behind me. I thought it was quite suitable for the day when my natural breasts—the killer Ta-Tas—were leaving me, and I could look forward to my new, belly-fat-built breasts. Dr. Esserman and I did our duet twice while Neal recorded it for posterity, and then I went into surgery.

The next thing I remember is waking up in the ICU, as expected. UCSF has multiple ICUs, and I was in the one used for plastic surgery patients. In the ICU, I had one-on-one nursing, so anything I needed happened quickly. I remember getting heparin shots and that the monitors beeped all night, keeping me from sleeping.

I was suitably annoyed by the constant beeping, but I wasn't in significant pain. As an experiment, I asked if I could forgo the opioids and try to manage the pain using over-the-counter painkillers and perhaps Ativan to sleep if needed. Dr. Esserman loved this idea and directed the nurses to mute the alerts in my room so I could sleep.

Dr. Piper had already left for her holiday, so on ICU rounds I met some of her fellows (doctors who have completed their plastic surgery residency and are studying with Dr. Piper in a fellowship for breast reconstruction).

During the surgery, the team discovered a giant lipoma (benign fatty deposit) in my lower right abdomen. To eliminate the possibility that it was cancerous, I raced through the halls the day after surgery for a CT scan. The hospital has two CT machines—one for adults and one for children. I went to the children's CT room. There were Disney character decals on the machine. When the CT tech asked me to put my hands over my head, I told her my surgeons didn't allow that. With some effort, she figured out how to fit my arms next to my body while sliding into the child-sized tube. The way I was moved from the gurney to the machine was wild. I was lying on top of an inflatable pad. At the CT machine, they inflated the pad, floated me over, and deflated it (still under me). The return to the gurney followed the same gentle process.

One of the downsides of scans is that people have all sorts of stuff going on below the surface, and most of it is irrelevant. Because of my family history, any anomaly detected must be thoroughly investigated. One of Dr. Piper's fellows came to tell me that the lipoma was completely benign—and that I had huge, benign kidney cysts. *Huge—the cysts were double the size of my kidneys.* I was advised to make an appointment with a urologist to evaluate them and a general surgeon to remove the lipoma when I had my revision surgery for the reconstruction. The medical term for discovering the lipoma and kidney cysts while treating my breast cancer is "an incidental finding."

With my cancer obliterated, the incidental findings were the most exciting thing about me, medically.

After the CT scan, I went back to the ICU, where I was very well cared for and was approved for an unrestricted diet on my second day. If only the choices were enticing. It's astounding that UCSF offers only one salad and three boiled vegetables while providing abundant synthetic food such as Beyond Burgers and Impossible Chicken Patties. Luckily, our home is near Copenhagen Bakery, and they make an excellent Chinese chicken salad that my husband could bring me for an appealing meal. A few friends visited me in the ICU, making time fly. I asked my mom to come after I was home because I didn't need her while in the hospital.

My doctors thought I might be able to go home early, skipping the general surgery floor. They either didn't know or forgot to mention that if I wanted to be discharged on Sunday, I had to decide this by Saturday night or very early Sunday morning because discharges could not be processed during the day on Sundays. I missed the deadline and spent another day and night in the sixth-floor general surgery unit. No more one-on-one nursing, but still excellent care. My night nurse pushed me to get myself out of bed unassisted. And the shower was set up for me to use—my exit papers allowed me to wash myself unassisted.

As we left the hospital, I felt relief. The hardest part of my cancer journey was behind me. The cancer guillotine had fallen, but it only took my breasts, and I was willing to give those up voluntarily. The cancers associated with my gene were all off the table. I wanted to focus on healing, seeing my kids, and taking an epic vacation with my husband.

I was granted life. Now, I wanted to live it.

LESSONS LEARNED

- [ ] Game day arrives swiftly once you are cleared for surgery and pick your line-up. Scrub in on surgical prep to be an informed, empowered patient. Train yourself for the marathon your body is about to run by eating properly, exercising as much and as hard as possible, and organizing your postsurgical support team.

- [ ] Prep your home for postsurgical supplies and know your limitations. For example, you might find it challenging to tackle stairs. You will need easy access to medication, food, and a bathroom. Stock your recovery garrison with pillows, comfy clothes, and nutritious groceries. You have a lot of control over your environment and how you prepare.

- [ ] Incidental findings are common when your body is being scanned. For a while after your cancer diagnosis, you may fear that every find is malignant. Don't be afraid to ask the doctors or nurses to explain the incidental finding and why they are concerned.

Andrea's Journey

Andrea expected the radiology department to call, but she wasn't expecting them to schedule her for additional tests immediately. She was suddenly anxious. She had just become an assistant principal at a new school. She was working insane hours and not getting much sleep. She was also recovering from a planned hysterectomy and was trying to focus on getting back into a routine.

Undeterred, Andrea underwent additional tests the very next day.

The medical assistant led Andrea to a different waiting area for the first time. Those extra tests led to biopsies and the placement of tiny metal clips on the suspicious areas.

The life-altering call came the next day while Andrea cared for her mother-in-law who was recovering from surgery. Andrea had DCIS—non-invasive, early-stage breast cancer.

"It was overwhelming," Andrea recalled with emotion. "Fresh out of a hysterectomy and now this. The recovery was more challenging than I expected, and being unable to exercise was frustrating." Andrea's family couldn't provide the support she needed at that moment, and Andrea scoured the Internet until she found the Peloton Breast Cancer Survivors group on Facebook.

Two days later, Andrea met with a breast surgeon. Andrea wanted to avoid radiation therapy because her mother had been treated with radiation therapy many years earlier and experienced permanent, long-term side effects. "My mom underwent a lumpectomy and then intense radiation therapy," she explained. "It had a significant impact on her health, resulting in back problems and other issues. I wasn't ready to subject my body to that." The doctor recommended genetic testing and a consultation with a plastic surgeon.

Andrea credits the women in her Peloton Breast Cancer Survivors group for their unwavering support. With her medical team and support network behind her, Andrea felt empowered to choose a bilateral mastectomy for the best chance at preventing recurrence and avoiding chemo or radiation. "If they're taking one, they might as well take both, right?" she concluded. However, her plastic surgeon demanded that she quit smoking before surgery. "He instructed me to go home, have a bottle of wine, smoke an entire pack of cigarettes, and then never touch one again," she recalled. "Yeah, it was a lot to process in such a short time."

Two days later, she had another meeting with the breast surgeon to discuss her decision. "At that point, I hadn't even met with an oncologist," she said. "Everything was happening so quickly." It wasn't until right before the surgery that Andrea finally met the oncologist recommended by her breast surgeon.

Blood work and genetic testing revealed that Andrea's tumor was triple negative. Andrea was seeking some explanation for why she developed cancer despite leading a healthy lifestyle. Triple-negative breast cancer is the most aggressive type, accounting for 10 to 15 percent of all breast cancers while disproportionately impacting Black and younger women. Andrea didn't have any genetic markers for breast cancer. There was no explanation—as is the case for 90 percent of breast cancers. It just happened.

Andrea heeded her doctor's advice and refrained from searching the Internet for information. "They warned me it would be overwhelming," she said. "So I had no idea what a double mastectomy would entail. I thought they'd remove the old ones and put in the new ones. But it wasn't that simple. What on earth are expanders?" Andrea pondered. She had assumed a straightforward transition from mastectomy to implants, but her surgeon had different plans. "You know, he started talking about sizes, and I was like, 'Dude, you're the expert here. You tell me.' I mean, I didn't have much to begin with," she said before chuckling. Andrea cherished her surgeon's honesty and dedication. Although renowned for mommy makeovers, he said, "Patients like you are where my heart lies." Those words resonated, particularly on the day of her surgery.

Andrea didn't want cancer to interfere with the exciting plans she had. Her medical team allowed her to proceed with planned trips, including a cruise and a visit to Denali. She returned the day after her stepdaughter's wedding for her pre-op appointment, to be followed by the surgery. Reassured by her doctor, Andrea anticipated a quick surgery to minimize the risk of hospital-acquired infections.

Amidst these activities, Andrea also saw her oncologist. To her surprise, the pathology results revealed that her cancer was progressing faster than expected. By the time of her surgery, she had already reached Stage I, fortunately without any signs of spreading further. "I made the right decision," Andrea confidently affirms regarding the mastectomy instead of lumpectomy.

Her choices, her medical team, and the Peloton group's support made her optimistic and empowered. Still, anxiety consumed her. The COVID-19 pandemic had just begun in the US, and hospital regulations were constantly changing. "It felt like navigating a maze blindfolded," Andrea recalled. However, her surgeon found a way to ease her apprehension. He held her hand, drew a smiley face on it with a Sharpie, and requested the anesthesiologist to administer a calming agent. "He set the tone for the entire ordeal," Andrea reflected. "Little did I know then that the journey would extend for nearly two more years."

Following the surgery, the surgeon decided to keep Andrea in the hospital overnight to monitor her progress closely and avoid delays, given how far away Andrea lived from the hospital. She had four drains inserted, which she struggled to comprehend until she experienced them firsthand. Her boyfriend also faced challenges with his feelings and ability to provide home nursing care. "I remember looking in the mirror when I got home and feeling … overwhelmed," she confessed. "It hit me harder than I expected. I've always had insecurities."

Then, another unexpected blow: on the day she returned home from her mastectomies, she received news of her son's near-fatal car accident. "It was a nightmare," Andrea recollected, her voice trembling. "It was just too much all at once."

Throughout her recovery, friends and acquaintances reached out to her boyfriend to inquire about her well-being, which left her unsettled. "They could have texted or called me directly," she expressed. "It felt like he was broadcasting my struggle. I know he was trying to cope, but it was difficult for me." Despite the hurdles, Andrea acknowledged her boyfriend's unwavering support. "He was my rock," she said. "He tended to my drains, assisted my mom, and was simply there."

Andrea faced complications during her reconstruction process, requiring multiple surgeries. She had fills for the expanders, where the doctor injects additional saline into the expander to gently stretch the skin—another process that Andrea didn't fully comprehend until she experienced it firsthand. The metal in the expanders triggered alarms in stores, resulting in uncomfortable situations where security meticulously searched her purse for theft. It wasn't until one of her fill appointments that the medical staff gave her a letter to present in such scenarios or while traveling.

Christmas felt different in 2019—devoid of festive preparations and elaborate meals, instead filled with the monotony of daytime television and the couch. Sleep eluded her, and when it finally came, it was in short spurts on the couch, with her feet propped up.

Doctors' appointments filled her calendar, including consultations with the oncologist and regular blood work.

There was only a single day without a visit to a clinic or hospital. "I practically lived there," Andrea exclaimed, shaking her head.

Then came the news: one of her implants had not taken as expected. By 2020, the COVID-19 pandemic was in full swing, postponing most non-emergency surgeries. Despite their best efforts, Andrea's surgery kept getting delayed. "It was so frustrating," she admitted. "I just wanted to get it over with."

Finally, when they received the green light, it was a whirlwind. "Can you have surgery in two days?" the doctor asked. Without hesitation, Andrea replied, "Yes!" The surgery involved replacing the faulty implant and adding more fat to ensure successful integration.

But there was another surprise in store. Andrea had not realized that she would not be getting her nipples yet. "It was a bit disappointing," she confessed. "But I trusted my surgeon." Amidst all of this, her relationship with her son suffered. Three weeks after her mastectomy, they argued. The details were hazy, but the aftermath was apparent—her son stopped talking to her for a year and a half. She attributed the strain in their relationship to the surgery, her emotional state, and the medications she was taking.

Things seemed to be on track until February 2020, when she developed an infection. It started during a weekend getaway at their ranch. "I just felt off," she remembered. "And then I looked down, and I was swollen like I was eight months pregnant. The pain was indescribable." Despite her discomfort, her main concern was for her boyfriend, now husband, whom she married on September 25, 2021. He was away hunting, and she did not want to spoil it for him. "I told him, 'No, we're not going to the hospital. Enjoy your weekend. I'll be fine.'"

Andrea knew things were far from fine. The pain was worsening, and she could not shake the feeling that something was seriously wrong. A nurse friend who was visiting their ranch noticed her condition and suspected complications from her surgery. Following her friend's advice, Andrea called her doctor Monday morning. His immediate response caught her off guard. He insisted she come in right away.

For a week, she visited her doctor daily for him to monitor her condition. Each time Andrea saw the plastic surgeon, he instructed her to arrive looking prepared for a night out. Initially, she found the requirement absurd, but they assured her it would boost her confidence. They also stressed the importance of keeping her arms active, cautioning that neglecting this could necessitate physical therapy. Having previously suffered a torn calf muscle, rendering her unable to walk for six months, Andrea was determined to avoid additional physical therapy. "It was the best advice they gave me," she conceded. She was grateful for his vigilance. Having already spent enough time in the hospital, she had no desire to return.

During her exchange surgery, transitioning from expanders to implants, a procedure typically done on an outpatient basis, things did not go as planned. The operation, which should have lasted four to five hours, lasted nearly ten. Given the length of the procedure and the distance from her home, her surgeon decided it would be best for her to stay overnight in the hospital. Her doctor performed liposuction to reconstruct the tissue. However, the aftermath of that procedure left Andrea pondering why anyone would willingly undergo liposuction. "I looked as if someone beat me with a baseball bat," she said. The complications of the surgery were something Andrea had not anticipated. The incisions from the fat grafting were not entirely closed, intentionally so to allow fluid drainage. The sight of blood and fluid was alarming, even to the hospital nurses unaccustomed to seeing patients in this post-procedure state.

When Andrea finally received her implants, no one told her she would have to wear a bra constantly for nearly three years. There was the discomfort of compression wear—Spanx and similar garments. Andrea found them so tight that she had to cut holes to use the bathroom without assistance. Medication posed another challenge. One drug intended to aid healing was too potent, so Andrea could only take it twice a day. She didn't appreciate the way pain medication made her feel.

Moreover, she had experienced post-anesthesia constipation after a previous surgery and was determined to avoid a recurrence of that discomfort. Anesthesia also had unexpected side effects, such as thinning hair and blurry close-up vision. "I had no idea anesthesia could cause these issues," she admitted.

Andrea felt a glimmer of hope when her son invited her to his high school graduation during the COVID-19 pandemic. However, he disappeared as quickly as he had reappeared, moving to Colorado without saying a word. While dealing with her health and the strained relationship with her son, Andrea cared for her mother-in-law while striving to keep everyone around her happy. She had put her work on hold, but the emotional toll was overwhelming.

Even her friendships suffered as some friends struggled to comprehend her emotional roller coaster.

Reflecting on her journey, Andrea can scarcely believe she endured it all. "It felt surreal," she remarked. "But you know what? Here I am. And if I can overcome that, I can conquer anything." Despite the setbacks, Andrea remained focused on her recovery. Even when she developed an allergic reaction to the tape used to secure the covers over her newly formed nipples, she maintained a positive attitude. During every checkup, Andrea would eagerly ask, "Can I take them off yet?" only to be told to wait another two weeks. Her journey was more complex than she had hoped, but her determination to see it through to the end never wavered.

Andrea realized her recovery was more of a marathon than a sprint. She found herself negotiating with her doctors about what she could and couldn't do and facing unexpected challenges. Humor became Andrea's coping mechanism. She would send playful emails to her doctors, framing her questions as if they were from a friend. This lighthearted approach helped to lighten the mood and navigate the ongoing challenges.

Finally, an opportunity to socialize presented itself—a concert at the ranch with friends. All Andrea wanted was to dance and feel normal again. She pleaded with her doctors, promising to be cautious. After a compromise, she was allowed to slow dance, but swing dancing was off-limits, and she had to keep her protective gear on for an additional week. "It may have been a small victory," Andrea recalled, "but it meant the world to me."

Then came 2021, and with it, the arrival of spring and a strong desire to be outdoors, swim, and lounge by the pool. However, Andrea's recovery, with its stitches and potential complications, did not allow for such activities. "I felt like I was missing out on so much," Andrea admitted.

On her birthday, instead of going out, Andrea decided to cook. Unfortunately, due to the lack of feeling in her chest, she accidentally burned herself. The smell of burning filled the air before she realized what had happened. The burn was severe, requiring a visit to her surgeon the next day. "You're lucky the plastic didn't catch fire," the surgeon remarked. But this setback meant another delay—the areola procedure would have to wait.

Despite the setback, Andrea remained determined to enjoy her summer. "I may not look my best in a bathing suit right now," she said, "but I want to swim with our grandkids." They agreed to postpone the areola procedure until September. The scars were a constant reminder of Andrea's battle, resembling a battlefield when she looked in the mirror. She diligently applied various scar creams recommended by her surgeon, finding solace in being able to control something amidst the chaos. However, as her scars faded, her health challenges persisted. Post-surgery complications seemed to accompany Andrea persistently. Without undergoing chemotherapy or radiation, she endured menopause-like symptoms every day. The relentless hot flashes made it feel as though her body was at war with itself.

Her Peloton bike, a Christmas gift from her husband, became her newfound workout routine, offering solace and enjoyment. Yet Andrea felt guilty that her difficult journey was comparatively more manageable than most. She didn't have to endure the nausea and exhaustion often associated with chemotherapy and radiation.

Finding solace in a survivors group on Peloton's Facebook community pages, she formed valuable friendships, even though they had never met in person. "I sometimes found it easier to open up to people I didn't know," Andrea revealed. She felt less judged and burdened. She recalled feeling like an inconvenience to her beloved mother-in-law during her challenging times.

After completing her treatment, Andrea began experiencing symptoms of post-traumatic stress disorder (PTSD). Her body was exhausted, and the medical issues persisted. Despite her attempts to explain, her husband struggled to comprehend the extent of the trauma she had endured. Even her doctors seemed to underestimate the toll it had taken on her. Amidst her battle, Andrea had to cope with her mother's illness and death. She missed her best friend's wedding. "So many aspects of my life were affected by this journey," she explained. Her choice to undergo surgery was prompt and resolute. She knew it was the right decision but didn't anticipate the emotional toll it would take.

"If I could talk to the me who had struggled through the surgeries and aftereffects, I'd say, 'Be patient with yourself,'" she added. "It's okay to feel frustrated, angry, or sad. It doesn't mean you're not strong."

LESSONS LEARNED

- [ ] Breast cancer treatment is important but not a 911 emergency. Slow down to think as you act. Consult with multiple teams. Ask questions about options, expectations, and side effects. Ask about how the different options will impact your life—exercise, clothing (compression garments are needed), and sexuality.

- [ ] If something doesn't feel or look right, escalate to your medical team sooner rather than later. Complications can happen, and they know what to do.

- [ ] Mastectomies result in loss of sensation in the breasts. Pain is a warning sign, and you need to be aware when cooking, grilling, and making a campfire so that you don't burn yourself without realizing it.

- [ ] Share your life plans with your medical team and partner to maximize your participation in all the good things in your life.

- [ ] A mastectomy is a major surgery. Ensure you understand what happens in the hospital, at home, and as a follow-up before your surgery.

Cindee's Journey

Cindee was thirty-seven and weaning her third and final baby when she felt a lump in her breast. She thought it was a clogged milk duct, but when it didn't subside after a month, her OB-GYN measured it as 3.5 by 3.5 centimeters and immediately ordered a mammogram and ultrasound. Her biopsy was the Tuesday before Thanksgiving, and the call came on the Monday following the holiday. The mistaken clogged milk duct was a monumental understatement—it was an eleven-centimeter-round tumor upon scanning.

Cindee felt her world shift beneath her feet as she received the call. Overwhelmed by the gravity of her situation, she broke down, fearing that she didn't have adequate health insurance, and then, thankfully, discovered she did. However, Cindee's policy required her to find and see a primary care physician to obtain the referral to an oncologist.

"I had a friend who was a nurse in Virginia, and she called oncologists for me," Cindee told me. "She found me two candidates. I picked one, and he recommended the plastic surgeon. I asked, 'Is this who you would send your wife to?' And he said, 'Yes.'"

Initially, the oncologist thought she had a Stage II or III tumor. He said, "We want to explore a trial for young women with large tumors. We'd do chemo first to see if we could shrink the tumor before surgery." To confirm her eligibility for the trial, Cindee had an MRI that looked good, but her tumor, at 5.5 by 5.5 centimeters, was larger than allowed by the trial criteria. Her dense breasts made it hard for the imaging procedure to fully detect her tumor. The UCLA-based trial team facilitated a genetic test through which Cindee discovered she had the CHEK2 genetic mutation (which increases one's risk for certain types of cancers, including breast cancer), inherited through her father, who was an adoptee and didn't know his family medical history. Cindee initially wanted a bilateral mastectomy, and her surgeon had planned on a unilateral one. The genetic mutation altered the recommendation to a bilateral mastectomy before chemotherapy.

It was early 2021, and COVID-19 was on the rise. Reduced hospital staff and a shortage of beds meant Cindee had to make some tough decisions on the fly. Adaptability became her new superpower. On January 29, the Friday before her scheduled surgery on Monday, Cindee was called while picking up all her pain meds. "I'm sorry," said the nurse, "but because of COVID, we can only do a single mastectomy, or you can wait and do a bilateral mastectomy when we have staffing." Her sister was flying out with her three kids, and Cindee elected to have the unilateral mastectomy. Her surgeon also took out eight lymph nodes. Seven out of eight had metastatic cancer, so they sent Cindee for a PET scan.

The PET scan showed the cancer had spread to Cindee's spine, sternum, and pelvis—Stage IV. Not only was Cindee devastated, but she also had limited support. "Due to COVID, I had to go through medical appointments, treatment, surgeries, and radiation alone," said Cindee.

Three days after surgery, with drains tucked into her pockets, she attended her eldest son's high school graduation—a poignant goal she silently vowed to achieve for all three of her children. What she anticipated might be one or two surgeries, turned into a series of daunting medical challenges. Cindee encountered not only the expected hurdles of cancer treatment but also an infection in one of her surgical sites. These setbacks resulted in additional surgeries, each one a blow to her morale and her resolve.

Opting out of an endless round of shots for chemical menopause, Cindee chose a hysterectomy, a procedure she described as a walk in the park compared to earlier trials. Harnessing the power of choice, she advocated for a hysterectomy to avoid indefinite hormone shots and embraced a simple but profound wish—to play soccer again. With unshaken confidence, Cindee refused to let her diagnosis keep her from returning to the field.

Facing severe radiation burns and the monumental task of thirty-five treatment sessions, she encountered every possible obstacle, and yet Cindee didn't back down. Amidst caring for her kids, aged four, nine, and nineteen, she completed her treatment, ringing the bell that symbolized the end of radiation, with triumph. "I tried my best not to stress over things I couldn't control," she said.

Just as Cindee grappled with the physical toll of cancer, she also navigated the baffling intricacies of the healthcare system. She found herself wrestling with insurance coverage issues and grappling with exorbitant medication costs, a sober reminder of the broader systemic challenges faced by many in her situation. Amidst these trials, when a blood clot was found, Cindee received a diagnosis of Factor V Leiden, a condition requiring her to take blood thinners, further complicating her therapy. The emotional and financial strains mounted, and yet she remained resolute.

Cindee found solace and strength in a community, discovering camaradery with fellow cancer fighters and survivors across various support groups, including a beloved group—"The club no one wants to join," she explained, then laughed. These connections provided a sanctuary of understanding—an oasis in the storm where experiences were shared and burdens eased.

Cindee's perspectives on friendship changed through her odyssey, and relationships evolved. "I'm terrible at asking for help," she said, adding, "I've gotten a lot better. I have a couple of very close friends. They would help me at the drop of a hat. I learned who I can lean on and who I can't. I did ask for help. And I do ask for help." She realized that her condition connected her to new allies and naturally siphoned off those less steadfast. Cindee's small circle of family and friends was her rock.

All this, yet Cindee doesn't tell a sob story. She tells a tale of aspiring to survive and maintain a quality of life. Rather than be defined by her illness, Cindee chose to see it as a chronic condition, akin to diabetes, focusing on maintenance rather than a definitive end. As a result, where many patients see only two years of efficacy with Kisqali (ribociclib), Cindee was at year three and has met a handful of people in year eight.

In the company of uncertainty, Cindee's philosophy evolved. Fear of the unknown morphed into a challenge met with positivity and action. The value she places on each day has skyrocketed, propelling her passion for travel and a mission to visit all fifty states with her kids. She enjoys simple pleasures, like playing soccer and embracing life's daily rhythms. Cindee learned about the depths of her strength, the value of a laugh when your skin is ablaze with pain, and the unexpected joy in the ordinary moments often taken for granted.

"I say yes to doing more things," she said. "I put myself out there more and try to make the best of life. It was a slap in the face that I didn't know I needed, and I wish everybody could have that without getting cancer."

LESSONS LEARNED

- [ ] Sometimes, you must make tough medical decisions on the fly. Do your best to make educated choices, then don't stress over things you can't control.

- [ ] Ensure you have health insurance and keep up-to-date paperwork you can refer to when needed. Calls to your insurance company or representative can also be helpful. Medical costs above insurance can be hard to deal with, so ensure your coverage alleviates as much of the financial burden as possible.

- [ ] Even when a tumor is caught early, there is always a chance the cancer has spread to other parts of the body. This is considered Stage IV cancer. While news such as this can be difficult, try to stay strong. Even Stage IV cancer is treatable.

- [ ] Even when precautionary steps are taken, infection can creep in after surgery. Communicating physical changes with your medical team is vital so infections are dealt with swiftly. Sometimes additional surgeries are required.

- [ ] Find joy in the simple pleasures of a life well lived.

Lesley's Journey

Lesley's watch buzzed urgently, a digital nudge amidst an ordinary day. Barely two days earlier, her world dipped into shades of gray at the news of another early pregnancy not taking hold. If that wasn't enough to bear, a lump had spiraled into a flurry of tests, culminating in a biopsy. Now, as she stood before her class in October, a cavern of teenage energy, her MyChart message blinked into existence on her computer screen. The words "invasive breast cancer" froze her mid-sentence.

Her student teacher, catching a glimpse of her ashen face, didn't hesitate. "Go," he urged softly but firmly. Lesley's hands barely remembered to clutch her keys before she found herself outside the classroom, the world tilting as she gasped for air, her daughter's name a plea on her lips.

Her school family, already bracing to support her, whisked her into the sanctuary of an empty classroom, reaching out to her mom as Lesley charted her course home. The next few hours blurred until a calm, reassuring voice crystallized the turmoil. "I'm Becky, your oncology nurse navigator," the voice said, sparking a sliver of hope. "This is the most common type of breast cancer, and it's the most treatable kind of breast cancer. You're going to be fine. From now on, if you need anything, you call me." Buoyed by naïveté, Lesley dreamed of a swift battle, envisioning a victory by Thanksgiving. Becky, her newfound guide in this uncharted territory, mapped out a strategy tailored just for Lesley, intertwining expert care teams by leveraging Becky's network of personal connections.

Becky's resolve extended beyond mere appointments; she orchestrated Lesley's treatment with a maestro's touch, delicately balancing oncology protocols with Lesley's wish to preserve hope for future family dreams.

Amidst the structured routine of chemotherapy, a remarkable transformation unfolded. Lesley began to shine even brighter. With a mindset focused on survival and swiftly moving past the treatment, she embraced the chemotherapy with positivity. Remarkably, after four rounds of AC, the lump was almost invisible, shrinking further before she transitioned to Taxol. Such was the progress that her oncologist even reduced the Taxol dosage for the final two cycles. "Instead of saying you *have to* do chemo," she said, "remember you *get to* do it to rid your body of the illness."

She dove headfirst into the sprawling, messy world of social media, seeking solace and kinship. And find it she did, in the shared stories and virtual nods of understanding that stitched together a tapestry of resilience. It was a space where saying "I've been there too" felt like a warm hug. One of her contacts evolved into a very close, lifelong bestie.

Lesley's battle marked her in unexpected ways. The once elusive lumps, now vanquished by medical alchemy, mirrored the internal transformation she underwent—a metamorphosis underscored by the support of her school community, which held an outdoor, school-wide parade and showered her in a blizzard of pink petals as she embarked on the surgical chapter of her saga. The unexpected acts of kindness from people were genuinely heartwarming surprises. The gesture of receiving handwritten cards touched Lesley. The diverse ways people showed their support, each reflecting their unique personalities, were fascinating and uplifting. For instance, school friends went out of their way to do amusing school-related activities, such as sending a singing gorilla Elvis telegram on a birthday. Another touching gesture was Lesley's cousin rallying a hundred friends and family members to create posters with supportive messages for her, assembling them into a banner, and displaying them in her home. Another cousin paid for a limo, full of her entire family, to collect her from her last chemo infusion. Moreover, the support extended beyond gestures to practical help. Lesley's sister organized a meal train that engaged friends.

During Lesley's lumpectomy surgery, a flattened tumor was discovered deep near the chest wall, which also had to be removed, revealing a total of three tumors. Despite this, the surgeons successfully performed the lumpectomy and bilateral breast reconstruction to match her breasts to each other. Her surgery included the removal of one lymph node. Her lymph nodes were negative for any trace of cancerous cells. After seven hours of surgery, Lesley was cancer-free, with a breast reduction.

Recovery unveiled a new Lesley, who vibrated with an infectious zest for life. She leaped into the realms of health and wellness with the enthusiasm of the newly awakened.

LESSONS LEARNED

- [ ] Approach each day one step at a time. Tackle each day with optimism and good vibes.

- [ ] There are multiple surgical approaches, ranging from no surgery (monitoring) to lumpectomy, unilateral mastectomy, and bilateral mastectomy. Each has pros and cons. In consultation with your medical team and loved ones, you choose what is best for you.

- [ ] If your treatment center has an oncology nurse navigator (ONN) service, ask to be connected and lean on your nurse navigator. They are experts who know how to guide you through this process.

- [ ] Reframing chemotherapy, from something you must do to something you get to do, powerfully shifts your mindset and mood.

- [ ] Your community wants to show you that they care and love you. Let them.

BATTER UP

Throughout cancer treatment and surgery, the support, love, and engagement I received from my community of family and friends was nothing short of incredible. I was blessed to be loved and connected. Some people texted me regularly. Some called. Some cooked excellent meals for my family and me. Some drove me to and from appointments, and some came to visit. Many prayed for me, lifting me and my family.

I couldn't have done it alone.

My friend shared a lesson from Rabbi Yudi Steiger of Chabad Lubavitch of Park City on *The Month of Healing*. We had just entered the Hebrew month of Iyar when my May 4 surgery was scheduled. It is also known as "the month of healing" since the Hebrew letters that spell the month of Iyar are an acronym for the phrase "Ani Hashem Rofecha"—*I am God, your Healer*. In 1977, the Lubavitcher Rebbe, Rabbi Menachem Mendel Schneerson (of blessed memory), met with Professor Mordechai Shani, the then-director of Sheba Hospital, the largest hospital in Israel. Rebbe Schneerson asked Professor Shani to consider changing the hospital's name. Instead of using the Hebrew term Beit Cholim, *a House of the Sick*, he wanted to introduce the name Beit Refuah, *a House of Healing*.

Following the meeting, the rebbe penned a letter to urge the professor to consider this name change. He provided two reasons why this name change was the right thing to do. First, it would positively impact the patients. They came to seek healing, not to be labeled as sick. "Even more importantly," the rebbe added, "this is a more fitting name for this institution since the purpose and the essence of this house are all about healing." Today, most hospitals in Israel are called Merkaz Refui, *Healing Centers*. And the word "health" has become an integral element of hospital names worldwide.

I was excited for Iyar. I was ready for the month of healing to put my cancer journey into the history books. My journey was about healing. It was about obliterating the cancer. In May, I dealt the cancer its final elimination knock-out with my surgery.

Part V:
Recovery

22. The Ninth Inning

I wasn't eager to see my body post-surgery. I knew the scars would be red and raw. I expected there would be bruising and swelling. Intellectually, I knew the indications of trauma would fade over time, but emotionally, I had no idea how I would react to what I would see.

Post-surgery, I was covered in bandages and gauze. The nurses checked the pulse of the flaps containing blood vessels from my abdomen—every hour in the ICU and every two hours when I moved to the general adult surgery ward. They could do this without me seeing my body. Even the mandatory shower that constituted my get-out-of-hospital card didn't require me to look in the mirror and see what my gifted surgeon had done.

So I waited.

I'd had three pregnancies and deliveries without a caesarian section, but now I would have a C-section scar. My breasts, which fed all three babies effortlessly and then surprisingly reverted to their original size and shape, were unlikely to look the same. My reconstructive surgeon, Dr. Piper, was honest in telling me that I should expect twelve months for my body to settle into its new shape. I figured, *what's the rush to peek?*

Although part of me wanted to know if I would remember my former body when I saw this new version, I wasn't sure if seeing the latest version would prompt grief or relief. I was balancing fear and curiosity. And for at least a week, fear won.

I eventually gave in to reality. I had to change my mindset. I told myself that my body has changed throughout my life, and this is just another stage. As a high school gymnast and sprinter, I had powerful legs, a tiny waist, and relatively flat abs. In my twenties, I was petite but muscular. In my thirties, I created three incredible people and marveled at what my body morphed into with each pregnancy. In my forties, I fought the belly pooch and battled with weight changes despite an active exercise regimen. So here I was in my fifties, and, hopefully, I had flatter abs and perkier boobs than I'd had in years.

After seven days, curiosity won out, and I stared into a mirror to inspect this new body. I felt like an explorer or scientist examining a specimen, but the specimen was me. The scars didn't look too bad. My breasts were broader, and the nipples were not pointing in quite the same direction. The bottom half of my abdomen was flat and tight. My surgeon did great work on the belly button, but there was a prominent bulge between my breasts and my new belly button. When I saw my surgeon for a follow-up appointment, she agreed my upper abdomen shouldn't look like that. She mentioned four possible causes:

1. Separation of the abdominal muscles due to pregnancy
2. Extra weight, particularly visceral fat (the fat that surrounds the organs)
3. A hernia
4. Something else

I was confident that my abdominal muscles had not separated due to pregnancy since this was the first time I had an abdominal bulge. The doctor examined me for a hernia and didn't find anything. My sister and her husband owned an impressive fitness facility and offered to measure my visceral fat. It was higher than it should be, so I knew I needed to shed some weight. My sister provided guidance and consulted with one of their nutritionists to re-engineer my diet. Middle age is not kind to women who want to lose ten to fifteen pounds.

While I accepted that I needed to lose a few pounds to flatten the bulge, it was too prominent after the surgery to be caused by visceral fat alone. I hadn't gained weight during chemo, and I didn't have that notable a bulge before surgery. My thesis was that the DIEP flap procedure restricted the distribution of my abdominal organs away from my lower abs, and my rib cage restricted distribution upward, leaving my five-foot-two body with no space for massive kidney cysts. I inquired whether the kidney cysts might be causing the bulge. My visit to the urologist confirmed they were vast and harmless—except they were likely causing the abdominal bulge.

My urologist offered to aspirate the cysts so we could determine whether eliminating their contents impacted the abdominal bulge. When he aspirated the left cyst, he drained 1.15 liters of fluid, and the bulge was materially reduced. A few weeks later, he drained the right cyst of 300 milliliters of liquid. We wanted to know whether the fluid was gone for good, so we would have to check if the cysts refilled in the future. If they did, I would ultimately need surgery to drain and cauterize the cysts so they would be permanently empty. They ultimately refilled, and in 2024, I elected to surgically cauterize the larger cysts on my left side.

Getting to know my new body turned out to be exciting and didn't trigger additional grief. I appreciated the incredible work my surgical team executed. My clothing still fit properly. A revision surgery would fix things that didn't settle quite right, and I felt confident the results would be attractive and familiar to me. My husband even liked this new, upgraded body as much as the old one.

Mainly, I was happy that my new breasts could not kill me.

The drains were a drag when I couldn't get all of them out after a few weeks. At week three, my left hip drain became excruciatingly painful. I spoke with the advice (aka telephone triage) nurse repeatedly, and we did a workaround, but it was often breathtakingly painful. At my four-week postsurgical check, I complained about "drain pain." The drain was still generating output, but the pain level was very high. I didn't want to use opioid painkillers for a drain! The nurse practitioner examined me and determined that the suture holding my drain in place had slipped inside my wound, and it was rubbing the underside of my skin. With a generous amount of lidocaine applied, she carefully pulled the suture out and provided me with adhesive rings to keep the tubing out of my body while I carried the drain around for two more weeks, six in total.

My first post-surgery goal was to be comfortable enough to participate in a brunch to enjoy a multigenerational Mother's Day with my parents, our children, and my sister's family, less than two weeks after my surgery. Because I wasn't taking any opioids, by week two after surgery, I was driving unassisted. Having a near-term goal to keep me focused and disciplined throughout my recovery was helpful. Surgery wasn't the end for me; it was a new beginning.

I had a lot to look forward to.

The pathology results were reassuring. There were no cancer cells in either my removed breasts or lymph nodes. Yet, surprisingly, no one called me with the good news.

It turned out the oncology team assumed the surgery team had told me of my final pathology outcome. When I sent a MyChart message requesting the results, the team was confused and horrified. With my breast surgeon starting her sabbatical the day after my surgery *and* my plastic surgeon leaving for a well-earned Brazilian vacation the night of my surgery, no one on the surgical team got a reminder to call me. The medical team called right after my email. *No need to apologize for giving me excellent news!* While it was astounding that that communication ball got dropped, and I was naturally annoyed that everything wasn't tightly coordinated, I chose to see it as humorous. The ball was dropped in the final inning.

LESSONS LEARNED

- [ ] Don't assume that no news is bad news. Bad news travels very fast. If you are expecting an update and don't receive it when planned, reach out and ask.

- [ ] Incidental findings are expected. If you have a pCR, you don't have metastatic disease. You're just a complex organism that's been studied under a microscope. None of my incidental findings threatened my health.

- [ ] If you aren't delighted with the results of your reconstruction, discuss options with your reconstructive surgeon. You can also consider artistic breast tattoos instead of nipple and areola reconstruction. Your body, your canvas.

- [ ] Set flexible goals for your post-surgery recovery. I wanted to minimize pain while limiting opioid usage. I was lucky that I could. My extended family's celebration of Mother's Day with my out-of-town parents and my college-bound kids was a goal and a gift. And if I were too tired, they'd bring the visit to me on the couch.

23. Next Season's Curveballs

While I was thrilled to be cancer-free, I knew there would always be a chance my breast cancer would reoccur. For triple-negative breast cancer like mine, the highest probability of recurrence is within the first three years and about 40 percent across the population. Yet I knew statistics were not predictive, and I believed my odds of experiencing a reoccurrence were low due to my specific circumstances. Recurrences are more common among triple-negative breast cancer survivors who meet the following criteria:

* People diagnosed under the age of thirty-five

* Large tumor size

* Surgery didn't successfully remove all the cancer

* No radiation therapy after lumpectomy

* Inflammatory triple-negative breast cancer

* Obesity

* Lack of a positive pathological complete response (pCR)

Different breast cancer pathologies have different recurrence rates. Invasive lobular carcinoma (ILC), for example, has a higher recurrence rate than triple-negative invasive ductal carcinoma (IDC). For triple-negative breast cancer, the chance of recurrence drops dramatically after three years and again after ten and fifteen years.

Every diagnosis is unique, and using population statistics to determine personal risk is statistical folly. The odds are favorable that I won't have a recurrence, but that's no guarantee. I still have the BRCA1 gene. My best bets are living as healthy as possible through diet, exercise, mental health, and humor. Without breast tissue, mammograms, ultrasounds, and MRIs are not effective. Manual exams by doctors and self-exams are the prescribed approach to monitoring.

Probability of recurrence and post-treatment monitoring protocols are excellent conversations to have with your oncologist and psycho-oncologist. Many people feel a great deal of anxiety about recurrence. Backaches or joint pain have new intensity when they can be a harbinger of metastatic disease. My approach is doing everything in my power to minimize the possibilities of recurrence while maximizing the monitoring available to ensure possible worries are found and treated early if I have a recurrence or a new primary, like my sister.

My mother was cancer-free when she recovered from multiple reconstructive surgeries. To her, her reconstructed breast never looked quite right, but she was still herself—vibrant, athletic, and engaged. Then, in March 1985, during a routine checkup, a bump my mom thought was something amiss in her implant turned out to be a small cancerous growth. The cancer was back.

As an adult, I would learn the difference between metastasis and loco-regional recurrence. My mother's repeat breast cancer was loco-regional, a second occurrence in the exact location, as opposed to a new primary tumor, and we are fortunate. The surgeon thought it was a remnant of her original tumor because it was along the incision line from her mastectomy. With BRCA1, even a lone cell can create a problem. I'm thankful for her vigilance and grateful that her recurrence was loco-regional.

My mother had gone to the plastic surgeon alone because she expected this to be a routine follow-up from her latest reconstructive procedure. She didn't want my father to take time off from running his real estate development company for something insignificant. My father battled traffic from his offices near our home in Holmdel, in central New Jersey, to Manhattan to be with her. He determined he would never again fail to attend a cancer-related doctor's appointment with her. At the time, I watched my parents cry, hold each other, and appear incredibly vulnerable and scared. My parents are like a planet, with my sister and me as the orbiting moons pulled close by gravity but held off from their tight-knit partnership.

My parents didn't want questions because they didn't have answers. Mom was reassuring us that it was a small thing, but Dad didn't believe she was out of the woods yet, despite having had aggressive surgery two years earlier to eradicate the disease. For this round, my mother would need a year of chemotherapy with a five-week break in the middle for radiation. My mom lost her hair and wore wigs and turbans, but we tried to make it no big deal. Mom and Dad were left to manage her side effects the best they could. They didn't want to upset my sister and me by sharing how she was feeling. Still, the hair loss, fatigue, and puffy face were impossible to hide. Mom faced her treatment with resolve, and most of the time, she was normal. She even played in her competitive tennis league and probably won throughout chemotherapy. She's fierce.

At fifteen, I focused on my belief that everything happening to her was temporary. My research habit helped alleviate my worries and anxieties because I understood that her chemotherapy and radiation were prophylactic to eliminate any microscopic remnants of cancer. The doctors had not seen any evidence that cancer cells remained in my mother's body, but since she was young and healthy, they and my parents wanted extra insurance. The worst part was eating dinner. On chemo days, my father, sister, and I sat at the table with Mom's seat vacant. My dad would torture himself, often out loud, with some version of *This is what life will be like if your mother dies.* My father didn't have tools, words, or friends to help him face his fears, so they came out at the dinner table. I learned to eat quickly and quietly to minimize the duration of this experience. I sympathized with him and what I'd determined were his unfounded fears. I learned to manage my emotions and argue my feelings into submission. During these Friday dinners, my dad and I were living a role inversion regarding who the supporter was and who was being supported.

I still eat too fast.

Even facing another round of cancer, my mother obliterated it. There was no evidence that her cancer had spread, and the chemo and radiation destroyed any undetected cancer cells. It was prophylactic but not optional. The steroids were to bolster her immune system against the chemo because that poison kills everything, not just cancer. Cancer cells are more susceptible, but chemo isn't a precision-targeted drug that only impacts cancer cells. Today's chemo regimens are more closely targeted to the pathology of cancer, get better results, and have lighter side effects. Still, chemo is about systemic treatment, and the drugs affect multiple body systems.

Looking back forty years later, we were fortunate. Now, I know many stories of women whose cancer returned undetected and spread. Their outcomes were not good. The fact that my mother diligently scheduled and attended her follow-up appointments and that the doctor palpated the mass and removed it before it spread was a tribute to my mother's determination and the doctor's attention to detail. Her diligence inspired me. I understood the benefits of detecting breast cancer early. I am infuriated when I talk to women with breast cancer whose doctors refused to screen them aggressively, despite their family history. In fact, when I was pregnant with my second child, my new OB refused to do a breast exam at every prenatal visit. I switched to a different OB whose appreciation of my breast cancer risk matched my own.

Although I was cancer-free, I knew I had no control over any future curveballs that breast cancer or any other cancer might throw at me. I decided it would be better to concentrate my energy on building my strengths and resources to make hitting future curveballs easier.

Simulating the feelings of the worst possible outcome only clouded my vision. When those feelings arose, I let them flow over me and out. Holding on to them handicaps my ability to generate viable solutions. I learned that happens because the limbic system's parasympathetic response becomes overactive or sustained. Neuroscience shows that adrenaline and cortisol surge in response to actual and imagined threats. Those hormones are terrific when you need to outrun a bear or lift a car off a loved one. But those survival reactions do not benefit prolonged skill building, critical thinking, or planning.

One night, early in my mom's chemo treatment, Dad and I were watching a TV show when his emotions overcame him, and he started to cry in the seat next to me. I cannot imagine feeling so alone and scared that you become emotionally vulnerable in front of your teenage daughter. I tried to offer comfort. I wasn't ashamed that he was emotional, and I didn't want him to feel embarrassed. Some part of me was honored that he was comfortable enough to let down his guard with me. Of course, I had also been worried about my mother, but I hadn't appreciated the depths of his fears and sadness. I held him as he cried. My mom was the love of his life. She was his person. He felt betrayed by cancer—several times. Cancer was supposed to be in the rearview mirror. Cancer was a curveball they believed they had swung at and hit out of the park.

Today, my mother is seventy-seven years old. She is vibrant, athletic, and as engaged as ever. She's amazing. I hold on to this when the fear of reoccurrence rears its ugly head. If I ever experience cancer's curveballs again, I have the tools and the wherewithal to crush it a second time.

LESSONS LEARNED

- [ ] Recurrence rates are based on large population statistics. They are not predictive of your risk.

- [ ] Consider the recurrence profile of your pathology when making treatment choices. My family's breast cancer diagnoses were all when we were young, and we weren't hoping for only five years. We wanted fifty or more years, so we elected aggressive treatments.

- [ ] Ask questions about post-treatment monitoring and diligently participate in it.

- [ ] A recurrence doesn't have to be a death sentence. There are new treatments, and cancer can be obliterated more than once. Ask my mom.

- [ ] A five-year survival rate means the percentage of patients who remain cancer-free for at least five years after successful cancer treatment. For many cancers, the probability of recurrence drops after five years. You should not expect to die five years after successful cancer treatment; plan to live.

Susan's Journey

In the bustling heart of the UK, Susan lived a life steeped in the vigorous demands of police work. Susan's journey began with a casual, unintentional brush of her arm against her chest. *It's probably just another cyst*, she'd thought, dismissing the gravity.

But in November 2014, at forty-nine, the cold, unexpected reality of a cancer diagnosis disrupted her life. Not one, but two breast tumors declared their unwelcome presence in her life—lobular and invasive.

Susan was no stranger to medical scares, with a history of biopsies and calcifications already under her belt. But this felt different—there was a certain weight to the steps she now found herself tracing down the familiar pathway of tests and scans. Susan's first reaction leaned toward dismissal—"A little bit of cancer," she mused, with a gallows humor that even she found ridiculous. In the thick of preparing for Christmas and simultaneously researching mastectomy options—*because, frankly, who has the time?*—Susan found herself halted by a diagnosis that threatened to redefine her. Yet, even with the harsh truths delivered by her doctors, her humor never waned. "I've got private healthcare," she quipped, which seemed to flip the script of her consultation. Her private insurance expedited her treatment; her team was more concerned about her after she told them she had it.

Chemotherapy was the uninvited guest that overstayed its welcome, casting shadows over her days. She had three cycles of Adriamycin and cyclophosphamide (AC) and three cycles of Taxol, each three weeks apart. The cold-capping method was a temporary shield, helping Susan hold on to strands of normalcy by preserving much of her hair until she decided enough was enough. Shaving her head became an act of liberation, her hair daring to sprout anew before chemo's end.

In the quiet sanctuary of her shower, Susan allowed herself to mourn, her tears mingling with water as a daily ritual of release. Yet each chemo cycle carved out a newfound understanding—a playbook for survival outlining when to rest, when to rally, and when to simply be. She didn't expect cancer to change her life; she interviewed for a new job on the morning of her mastectomy because she focused on living.

Recovering from her mastectomy over Christmas, Susan wanted to explore going on holiday. "The weather was bad, so I just started researching things online," she said. "That's the worst thing you can do."

"Did I ponder the mortality bit? Nope, not once," Susan said, dismissing the thought as quickly as it came.

Two years passed before she could seek reconstruction—a journey of self-reclamation as surgeons reshaped the landscape of her body, drawing upon her resilience to mold her once again. The rebuilding—a saga of its own—was a testament to her determination to feel whole again. From the muscle being wrapped around her back to the final placement of the implants, Susan embraced her transformed spirit as much as her transformed body.

She emerged from her trials, not just surviving but thriving, with an unshakable resolve and a body she's not afraid to bear. "Scars? Yeah, I've got them. They're my badges of survival." Susan is proud of the tattoos she co-designed for her new breasts as an expression of her new body and her identity.

Jovially, she speaks of her decision to work as a desk police officer for five years and then leave the police ranks. She embarked on far-flung adventures, from India to Cambodia, recapturing life with an avid thirst as she nestled into the joy of playing with grandchildren, embracing the rush of gym workouts, and shedding pounds.

The echo of recurrence occasionally whispers its haunting doubt, but Susan dashes it away with a determined flick. With the passage of each day, concern ebbs away, surrendering to a mantra that reverberates through her very being: *Cancer is not a death sentence.*

As she might tell you, outrageously candid as ever, the barrage of "be positive" felt more like a well-meaning missive fired from the uninformed. Ignorance may be bliss, but realism packs a punch in this gritty narrative of survival. Today, nearly a decade since the odyssey began, Susan paints the picture of her life with broad, confident strokes—filled with color and bursting with vitality. She's a living testament to the resilience etched in the human spirit through trials and pain, laughter and triumph.

Susan carves out a life post-cancer that embodies living—surviving and thriving. She values honesty, wearing her experiences unapologetically, honoring the body that carried her through the storm. "Pain?" she scoffs. "After all that? Just bring it on!"

LESSONS LEARNED

- ☐ Reconstruction is not always possible immediately after surgery. Prepare yourself to be patient to achieve the best outcome.

- ☐ Breast tattoos can be a beautiful way to embrace your post-cancer body.

- ☐ The specter of recurrence remains in the back of most cancer patients' minds, but you can use it as a catalyst for both diligent monitoring and seizing life's great adventures.

- ☐ Obliterating cancer often makes people feel more powerful than they were before. Embrace this new confidence. You can face any curveball.

24. The Win

I will never forget the day I danced in a medical procedure room. The last drain was pulled, and I was officially free to move about without consideration of yanking, kinking, or otherwise interfering with the vital work this last drain had to do. My body was rejecting the thing—it turns out that my great healing powers were annoyed to be thwarted in scar recovery by a plastic tube. I could still remember the pain when my body pulled the suture into itself (Chapter 22: The Ninth Inning). That explained the excruciating pain every time the tube moved, and with extensive lidocaine and a light touch, the nurse practitioner had re-situated the suture. When this last drain was removed, I got Stephanie, the nurse practitioner, to dance with me.

Share the joy—right?

Untethered from drains, it was time to embrace life and travel. My consulting practice had been gaining momentum, and exciting new opportunities were forming creatively and compellingly. We were very lucky that our work and finances afforded us the option to indulge in a celebration of being cancer-free. My family was looking forward to celebrating life by taking what we called our Cancer-Free World Tour.

Our tour started separately. Neal left first to join one of his best friends from high school to go to her fifty-fifth birthday party in New Jersey. Ariel and I joined him later, during which journey we got caught in a travel disaster. Our Newark-bound flight was diverted to Dulles Airport in DC. After nine and a half hours of trying to get off the ground, friends from DC suggested we take the train instead. Off Ariel and I went for a 2:30 a.m. Lyft tour of Washington, DC, en route to the train station. It was her first time seeing our capital, since COVID deprived her of our public middle school's eighth-grade DC trip that both her brothers had experienced. She was mesmerized. And Amtrak between DC and Penn Station was a breeze.

The Manhattan leg of the trip included the Tenement Museum, the musical *Shucked*, delicious dinners, visiting with Neal's mother and her partner, sending Ariel off on her teen tour summer travel adventure, Alex Edelman's play *Just for Us* with friends, more eating, and picking up the muscle car (Dodge Challenger) that transported us to upstate New York. Spending time with Ariel and watching her connect with her camp friends in New York City before their departure on their summer adventure, with eyes pointed forward and eagerly embracing the future, made my heart brim with happiness. I was grateful to everyone who helped me survive cancer.

Neal and I drove to Utica, New York, and stayed in Sylvan Beach, New York. Mostly, we watched baseball. Watching our son play was a joy. We were there for the start of his team's winning streak—winning is more fun than losing. We learned about the best restaurants in and around Utica from the fans who came to game after game. We were there when Taylor was named Player of the Game. We watched with pride as kids asked him to sign their baseballs, Blue Sox programs, and mini-bats, and we got to know his teammates. It was so much fun.

After we left Utica, we headed to France. We didn't spend time in Paris; instead, we went straight to Burgundy. We biked through vineyards and stopped in different towns to wine and dine. We discovered that a Michelin one-star restaurant was three doors down from our *hostellerie* and made reservations as a treat. In Beaune, we watched the Collegiate Church Notre-Dame and the Hospices de Beaune light up with images in a beautiful and magical presentation. My e-bike was a breeze, and Neal, who had determined his spirit animal was the ox, powered through all the ups and downs. *A metaphor for the year, no?*

From Beaune, we drove to Nice, where we embarked on a day's sailing trip during a heat wave. We enjoyed a delightful French lunch on the water, then escaped to an air-conditioned Airbnb property for the evening, where we cooked the food we would have had for dinner on the sailboat. *One must be flexible.*

From there, Christian and Angela, friends from business school, welcomed us to Corsica and their stunning home.

We had views of the Mediterranean and surrounding islands. Captain Christian skillfully navigated us on his speedboat to Porto di Cavallo, where we enjoyed ... you got it ... a fabulous meal, and then a hidden beach and cove. Food is even more delicious when you have no concerns about mouth sores, nausea, or dry mouth. Corsican sounds a lot like Italian. (Corsica was part of Genoa before becoming part of France and was Napoleon's mother country.) Meeting their children and friends and exploring a new place was a treat.

From Corsica, we flew via Paris to Austin, Texas, to spend time with our son Ben and visit my cousin's family as well as friends Matt and Hillary, who'd moved there from the Bay Area. Once again, the highlight was eating—every night was a treat with Ben. My cousins Jennifer and Trent were gracious hosts in their beautiful Lake Austin riverfront home. We got to see Gleeson, another business school classmate, for dinner, and Matt and Hillary. We spent our time socializing at night and staying cool during the day. After a scorching day with Ben, I flew to Los Angeles to meet up with Ariel for our Disneyland and Taylor Swift finale, accompanied by more family visits.

It was, by all accounts, a great way to celebrate my cancer obliteration. I was a new person, changed in unfounded ways, and eager to embrace life. My appreciation for life and those in my world had only expanded. The second half of 2023 was my season of saying yes to everything.

After crushing the cancer curveball, I realized I had unwittingly pledged to a sorority that no one willingly rushes—yet its members hold their heads high with pride. My sister and mother donned their pins long before I understood the depth of what membership meant. This sorority's roster read far too long; its ranks swelled by the common thread of cancer touching lives indiscriminately. Yet, within this community, there was a boundless wealth of wisdom and hope—qualities I clung to as I navigated my cancer journey. I drew insight, comfort, and courage from conversations with family members who had weathered this storm before me. But beyond bloodlines, I connected with "sorority sisters" whose experiences had been beacons on my path. Among them were women I'd never encountered until cancer narrowed our worlds—plus a dear expat friend from when Neal and I lived in Brazil from 1997 to 1999. Despite time and space pushing us apart, cancer's visceral thread stitched us back together—a solidarity among survivors that knows no bounds.

These sisters stood as living miracles, victors who stared down a terrifying breast cancer prognosis. They participated in clinical trials and underwent chemo and radiation treatment in addition to surgeries. They not only battled cancer but also willingly shared their stories with me, a then-stranger. Between them was a wealth of divergent experiences. They freely offered insights and a kinship in the struggle for survival. Their counsel formulated a mantra, preaching patience and support, all while keeping laughter close as we danced around cancer's unpredictable pitches.

Our conversations, many of which are summarized in this book, are sprinkled with my marvel at their resilience, grace, and renewed health. They brought me solace and gratitude. Action had always been my balm, yet these strong women reminded me that feeling, too, is part of the healing process. We raised a toast to birthdays, new beginnings, exercise PRs (personal records), and the luxury of free-flowing laughter, all garnished with a hint of normalcy. As cancer threatened to script its narrative with my hair, I took comfort in the promise of regrowth, buoyed by these incredible women's arsenal of care tips.

    I am beyond thankful to every sorority member who has extended a hand, a thought, a sliver of hope. To those who volunteered their time and energy to walk this stretch of the path with me, your compassion leaves me speechless. My gratitude is immeasurable for those whose daily humor stitched joy unabashedly into the fabric of my life. I am profoundly grateful to this entire community, whose love billows as a steadfast sail through choppy seas.

    I crushed cancer's curveball with the power of the masses.

LESSONS LEARNED

- [ ] Whatever you feel when you reach the end of treatment is exactly right. I felt joy, so I danced. Others may feel anger, exhaustion, or relief. Embrace what you feel and go with it.

- [ ] After treatment, try saying yes to everything for a while. When you are open, the universe can deliver amazing gifts.

- [ ] Share your story. Even if you are the only reader, your story matters. If you share with other people, you will make their journey easier. Please pay it forward.

- [ ] The survivor sorority is full of incredible people who offer unique camaraderie. I imagine it's like the camaraderie of war veterans. We've seen some stuff.

BATTER UP

Like virtually every cancer survivor I'd known, when I received the news that I was cancer-free, I felt massive relief. But what followed was a void. The center of my universe was no longer UCSF, cancer treatment, and surgeries. The gigantic, gravitational pull of cancer was lifted, leaving me in a space of not-knowing and not-being-busy as my body used its energy to heal and my mind processed *WTF just happened?* Despite feeling truly fortunate, deeply grateful, and very healthy, it was certainly not how I thought I would spend my time on this planet. My sister felt the same way when she, thankfully, was declared cancer-free—twice. In her words:

> *People expect to feel relieved at the end of their cancer journey or treatment. And so I think I was surprised when I didn't. The doctors tell you that you are healthy. Don't smoke. Exercise regularly. Good luck to you. Which, after being in the thick of the fight, feels like a little bit of a letdown.*

The void left by cancer felt peculiar. I recognized cancer itself lacked inherent meaning—it was merely an occurrence in my life (and my friends' and family's lives) and not an unforeseen one at that. While there were numerous aspects of the healthcare delivery system I would have liked to enhance, I was overwhelmed with gratitude for the remarkable advancements in treatment, side effect management, and surgical procedures. My journey starkly contrasted with those of my mother and sister.

Post-treatment, a handful of medical activities lingered for a few months. Weekly follow-ups from the surgery indicated promising healing trajectories; tinkering with the immunotherapy regimen ensured maximum benefits while granting Neal and me the liberty to travel; other medical appointments addressed issues discovered or suggested post-surgery. These activities consumed hours each week, a stark contrast to the total days spent in the past grappling with the anxiety of uncertainty.

The worst was now a memory.

Satisfaction often comes from joy after a struggle, and Viktor Frankl's book *Man's Search for Meaning* is the penultimate example of finding joy in the most difficult of situations. When I read Frankl after my treatment, his philosophy that both struggle and love are viable creators of meaning resonated deeply with me. Enduring the struggle of chemotherapy and treatment gave me a new focus and purpose. Amidst the happiness of being cancer-free, I felt unmoored when all the therapy ended. The continued opportunity to love and be loved by people is the hot air balloon that lifts my spirits and focuses my energy.

Arthur C. Brooks—a Harvard professor, bestselling author and international thought leader on the science of happiness—emphasizes that satisfaction is a formula that divides what you have by what you want. Every philosophy and faith has a version of this lesson: *He who is rich is happy with what he has.*

Cancer is a struggle. For those of us who required chemotherapy, immunotherapy, surgery, and radiation, it wasn't fast or easy. I didn't know if the treatment was working until my oncologist examined me and felt the tumor had shrunk. Shrunk wasn't *gone*, so I looked forward to seeing Dr. Chien every three weeks, chatting about what I was experiencing, and learning what she could feel from examining me. Cancer also impacts time because, during treatment, someone else dictated my calendar. So I focused on the days I could control and what I wanted to do with my time outside of UCSF. I didn't know the cancer was gone entirely until the pathology from my surgery was complete.

My mini-milestones of going to Florida to watch my son play spring baseball, attending my daughter's lacrosse games after surgery, and being healthy enough to ride a bicycle through Burgundy over the summer were all pursuits of joy after a struggle. I filled my life with new memory making. I'd fronted a rock cover band for a decade and continued rehearsing during treatment. Then, after treatment, I resumed playing gigs. I went to Disneyland with my daughter. I celebrated my birthday with a fabulous group of women, enjoying a great weekend on a lake. I wakeboarded two days after Dr. Piper cleared me for all activities. My Michigan Wolverines won the Big Ten and went on to win a National Championship while I wore my custom Fuck Cancer #63 maize-and-blue jersey. I marched in Washington for the first time in my life. Both my sons and my best friend from college marched with me. I have no intention of slowing the pace anytime in the future. These experiences brought me enjoyment and satisfaction because I shared them with people I love. After all, I was staying strong and healthy enough to do them. My love for those around me was an endless reservoir of faith and power.

And I'd learned from the best. One of the life lessons of my mother's cancer was that most *stuff* is *small stuff*.

Cancer is big stuff. Cancer can alter the trajectory of your life. I realized at fifteen that in comparison to cancer, a bad grade didn't feel that important because there would be another test. It's the same with competition. Or a date. Cancer offers a gift of perspective and gratitude. I'd still rather no one I love ever be diagnosed with cancer, but that's not an available choice.

Wisdom guided me to pause within this vacuum, to dwell in the space where there was neither urgency to propel forward nor the battles of past orbits. At the same time, my body recovered while my mind reset. Remarkably, within this calm, away from the frenzy of the central star now set on a different course, new possibilities began to form. The aftermath is a landscape rife with new beginnings and clarity. I tread softly into this open expanse, realizing I needed to drift a while before charging on to the new course ahead.

I crossed into survivorship, a term whose genesis I couldn't pinpoint. With my pledge year to the survivor sorority complete, I was now an official member of this resilient fraternity. When the phone rings, text pings, or email dings, I offer reassurance, a calm ear, and friendship to anyone left reeling from the shock of a recent diagnosis, adrift in the turbulent seas between diagnosis and treatment. I aim to instill confidence that they can confront cancer and that the experience will surpass their expectations. Surprisingly, the journey with cancer is interspersed with moments of joy, often sprouting in response to the struggles and discomforts that cancer brings. The familiar faces around you and the new ones you encounter can fortify you with love, prayers, and humor—if only you let them in. Cancer is a potent reminder to cherish every day, every person, and every word. The cancer filter helps every person touched by cancer see these reminders. As I peer into the future, I'm intrigued by the opportunities that might unfold and what I might conceive in my subsequent chapter. So far, it's been a journey of profound gratification.

    I wish you such a journey.

Conclusion

Cancer has all the ingredients for victimhood or happiness, sometimes simultaneously and often alternating between the two. Every cancer patient likely spends some time feeling like a victim because cancer sucks and derails your life. Adequate health insurance and access to care are blessings that should be available to everyone, yet I am aware they are not, and I was lucky to have them. Still, it's easy to feel like a victim of cancer. Initially, I tried to reverse engineer what I could have done differently in my life so that I didn't become a cancer patient. I lamented delaying my prophylactic surgery. I questioned whether I should have done a single surgery rather than a breast reduction first to reduce my risk of skin necrosis. Lacking time travel technology, I had to let go of what-ifs and focus on what I needed to do to survive.

Many cancer patients lose sight of their power in the turbulence of tests, biopsies, doctors' appointments, scheduling, insurance, and fear. These are life's big, scary moments, and emotions are high. At times, choosing to focus on things that made me happy while facing cancer felt like condoning cancer—like saying it was okay that I have cancer. It wasn't okay, but that didn't matter. News alert: *Cancer doesn't care if you approve or not*. Cancer is nothing but mutant cells causing trouble. It's not conscious. I didn't do or not do anything to welcome it. Cancer just happened.

Your cancer is no different.

After experiencing all the emotions and shock you naturally feel when a doctor tells you, "I'm sorry. It's malignant," step up to the plate. There are medical teams to organize and treatment choices to make. You can do this. You are stronger than you think. I learned a lot through my personal and family cancer experiences, and I'm honored to share my insights regarding the five stages of my breast cancer journey with you.

PREVENTION

Cancers are malfunctions in the body, and early detection is vital to increasing the chances of successful treatment and a long life. Five things to remember about prevention are:

1. Early detection is crucial in the fight against cancer. Regular screenings and self-examinations can help catch cancer at an early stage.

2. While conventionally, yearly mammograms are recommended for individuals over forty, screening should be personalized to your risk profile. Consider joining the wisdomstudy (https://www.thewisdomstudy.org/—and it's free) to understand your risk and the best screening for you.

3. Knowledge is a powerful tool. Using information from medical screening and testing leads to rational and educated decisions. Stay informed about screening options and preventative surgeries and discuss them with your medical specialists.

4. Access to quality medical care may vary but be proactive and persistent in advocating for your health.

5. While most cancers are not preventable, healthy lifestyle choices can improve your odds of avoiding cancer and fighting it when you can't. Protect yourself from the sun, sleep well, don't smoke, exercise, get vaccinated for HPV and hepatitis B virus (HBV), and eat healthy.

DIAGNOSIS

When you hear those dreaded words, "You've got breast cancer," know they don't mean an end but a beginning. Tap into your confidence, gather support, and approach your diagnosis with courage and hope. And don't forget these five tips:

1. Gather your medical team and ask questions. They exist to help you.

2. A cancer diagnosis can be scary, and it is not unusual to fear death or consider your mortality. Be kind to yourself while you work through emotions.

3. Communicate your diagnosis with friends and family and organize help where needed.

4. Be proactive in advocating for your personal and medical needs.

5. Find therapists, cancer survivors, and fellow cancer patients who can provide you with moral support and practical advice.

TREATMENT

There are various treatment options available for cancer patients, such as surgery, chemotherapy, radiation therapy, targeted therapy, and immunotherapy, as well as management strategies for the potential side effects of these treatments. Make informed decisions about your treatment, anticipate the financial burden, and seek support from healthcare professionals, like-minded groups, and family and friends. When contemplating treatment, don't forget the following:

1. Educate yourself so you understand your treatment options. Gathering information, asking questions, and seeking additional opinions actively involves you in your cancer outcome. Remember, there are many variations in cancer pathology, and compared to survivors, your medical team is more current on the best treatment protocols.

2. Be on time and prepared for treatment sessions. Create happiness tripwire rituals that bring you joy and comfort.

3. Use the tools, strategies, and medications available to minimize and manage your specific cancer treatment side effects. Stay ahead of the nausea, pain, hair loss, neuropathy, etc. If you can, proactively minimize side effects instead of suffering. Use the tools, strategies, and medications available to minimize and manage your specific cancer treatment side effects.

4. Cancer treatment can be disruptive to your life. Plan for financial changes, review your health coverage, and communicate with your employer.

5. Gather the troops. Family and friends can be recruited to help you and your family during cancer treatment.

SURGERY

For many cancer patients, treatment is followed by surgery. When surgery is part of your cancer journey, consider these five points:

1. When selecting your surgical team, look for breast and plastic surgeons who specialize in your cancer type and reconstruction approach. You might need to travel to find doctors best suited for your situation.

2. Prepare your home environment for postsurgical needs, such as avoiding stairs, managing surgical drains, accessing medications and food, and staying comfortable with essential supplies like pillows, loose clothing, and nutritious food.

3. Have a plan for postsurgical pain management. Consider using a medication tracking app if you manage multiple meds on a strict schedule. Stay ahead of the pain.

4. While reconstruction can restore breasts cosmetically, it's normal and valid to mourn the loss of sensation and the complex feelings of parting with your original breasts. Honor those emotions.

5. Friends and family will want to help and offer support. Let them.

RECOVERY

Since 99 percent of localized breast cancer patients become cancer survivors, chances are you'll have to get to know your post-cancer body, celebrate being cancer-free, and contemplate the possibility of recurrence. Here are five details to remember when navigating the complex emotions of this transitional time:

1. Unexpected surgical complications, such as infections, may happen. Give your body time to recover. Don't rush to remove drains or bandages. Don't hesitate to alert your medical team if something looks or feels off during recovery. They know what to look for and how to intervene promptly.

2. Don't assume no news is bad news if you're waiting for results or reports. If you expect an update and don't receive it, proactively reach out and ask your care team. Bad news tends to travel fast.

3. Incidental findings on scans are common as you get to know your post-cancer body. A pathological complete response (pCR) means you don't have metastatic disease, even if scans pick up other non-threatening abnormalities.

4. Ask questions about your unique post-surgery monitoring plan and follow it diligently. Again, feel free to alert your team if anything looks or feels off; they're experts in prompt intervention.

5. A cancer recurrence, while scary, is not necessarily a death sentence. Today, there are often multiple options to obliterate cancer if it returns. Breast cancer survival rates continue to improve.

You can also choose happiness. According to Oprah Winfrey and Professor Arthur C. Brooks, happiness is not a destination; it's an ongoing, lifelong quest. It isn't a feeling; instead, feelings are evidence of happiness. And the best news—it's contagious. This state of mind started with my family and good friends, followed by my professional impact. I didn't procrastinate because I knew a cancer curveball could knock my plans out of the park. I also found my purpose, which was to recast the cancer narrative and give every person experiencing a breast cancer diagnosis the confidence not only to handle what's to come but to live life to the fullest. Reflecting on my year as a cancer patient, I can honestly say it was one of the happiest years of my life.

Yours can be, too.

I hope my approach becomes a first-day memo for cancer patients. I hope my story illuminates a path so you or your loved one's cancer journey includes joy, satisfaction, and meaning wherever possible. Your journey might be different than mine, and it might be similar or vastly unique compared to the experiences of those shared within these pages. That's okay. No two paths are alike, yet there is an abundance to be learned from the trials of others. Cancer survivors discover an appreciation for life.

My wish is that my story, coupled with the narratives generously shared by others, guides you in devising your approach, helps you lean on your strengths, brings a smile to your face, and ensures you crush cancer's curveball. It is more than just a wish—recognizing that life is full of curveballs and many opportunities to thrive is a testament to resilience, a beacon of hope, and a compelling call to action that will serve you well.

Cancer knocked you down, but you are not out. And you are not in this alone. Let's build a new cancer narrative with stories of hope, humor, setbacks, perseverance, and joy. Visit www.joellekaufman.com to share your story or find more tools to help you crush the cancer curveball.

Acknowledgments

Crushing the Cancer Curveball would not have been possible without the support, love, and expertise of many individuals and organizations. I am deeply grateful to everyone who contributed to my story.

My gratitude begins with Dr. Eugene Nowak and Dr. Eugene Resnick of Cornell Medical Center, whose successful treatment of my mother's cancer so long ago marked the beginning of this journey. Their expertise and care set the foundation for my battle years later and ensured that my mother would be with me when I faced cancer's curveball.

Throughout my treatment, I was blessed with an incredible medical team. The UCSF Breast Cancer Center and the UCSF Genetic Cancer Clinic provided world-class care and expertise. Drs. Amy Jo Chien, Laura Esserman, and Merisa Piper offered exceptional guidance and treatment. Drs. Susan Lee Shar and Rudolph Buntic of CPMC and the Bunkhe Clinic were wonderful caregivers in the early part of my journey toward the prophylactic mastectomy that never happened.

I want to express my profound gratitude to Dr. Harriet Borofsky for her twenty years of dedicated care for my breast health, her expert imaging, calming support, and crucial referrals. Your longstanding care and expertise were invaluable.

I'm also profoundly thankful to Karen Kemby, Brooke Byers, and Harry Hagey for their assistance at UCSF. I truly appreciated your support in navigating the complexities of care.

I'm also thankful for all the medical assistants, physician assistants, nurses, and nurse practitioners who were part of my care team, including Dr. Sadie Phillips, my psycho-oncologist, whose mental health care was on target. I appreciate Dr. Peter Kuhn and his research lab at USC for their invaluable feedback and support. I believe your work will radically redefine how we discover breast cancer and help countless women.

A special thank-you to Meryl, my Anthem cancer care navigator, for her cheerful check-ins and resources. I want to thank Sharsheret for its resources for women facing breast and ovarian cancer, including the excellent resources for those of us with genetic cancers. Your work makes a significant difference in the lives of so many. Additionally, Aimee Sax of Sharsheret always had good ideas for improving my approach. You all contributed to the shape of this book.

I want to express my gratitude to Dignitana, the makers of the DigniCap. This innovative technology allowed me to keep my hair during treatment, which was incredibly important. You helped me maintain a sense of normalcy and dignity throughout my journey.

My friends and community rallied around me in ways I could never have imagined. My sister-by-choice and dear friend, Jessica Rosenbaum, coordinated support, food, and rides like a true logistics champion. I'm deeply grateful for the meals prepared with love, the rides to appointments, and the particular group of friends who sat with me during chemo treatments and brought me lunch in the hospital. Your presence and care made those challenging times more bearable. Shira Goodman and Julie Gupta traveled across the country to be with me, offering comfort and companionship when I needed it most. The Hamilton Baseball community welcomed us warmly in Orlando during treatment and on our visits, providing a sense of normalcy and joy. My entire Harvard Business School (HBS) Class of '96, Section B, showed me love and support through our WhatsApp group, reminding me of the strength of long-lasting friendships. I'm also profoundly grateful to all the friends and colleagues who sent notes, flowers, cards, and jokes, and to those who called to see how I was doing. Your thoughtfulness and care lifted my spirits. Thank you to all who read my posts on CaringBridge and Substack. Your engagement and support meant the world to me.

I want to thank a few friends whose unique support touched me deeply. Julian, your text messages before every chemo session were a constant source of encouragement and reminders that I wasn't alone. Gleeson, your funny chemo-fighting cards never failed to make me smile, even on the most challenging days. Justin, your collection of mistaken emails and funny replies brought a daily smile to my face. Jonathan, your generosity in ensuring I traveled safely during treatment was extraordinary and deeply appreciated. Your kindness made a significant difference.

I want to extend a special thank-you to my new friend, Jacqueline Steele, who was going through her cancer journey at the same time as me. Jacqueline, you became an excellent peer and a dear friend during this time. You are a gift to my life.

I'm grateful for Rabbi Rebecca Schatz's support, which included prayers and music that added spirituality to my journey. I also want to thank Rabbi Didy Waks for supporting my son Taylor and including me in his prayers. Thanks to Rabbi Yossi Greenberg for supporting my son Ben and keeping me in his prayers. Your spiritual guidance and support for our family were deeply appreciated.

I want to thank the incredible staff and counselors at the Menlo School for their unwavering support of my daughter, Ariel, during this challenging time. Your care and understanding made a world of difference. A special thank-you to the Menlo School boys' and girls' lacrosse teams for their Play for Pink initiative. Your generous support touched our hearts.

I'm particularly grateful to Dr. Jeremy Wilkinson for his continued support of my daughter's mental health throughout this process. Your expertise and care were invaluable.

I want to thank the women who bravely shared their stories with me. Your experiences and insights have enriched this book immeasurably. Thank you to my sister, Tracey Downing, and to Alysia Andrikopoulos, Heather

Albrecht, Andrea Jones, Irit Ingel, Josie, Jessica Gravel, Lesley Kaminski, Michelle Audion, Susan Sooner, and Cindee Yandow. Your courage and openness will help countless others. Thanks to the Peloton Breast Cancer Survivors group for the support they all show each other.

I am writing to express my sincere gratitude to Charlene Li for insisting I make this book bigger than I dreamed. Your encouragement pushed me to create something that could change many people's lives.

I'm deeply grateful to the Greenleaf Book Group team for their expertise and dedication. A special thank-you to my wonderful and patient developmental editor, Denise Willson, who reinvented the book to be more valuable to every reader. Your insights and guidance were invaluable. Thank you to Dee Kerr for your unabashed enthusiasm for the book.

To my family, your love has been my fountain of strength. Benjamin, Taylor, and Ariel, you brought joy and laughter during this challenging time. To my parents, my sister, Tracey, and her family (Thom, Jake, and Emma), my mother-in-law, Connee Kaufman, Connee's partner, Michael Mashberg, and the extended Weintraub family, your support meant the world to me. You brought me endless smiles and filled my heart with love.

I am incredibly grateful to my sisters-in-law, Heather Stein and Michele Traeger Kaufman, who traveled from their homes to California to support me and my family during this challenging time. Dr. Heather Stein's medical expertise was invaluable; she served as another voice, asking crucial questions of the medical team and reassuring us of the quality of treatment I was receiving.

Your presence and support were a source of great comfort and strength.

Last, I want to express my love and appreciation to my husband, Neal. He genuinely felt thankful that my tumor was detected early, and his optimism was uplifting. He kept our lives normal, ensuring I felt treasured, beautiful, and loved. Neal managed his anxiety to be a pillar of strength for me. He attended all key appointments and became my voice when I was tired of sharing the same updates. His unwavering support and love were instrumental in helping me face each day with courage and confidence.

To everyone who played a part in my story, your support has been appreciated, whether named here or not. You've all contributed to helping me crush this cancer curveball, and I am eternally grateful.

Joelle Kaufman, California, USA, 2024

Endnotes

1 https://pubmed.ncbi.nlm.nih.gov/19440188/

2 https://www.cancer.org/cancer/types/breast-cancer/understanding-a-breast-cancer-diagnosis/breast-cancer-survival-rates.html

3 https://www.hopkinsmedicine.org/health/conditions-and-diseases/breast-cancer/inherited-cancer-risk-brca-mutation

4 https://www.healthline.com/health/breast-cancer/survival-facts-statistics

5 Josie's name has been changed, per her request, to respect her privacy.

6 https://www.cancer.gov/about-cancer/diagnosis-staging/staging/sentinel-node-biopsy-fact-sheet

Index

AC (Adriamycin and cyclophosphamide): *140, 199, 223, 227-233, 286, 305*

Advocacy: *47, 97-105, 161-169, 265-275, 326-328*

Anxiety: *89-95, 143-150, 171-181, 299-303*

Aromatherapy: *161-169*

BRCA1 gene: *17-25, 31-36, 197-208, 223-233, 299-303*

Breast reconstruction: *243-250, 255-262, 265-275, 277-281, 329-330*

Cancer diagnosis:

    Coping with: *57-62, 63-67, 69-75*

    Emotional impact: *83-87, 89-95*

    Initial response: *27-29, 63-67*

    Sharing news: *77-82*

    Support systems: *171-181*

    CaringBridge: *79-82, 333, 335*

Chemotherapy:

    First treatment: *151-159*

    Managing side effects: *161-169, 183-194*

    Preparation: *143-150*

    Protocol: *197-208*

    Recovery: *291-295*

Cold capping: *161-169, 187-194, 305-308*

Communication:

    With doctors: *97-105, 255-262*

    With family: *69-75, 171-181*

    With friends: *77-82*

Diagnosis stages:
- **Initial tests:** *17-25*
- **Prevention:** *31-36*
- **Screening:** *27-29*

DIEP flap surgery: *243-250, 255-262, 291-295*
DigniCap: *151-159, 161-169, 187-194*
Emotional support:
- **Family:** *69-75, 171-181*
- **Mental health professionals:** *89-95*
- **Support groups:** *83-87, 197-208*

Exercise: *161-169, 291-295*
Family support: *69-75, 77-82, 171-181, 223-233, 331-338*
Financial impact: *133-141, 171-181, 239-242*
Genetic testing: *17-25, 305-308*
Hair loss: *183-194, 305-308*
Healthcare navigation:
- **Insurance:** *133-141*
- **Medical team:** *97-105*
- **Treatment decisions:** *143-150*

Immune system: *151-159, 297-303*
Infusion treatment: *151-159, 161-169, 197-208*
Life after cancer: *311-316, 323-332*
Lymph nodes: *97-105, 255-262, 291-295*
Mastectomy: *243-250, 255-262, 265-275, 277-281*
Mental health:
- **Anxiety management:** *89-95*
- **Coping strategies:** *143-150*
- **Support resources:** *161-169*

Nausea management: *161-169, 183-194*
Oncologist: *97-105, 133-141, 151-159, 161-169*

Pain management: *255-262, 291-295*
Patient stories:
    Alysia: *107-114*
    Andrea: *265-275*
    Cindee: *277-283*
    Heather A.: *123-128*
    Jacqueline: *217-222*
    Jessica G.: *47-52*
    Josie: *115-121*
    Lesley: *283-288*
    Susan: *305-310*
    Tracey: *223-235*
PET scan: *97-105, 133-141, 151-159*
Port (medical): *97-105, 151-159, 161-169*
Prevention: *17-25, 27-29, 31-36, 326-327*
Radiation therapy: *297-303, 305-308*
Recovery:
    Emotional: *323-332*
    Physical: *291-295*
    Transition: *311-316*
Recurrence: *297-303, 305-308*
Side effects management: *151-159, 161-169, 183-194, 197-208*
Support systems:
    Family and friends: *171-181*
    Medical team: *97-105*
    Support groups: *83-87, 197-208*
Surgery:
    Preparation: *243-250*
    Procedure: *255-262*
    Recovery: *291-295*
    Types: *265-275, 277-281*

Survivorship: *311-316, 323-332*

Treatment:

    Decision-making: *133-141*

    Planning: *143-150*

    Protocols: *151-159*

    Side effects: *161-169*

Triple-negative breast cancer: *197-208, 297-303, 311-316*

About the Author

Joelle's 2023 triple-negative, Stage IIA cancer diagnosis was the fourth identical diagnosis in her immediate family since age thirteen, when her mother was first diagnosed and, fortunately, survived. Her sister, too, survived breast cancer, diagnosed at age twenty-nine, and then again in the summer after Joelle's successful treatment. Breast cancer shaped Joelle's adult life by informing her healthcare choices, family planning, and mindset. Using her forty years of experience with breast cancer, Joelle created a unique approach to her treatment that unexpectedly resulted in the happiest year of her life.

Joelle is a UCSF Patient Experience Council member and sits on the Advisory Board of USC's The Pink Test. Sharsheret's October 2023 breast cancer newsletter featured Joelle's advice. She's been quoted in *The New York Times*, *The Wall Street Journal*, *Fortune* magazine, *Business Insider*, *TechCrunch*, and more in her leadership roles during her twenty-five-year career in Silicon Valley.

More information about *Crushing the Cancer Curveball* and Joelle's free resources for breast cancer patients can be found online at www.joellekaufman.com.

www.ingramcontent.com/pod-product-compliance
Lightning Source LLC
Chambersburg PA
CBHW030510080526
44586CB00011B/136